The Last Legionary

Life as a Roman Soldier in Britain AD 400

THE LAST LEGIONARY

LIFE AS A ROMAN SOLDIER IN BRITAIN
AD 400

Paul Elliott

SPELLMOUNT

First published 2007

This edition published 2011 by
Spellmount Publishers, an imprint of
The History Press Ltd
The Mill, Brimscombe Port
Stroud, Gloucestershire, GL5 2QG
www.thehistorypress.co.uk

Reprinted 2012

British Library Cataloguing in Publication Data.
A catalogue record for this book is available from the British Library.

ISBN 978 0 7524 5927 1
Typesetting and origination by The History Press Ltd.
Printed in Great Britain

Contents

About the author

Paul Elliott has a degree in Ancient History and Archaeology. His interests include collecting Roman artefacts and he is closely involved with a number of international Late Roman re-enactment groups. Amongst his previous publications are, *Warrior Cults, Brotherhoods of Fear, Assassin!*, and *Vietnam: Conflict and Controversy*. He lives in Yorkshire.

List of Illustrations

Text Images

Plates

Acknowledgements

My long fascination with Rome began at school under the tutelage of a welcoming, 'old-school' Classics teacher. The syllabus focussed on the drama of the Second Triumvirate, but I believe it was the field trip to the fort at Vindolanda, south of Hadrian's Wall, that actually caught my imagination. At that time the visible remains were concentrated around the village outside of the fort, and it was the daily lives of the civilian population that I could see in my mind's eye. I marvelled at the road surface, the little aqueduct, the drain in the butcher's shop, the inn with its open courtyard. I imagined the butcher washing blood into the drain, I imagined riders dismounting, breathlessly, from their horses in the yard, I imagined slaves skulking in the alleys, off to stoke the furnace for the inn's one heated room.

That visit, twenty years ago, certainly inspired me to study Roman history at degree level, but it also inspired me to look at the little people, the common man – Mr. Average. And the glory of Rome soon faded. I wanted to see the tarnish and the chaos, and my mind's eye was drawn to the struggles of the common man in the desperate days of the third century, and again in the fourth.

My experiments in creating replica artefacts several years ago was an expression of my desire to 'get closer' to the Roman people. They began with slings and slinging, but moved on to tunics and wax tablets. It was at that point I discovered that there were a number of living history organisations in Britain that had a huge amount of experience handling and manufacturing Roman artefacts. To two of these groups I am indebted; Cohors Quinta Gallorum ('Quinta') based at the Arbeia Roman fort at South Shields, and Comitatus, based in the north of England.

I'd especially like to thank the members of Comitatus, all of whom have been extremely patient with my constant questioning over the past three years! This group of re-enactors prides itself on a wholly authentic approach, an approach that I certainly feel at home with. Their clothing, furniture, weaponry and daily items are often made of authentic materials and reconstructed according to known Late Roman finds. By joining Comitatus I felt I was stepping as close to the material culture of Late Roman Britain as I was ever likely to get!

A great many people around the world have also given me assistance in trying to recreate the tiniest details of life for a Late Roman infantryman. I owe thanks to Florian Himmler for allowing me access to his thesis analysing wear and tear on Roman boots (prior to publication), as well as his experiences on board the *Lusoria*; to Aitor Irirate for discussions of shoes and tents; to D.B. Campbell and Graham Sumner; to Volker Bach for sharing his insights on Roman rations; to Robert Vermaat; and to Paul Carrick for sharing his knowledge of boot and shield manufacture.

Anton Powell (University of Wales) taught me the value of beginning any investigation in the presence of a reliable historical source, Dr. K. Gilliver (University of Cardiff) cautioned me on the use of Vegetius as a primary source, and Dr. Alison Griffith (University of Canterbury, Christchurch, New Zealand) helped me to solve a Mithraic puzzle. Kurt Hunter-Mann of the York Archaeological Trust generously gave up his time to talk me through the extant Roman finds in the Bridlington area, and to look into some of the questions I had related to crop marks and recent local finds. John Conyard has borne the brunt of many of my questions. I'd like to thank him for being open and free with his knowledge of the period and with the difficult business of recreating life in the past. Our desire to 'experience the past' is mutual. We marched together on several experimental Roman marches, in period clothing, eating period rations… and we marched in step.

I am indebted to my wife, Christine, who first encouraged me to begin this project and who has been unflinching in her support of my work; and to my son Bradley, who took a number of photographs for the book and who tasted all of the Roman recipes.

Of course, none of those named above is responsible for the book that follows or the assumptions I have had to make, it is my work, and the story of Gaius that illuminates the text, is my story.

Timeline

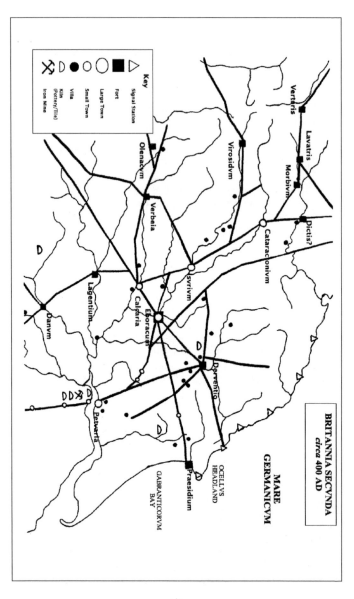

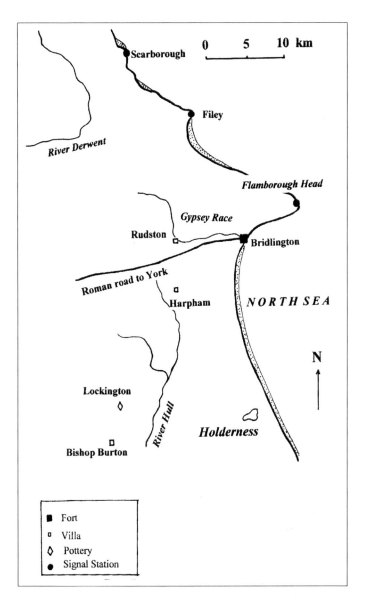

Fresh Roman coinage is not imported into Britain after this date.

403   Battle of Verona; the Visigoths are forced back into Illyricum.

404   Fearing more Gothic attacks, the young Emperor Honorius transfers the imperial court further south from Milan (Mediolanum) to Ravenna.

406   German tribes cross the Rhine and begin a destructive campaign across Gaul.

407   Constantine (proclaiming himself 'the Third') is proclaimed Western Emperor by the last remaining forces in Britain. He leads them into Gaul to engage the barbarians.

407–411   Constantine III rules parts of Britain, Gaul and Spain from Arles (Arelate).

409   British cities expel all imperial officials and sever ties with Constantine III.

410   Rome is sacked by Alaric and the Visigoths; Rescript of Honorius ordering the cities of Britain to look to their own defence.

411   The fall of Constantine III.

414   Visigoths settled in southern Gaul.

451   Battle of Catalaunian Plains; Roman forces under Aetius repulse the Huns led by Attila.

452   The Huns rampage through northern Italy.

454   Murder of Aetius; the final days of the western legions begin.

476   Romulus Augustus, last Emperor of the west, is deposed from his throne at Ravenna by the Germanic mercenary general, Odoacer.

CHAPTER I

Introduction

'Ad spathas et ad pila'
To broadswords and to javelins!
Vegetius 3.4

The wording for the sub-title of this book was chosen with care. This book concerns an individually named Roman soldier. There are few of those mentioned by the ancient historians, and of those we know nothing about their lives. Other names come to light in written records preserved by the sands of Egypt, by the anaerobic soil of Vindolanda or by chance in other places, but little, again, can be discovered about the careers and individuals of named soldiers. At best they provide snapshots of many separate lives. My greatest desire has been to build up a broad picture of the typical life of a legionary. Selecting a time and a place, deciding upon a soldier's origins, and following that legionary using historical texts and archaeological finds to piece together a hypothetical career – a kind of patchwork life.

The book covers all aspects of Late Roman military life, from recruitment to weaponry, marriage to wages, warfare to religion. We follow the career of a new recruit, Gaius, who stands as an 'everyman' figure stationed at a coastal fort in the north of England. His career becomes the backbone of the book, and as he encounters new aspects of life in AD 400, the reader shares in that information.

Gaius' narrative gives structure to the book, but it also becomes a reflection of the information being presented. Other books pass on their information discretely, discussing inflation, tunics and invasions separately, with some occasional cross-referencing. In *The Last Legionary*, the brief sections of fictionalised text allow the reader to see how all these separate strands come together to impact on one man's life: how one thing can lead to another and how lives are affected, even in small ways.

The evidence used to create Gaius' life has been gathered from several sources. By far the most prolific source is archaeology, which should be expected in a book that seeks to illuminate daily life. By focussing on military life in Britain specifically, I have been able to draw on the vast amount of archaeological work that exists today, equalled only, perhaps, by the finds made in Germany on the Rhine frontier. The written sources, ancient authors such as Ammianus Marcellinus, Zozimus and Procopius, are of inestimable value in putting archaeology into context and providing a firm framework of events, and also of describing cause and effect in the ancient world. Much about military life in AD 400 can also be gleaned from the detailed writings of a contemporary writer named Vegetius, and also Maurice, a sixth century Byzantine Emperor.

But gaps remain. In reconstructing the details of a life, one finds unanswered questions at every turn. What was Scarborough signal station called? Did Late Roman soldiers have tents? How did Gaius light a fire? Did the soldiers use their spears under-arm, crouching low; or over-arm, standing on tip-toe? What is one to do? The historical novelist can simply invent a likely answer that fits the genre, but in trying to create the life of one man using evidence, that route isn't an option. Living history can instead provide those answers that archaeology cannot, and that the ancient texts *do* not. Living history interpretation is the modern recreation of archaeological finds with the aim of exploring the use of those finds, whether it be a spindle whorl, spearhead, wicker chair or bread oven. In order to answer many of the questions that arose, I turned to living history. First I began to experiment with the material world of the Late Roman army: I hand-stitched Late Roman tunics, made shields, mixed authentic paints and (amongst other things) made a set of Roman hobnailed boots. Next I turned to a number of well-established Late Roman historical research groups that were very well thought of by the academic community. Their practical and common-sense help in filling in the missing details of Gaius' life was extremely valuable.

The Last Legionary focuses on one man in a unit of border guards, on the fringes of empire. Is that representative? Does Gaius give us a true example of what life was like in AD 400 for a Roman soldier? The frontier forces, the *limitanei*, were once the great legions of the Principate, the legions that conquered half the world. At the beginning of the fourth century these proud legions became static frontier forces, over time farming land and carrying on crafts and trades around the fort. Other more mobile units were created that quickly overtook and outshone the old legions. The *limitanei* are attractive to explore here, firstly, because they were so ubiquitous, and secondly, because their troops blurred the distinction between military and civilian life. And in fact, the unit detailed, the Legio Praesidiensis, was later transferred from Britain *to* a regional field army, and this 'elevation' to the mobile reserve allows us to explore something of life in that type of military unit, too.

Gaius is also representative of his age. This period was a time of great upheaval, yet there are no eyewitness accounts of legions marching onto boats to cross the Channel, never to return. There are no accounts of Saxon attacks on Romano-British farms or towns. No accounts of soldiers marched from the frontier all the way to Italy to defend it against vast armies of Visigoths. What was it like to be there? What was it like to be one of the last soldiers to leave Britain? What was life like for the last legionary?

CHAPTER II
Joining Up: 383 AD

I am writing to you about my wife's brother. He is a soldier's son, and he has been enrolled to go for a soldier. If you can release him again it is a fine thing you do ... since his mother is a widow and has none but him. But if he must serve, please safeguard from him going abroad with the draft for the field army...

The Abinnaeus Archive

Gaius was born in AD 362 to a Romano-British father and mother. His father was a legionary and stationed at a fort on the coast. His mother lived in the *vicus*, the small settlement just outside the walls of this fort. Now that she is widowed, she lives with Gaius in Eboracum, the greatest city of northern Britannia. Diocletian, who ruled the empire in his grandfather's day, made it law that in many trades and professions, the son should follow the father. Gaius has little choice but to join up and join the legions. His friends are also the sons of veterans, and some of these are planning to go into hiding, to dodge the conscription and avoid the army. The Code of Theodosius states that all veterans' sons between the age of twenty and twenty-five were eligible for recruitment. If only these lads could lay low, move away, take up another trade (albeit illegally) until they reached their twenty-fifth birthday, they might avoid the fate of their fathers. Later edicts would broaden this age range to try and catch the draft dodgers, sons between the ages of eighteen and thirty-five were later forced to join their father's unit.

The legions still had willing recruits, of course, but many legionaries had been obliged to join the ranks. A life in the legions was no longer the prized career-of-choice that it had been a century or two ago. The official height regulation of 5ft 10in was regularly flouted, and the preferred candidates for the ranks (farm-workers, labourers, craftsmen, hunters and butchers, for example) were sometimes in short enough supply that city-folk were instead recruited. This of course meant that the basic training and toughening-up process took longer than normal – up to four months, according to Vegetius. Prisoners of war, captured Picts, Scots or Saxons, were a good source of recruits, and foreign tribes that were not at war with Rome might also provide recruits. To these hardy barbarians, a life in the legions was not a penance, but a prize.

Many conscripts came from agricultural estates, the villa-farms that dotted the rich rural landscape of the Western Roman Empire. Landowners were forced to supply a suitable recruit (usually a tenant farmer or his son). Since the cost was so high, several landowners could club together, taking it in turns to furnish a candidate for the legionary recruiters. Recruiting officers were always wary of being fobbed off with a stand-in, perhaps a vagrant or a slave, or with a troublesome and unproductive tenant that the landowner was keen to get rid of. Alternatively, a levy of thirty-six *solidi* could be paid to the government instead. Not all the recruits went willingly. Self-mutilation was frequent enough to be legislated against. The hacking off of a thumb rendered a conscript useless as an infantryman, and for the past fifteen years the offender was punished by being burned alive. Only two years ago, however, the Emperor Theodosius, desperate for manpower, decreed that two 'thumbless' recruits can stand in for one unmutilated candidate.

Accompanied by his friend Severus, also a veteran's son, Gaius answers the call-up and is sworn in at the gigantic legionary fortress in Eboracum with all of the gravitas of a solemn religious ceremony.

> We swear by God, Christ and the Holy Spirit, and by the Majesty of the Emperor which second to God is to be loved and worshipped by the human race … we swear that we will strenuously do all that the Emperor may command, will never desert the service, nor refuse to die for the Roman State.
>
> Vegetius 2.5

Once enlisted, Gaius and Severus are herded together with seven other conscripts (all unwilling draftees from the local farms) and marched off to the fort of Praesidium which may have been situated on the east coast. It is a three day journey, and each night the nine recruits are chained together, or, if the travellers sheltered at a villa, locked in a single room, with a guard posted outside.

The fort of Praesidium (if it was indeed sited on the coast) guarded the beaches of Gabranticorum, a wide curving bay with a series of stone signal stations at regular intervals to warn of sea-borne raiders. The Roman road from Eboracum ended here. Gaius, Severus and the other recruits were taken immediately through the big double gates into the fortified compound and settled into one of the barrack rooms.

Praesidium would have been one of many stone-built forts that were constructed in the first century AD. In AD 383 these forts still served to garrison troops ready to defend against attacks from barbarian invaders, or from disgruntled rebels. Much of northern Britannia had been heavily fortified and garrisoned following the invasion, and it remained so through to the fourth century AD. Britain was actually made up of four separate provinces at this date. What had previously been 'Upper Britain' (Wales, the West Country and the South East) became Britannia Prima, with its capital at Cirencester; and Maxima Caesariensis, with its capital at Londinium. Further north, what had once been 'Lower Britain' (the Midlands and East Anglia, and the North as far as Hadrian's Wall) became Britannia Secunda, with its capital at Eboracum; and Flavia Caesariensis, with its capital at Lindum.

The fort of Praesidium was home to the Praesidiensis legion, an infantry unit of around 1,000 men tasked with frontier defence.[1] The red star on the blue field was the shield emblem of the Legio Praesidiensis, but it is still a mystery where this legion might have been based. It could have been Bridlington on the East Yorkshire coast, or Newton Kyme near Tadcaster, or elsewhere. A barely known legion, a footnote to history, is barracked in a lost Roman fortress somewhere in the north-east of England. Where was it? And what was it actually like?

The Legio Praesidiensis is mentioned only once in the *Notitia Dignitatum*, a list of all units and officers of the empire *circa* AD 400. The Praesidiensis appears in the listing for the mobile field army of Gaul (one of the powerful *comitatenses*), under the command of the Master of Infantry. So was it a Gallic unit? Many of the unit names give an indication of their origins, and in Britain there are three historical accounts of a fort called 'Praesidium' or 'Praetorio'. With so many British units being marched across the Channel to fight in Gaul (Magnus Maximus, Constantine III and Stilicho all took troops to join the field army in Gaul), it is reasonable to assume that the Praesidiensis came from Praesidium. So it is a British unit, but where is this Praesidium?

Lots of Roman forts in Britain have been only tentatively identified. We know for certain that South Shields is Arbeia, that Doncaster is Danum, that York is Eboracum; but some forts remain unidentified. We have no epigraphical evidence of their Roman name. In other cases, we know the names of several Roman forts, but are in the dark as to their whereabouts. Praesidium is one of these.

The name of the fort occurs in the Antonine Itinerary of the second century (essentially a list of stopping points on journeys across Roman Britain). It is also mentioned in the *Notitia Dignitatum* as a base for a cohort of Dalmatian cavalry. Lastly, the mysterious fort of Praesidium is mentioned in the seventh century Ravenna Cosmology between two other unidentified entries, Camulosessa and Brigomono. Praesidium is also referred to as 'Praetorio'.

The First Antonine Itinerary (Iter I), plots a course from Bremenium (High Rochester, north of the Wall) to Praetorio, a distance of 161,000 paces: *'A limite id est a vallo Praetorio usque mpm clvi'* (From the frontier, that is, from the entrenchments [i.e. Hadrian's Wall], all the way to Praetorio one-hundred and fifty-six thousand paces).

The list of stopping points is as follows: Bremenium (High Rochester), Corstopitum (Corbridge), Vindomora (Ebchester), Vinovivum (Binchester), Cataractoni (Catterick), Isurium (Aldborough), Eboracum (York), Derventione (Malton), Delgovicia (suspected posting station near Millington, East Yorkshire), Praetorio. Delgovicia is listed some thirteen miles from Derventio (Malton) and twenty-five miles from Praetorio. Tracing this route on a map one finds that it is straight-line travel to York, followed by a North East trip up to Malton, a southerly trip to Millington and then…? Praetorio or Praesidium is in the area somewhere.

The next stage of this investigation is to identify a suitable unnamed fort in the area. This task is not too difficult. Newton Kyme near Tadcaster has been identified by crop marks as a Roman fort of the period. It is unattributed and could be a candidate for Praesidium, but it lies west of York, which means that the Iter I would have to back-track through Eboracum to get there. Also, is Newton Kyme a suitable stopping place for a route? Would not York or Brough or somewhere on the coast make more sense? There are no other suitable forts in the East Riding. The fort at Brough-on-Humber was abandoned AD 125. The fort at Lease Rigg in North Yorkshire was abandoned AD 120. There are unattributed forts at Hayton and also Roall Manor Farm (discovered 1991) but both are under 1.5 hectares, suitable in size only for a quingenary cohort of 500 men). Praesidium was probably constructed for a milliary cohort (1,000 men), since our thousand-strong Legio Praesidiensis must have been accommodated there. Note that the fort at Newton Kyme is, at 4 hectares, easily big enough to hold the Praesidiensis.

But the Iter I route is moving eastwards, and the Roman roads head east too, straight toward Bridlington and Flamborough Head. There are no Roman remains in the vicinity, however, so why do two roads converge here? Ptolemy's Geography (early second century) describes Bridlington

Bay as *'Gabranticorum Sinus'* (with many harbours). None have been found, and it is thought that coastal erosion has destroyed all trace of these ports as well as a possible Theodosian signal station at Flamborough and a fort in the general vicinity of the harbour or beyond. Could this be Praesidium, now lost to the North Sea? If the Praesidiensis *was* based at a now missing fort at Bridlington, what did it do there? What did the fort look like?

Praesidium/Praetorio was most likely a Flavian construction, of standard playing card shape, built to hold a milliary cohort (double cohort) of 1,000 men. Like Housesteads, Birrens, Crammond, Lyne and Chesters, it would cover at least 2.1 hectares, possibly 2.3 or more, and have dimensions somewhere in the region of 200m x 130m. As with most milliary forts it would have ten barracks blocks, not six (for a standard quingenary cohort). Its fortifications and inner buildings would be of stone, and would follow the plan of other forts of the same size. Look to Housesteads, which has many outstanding remains, and which has been faithfully reconstructed by Peter Connolly and Ronald Embleton. Praesidium was of the same size and must have looked very similar.

In the fourth century, Count Theodosius established signal stations on the North Yorkshire coast to warn of Saxon raids. Many believe that Flamborough Head would also have had one of these stations (probably on Beacon Hill, now a gravel quarry). From the Headland you can see Filey, Scarborough Castle and the Whitby promontory.

A fort at Bridlington would be well placed to act as centre of operations for these forts. A network of signal stations stretching *south* around the broad Bridlington Bay has also been suggested. This counterpart to the northern chain would guard this huge and accessible anchorage from barbarian piracy. Would Praesidium have some part to play in manning and supplying these southerly stations? Unfortunately, all of Bridlington's Roman remains (except a little pottery and several coin hoards) have gone into the sea, and Scarborough's signal station is headed the same way (figure 1).

Gaius' new home of Praesidium, then, is a large auxiliary fort of Flavian date, on flat ground out past the present-day Bridlington harbour where the Gypsey Race stream meets the sea. This position is a reflection of the forts at Ravenglass, Dover, Porchester and elsewhere, which don't dominate from cliff tops, but place themselves directly where people, vessels and supplies will congregate: by the seashore, near fresh water. Troops of the Praesidiensis like Gaius and Severus might be assigned to signal stations, to inland or cliff-top patrols, to guarding warehouses, or searching ships. They might be sent to chase rebels in the North Yorkshire Moors or reinforce northern units on the Wall ready for raids into Pictland. Swan-necked cargo vessels might transport supplies out to the harbours and signal stations along the southern stretch of coast as far as Spurn Point. The beacon might sit ready at the top of Flamborough's own signal station, a towered fortlet that would resemble the Scarborough station in many ways.

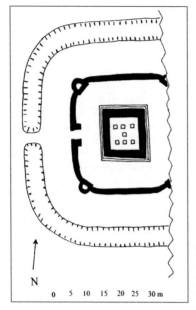

N

0   5   10   15   20   25   30 m

Figure 1. Plan of the Scarborough signal station. The north-eastern portion has gradually been lost as the cliff has eroded away.

Finally, a bustling vicus on the landward side of the fort, with small temples, perhaps inns, tradesmen and a bath-house fill in the picture.

The British provinces ('the Britains') were proving difficult to defend. A generation ago, when Gaius was a boy (AD 367), a combined attack by tribes of the Picts, the Scots, Saxons and the Attacotti brought the island's defences to its knees. Gaius remembered the flights of refugees, the burning of villages and farms, the butchery and the chaos. His father, Maritus, had deserted the legion to get his family further south to the capital city of Londinium.

> ...at that time the Picts ... together with the warlike people of the Attacotti and the Scotti, were roving at large and causing great devastation.
>
> Ammianus Marcellinus 27.8

As with previous raids, the barbarians had not been interested in settlement or conquest, but in booty and in prisoners. With forts on fire, populations enslaved and refugees crammed into the southern towns, no-one could believe that Britain could be ever be restored. But troops came from the mainland. Count Theodosius, with senior officers including a certain Magnus Maximus, routed the barbarian raiding parties and seized their spoils. Theodosius then freed the desperate people of Londinium and brought order to the south. Gaius was suddenly forced to say goodbye to his father, Maritus. With the arrival of Theodosius and four legions of the Gallic field army, many of the deserters from the ruined forts went into hiding. If found away from their units, they would be summarily executed. His father threw away the wide military belt that marked him out as a legionary, threw off his military cloak (*sagum*), and pulled on a baggy, hooded cloak more commonly used by civilians. The vast numbers of deserters, however, meant that it was impossible for the relief force to execute every man they found who had left his post. To do so would leave the British provinces without any viable military force once the relieving troops had departed. Maritus was finally discovered hiding in a cellar, but the gods were with him:

> [Theodosius] issued a proclamation promising immunity to deserters who returned to the colours and summoning many others who were dispersed in various places on furlough. This secured the return of the majority.
>
> Ammianus Marcellinus 27.8

With a reconstituted force of British troops to join his four legions, Theodosius and his officers moved northwards to drive out, kill or enslave any barbarian raiders they found. Families of the British troops, including Gaius and his mother, followed the army as part of the baggage train. Seven months after they had fled Praesidium, Gaius and his family returned. The rebuilding began in earnest, but Theodosius was not content just to rebuild; he was intent on improving the island's defences, and toured the provinces for almost a year directing new building work.

Forts along Hadrian's Wall had been overrun and torched, Fullofaudes, the military commander in charge of the frontier forces (the '*dux*' or 'duke') had been besieged at Eboracum. Nectaridus, the '*Comes*', or Count, of the Saxon Shore had been killed in action. These two military posts illustrate the way in which Britain had so far tackled the barbarian problem. A Roman *dux* was a general in charge of defensive frontier forces. These *limitanei* troops were static and garrisoned in legionary forts and watchtowers and ranged along the frontiers. In Britain, Hadrian's Wall and the forts in the north of Britain that supported it, were all manned by *limitanei* troops. Gaius and Severus, and the other soldiers of the Legio Praesidiensis were all *limitanei*. They did the job of the old-style legions, standing guard against barbarian attacks. There were Dukes all over the empire commanding *limitanei* soldiers. A Roman *comes* was a general with greater powers. Theodosius had been a count and he had led several legions of the Gallic field army across the Channel to relieve a beleaguered Britain. The Count of the Saxon Shore, meanwhile, had the responsibility to garrison the heavily defended forts dotting the south-east coast of Britain.

Figure **2**. Ravenscar. Inscription discovered at the Ravenscar signal station. One translation of this text records that Justinianus, the commander and Vindicianus, the magister, constructed the tower (*burgus*) (after R.P. Wright).

These were placed to deter Saxon raids on northern Gaul and southern Britain. Forts like Rutupiae (Richborough), Regulbium (Reculver), Branodunum (Brancaster), Portus Adurni (Porchester) and Dubris (Dover) were massively constructed and well garrisoned. They may also have serviced the Channel fleet.

Count Theodosius did not leave the British provinces until after he had restored and re-garrisoned its forts. It is likely that the chain of fortified signal stations on the North Yorkshire coast were commissioned by Theodosius, and, as already mentioned, there may have been a similar chain of stations stretching south to Spurn Head. Remains of signal stations have been found at Huntcliff, Goldsborough, Ravenscar, Scarborough and Filey (figure 2). A sixth is likely to have been built on Flamborough Head, from where four of the others could be seen. The station at Scarborough is the best preserved, although some of the building has already vanished over the cliff. In AD 383 a central watchtower stands in a courtyard defended by a ditch and circuit of stone walls with corner towers. They are in effect small forts with the addition of a watchtower. Presumably a beacon fire was kept ready atop the tower, ready to be lit when Saxon or Pictish boats were spotted (plate 39). Some reconstructions have estimated the height of the stone tower at 20m.

How these forts and their beacon fires operated is a mystery. They may have been used to send a signal inland to the cavalry fort at Derventio (Malton) which might then dispatch a rapid reaction force. Alternatively, the beacons may only have signalled a warning to local settlements inland. One theory is that the signals passed along the coast to warn ships of the Roman fleet docked along the Holderness coast or in the Humber estuary. Perhaps all of these theories are correct and the signal stations could serve several purposes at once. The garrisons were small, but seem to have been purely military. The fortifications were significant enough, and must have easily deterred Saxon raiders from besieging and then disabling them.

Members of the Praesidiensis legion, including Gaius' father, Maritus, built the stations over the next few years. Peace and prosperity returned to the British provinces. The legion had fresh recruits to replace men killed or enslaved by the barbarian invaders. Many were locals, but some were in fact Picts and Saxons, barbarians captured by Theodosius and drafted into the *limitanei* frontier force. They became willing legionaries and were eager to embrace Romano-British culture. As had been the custom for centuries, some took Roman names to ease the transition into Roman life. Others retained their foreign-sounding name. No stigma was attached to this; the general Fullofaudes who had been killed in the attacks had carried a barbarian name. Recruits from the Germanic tribes had been accepted into the legions for many years, and their numbers had steadily increased until, by the fourth century, it is estimated that a third of the total legionary numbers were made up of men of Germanic origin. In Britannia the ratio is not that high, but the influence of Germanic culture is evident everywhere, in the clothing, in the style of leather belts, in the types of knives and weapons preferred by the legions. Once the barbarians embraced the legions, there was no longer a 'them and us' attitude. The men of the legions stuck together, lived together and fought together. Their origins were irrelevant.

Within five years of the barbarian attacks and the restoration of the province by Count Theodosius, Gaius' father was struck down by disease. Both his widow and ten-year-old son left the small village outside Praesidium to live with relatives in Eboracum (York). There Gaius was brought up by his uncle Augustus, a butcher, until his twentieth birthday. Events were in motion, however, that would change Gaius' life, the fate of the British provinces, and possibly the future of the entire Western Empire forever. The Picts had come once more out of the Highlands to raid settlements on the Wall. Scotti from across the waters in Hibernia, Land of Winter, were landing on the west coast, south of the Wall, and attacking in force.

In AD 382, as the corn ripened, the Duke of the Britains, who had his headquarters at Eboracum, gathered together a large army to face this threat. The city bustled with military activity. Mules, ponies and oxen were procured. Rations were shipped in and loaded onto wagons. Skirmish troops and cavalry units arrived from forts across the northern provinces to swell the ranks of the mighty Sixth Legion. At the head of this great army rode Magnus Maximus, the junior officer from Hispania (Spain) that had accompanied Count Theodosius to Britain fifteen years previously. Maximus had been sent to organize the province's defences only three years ago, after Theodosius' own son had gained the imperial throne.

The entire city turned out to see the legion assemble and large crowds of local people waved the soldiers off. There was much lamenting. The people of Eboracum worried that this war might end as catastrophically as the last one. Gaius and his uncle watched the soldiers file past with a look of grim determination on their faces, wearing ringmail, and carrying large oval shields.

Days passed. News came in of attacks on the east coast by Pictish raiders. And then messengers began to arrive at Eboracum from the north. Victory over the Picts and Scotti! Magnus Maximus had been victorious. Fear and anticipation of what might have befallen the army, of what had occurred fifteen years earlier, and that was still fresh in the memory of many, turned quickly into ecstatic relief. And it was a deep and overwhelming relief. The people of the city were grateful beyond measure – a festival was suggested, with honours for the conquering general. Celebrations across the city were being planned for the Duke's arrival and Gaius and his uncle Augustus rushed to meet the demand for fresh meat. As Maximus neared the city, envoys from the town council (*curia*) along with the commander of the city's garrison, were dispatched to meet him. Magnus' troops, however, relieved and overjoyed, were proclaiming him 'Caesar', 'Augustus' and 'Imperator'. The Sixth Legion had proclaimed its own emperor, in defiance of the Emperor Gratian who sat on the throne of the Western Empire and Theodosius, Emperor of the East.

Peeved because Theodosius [son of his old commander by the same name] was considered worthy of the throne while he himself had not been promoted even to an honorific office, Maximus further roused the soldiers to hatred against the Emperor. They for their part were quick to rebel and proclaim Maximus Emperor.

Zosimus

When the Sixth legion did return with prisoners, recaptured booty and the Dux Britannium (Duke of the Britains) at the head of the column, it knew not what the reaction might be. Garrison troops inside the fortress were already proclaiming Maximus the saviour of Britannia. Some even dared to call him Emperor! Maximus was relieved to find that his Praefectus Praetorium, the garrison commander, welcomed him as Emperor with open arms.

For Gaius, the next few months proved to be business as usual. He kept his head down through the autumn and winter and worked hard in his uncle's slaughterhouse. Magnus Maximus was preparing to cross to Gaul with the majority of the Sixth Legion as well as a number of other units. Gaius, naturally enough, did not want to be drafted into this army, destined for foreign lands and foreign wars. His friends, the sons of veterans like himself, were being recruited for the campaign. He doubted that he

Figure 3. A coin minted by Magnus Maximus. He is depicted wearing a Late Roman diadem and wears an imperial cloak over his armour.

would ever see them again. Now aged twenty years, Gaius was eligible to be conscripted into the legions to follow in his father's footsteps.

Eboracum was now home to an imperial throne. Ambassadors from sympathisers and like-minded rebel generals came and went. Again the city prepared for a massive assault. This time on Rome itself. With the lambing season underway, the new emperor led the vast army south to Londonium and ultimately Dubris where it prepared to sail to Gaul. It was AD 383 (figure 3).

> … Maximus maintained that he had not of his own accord assumed the sovereignty, but that he had simply defended by arms the necessary requirements of the empire, regard to which had been imposed upon him by the soldiers, according to the Divine appointment, and that the favour of God did not seem wanting to him who, by an event seemingly so incredible, had secured the victory. Adding to that the statement that none of his adversaries had been slain except in the open field of battle …
>
> Sulpitius Severus, *Life of St Martin*

Within months, things in Britannia began to change. Despite the huge loss of military manpower, and flouting the predictions of many, the northern frontier on Hadrian's Wall held. However, piratical raids on the east coast (by Picts) and on the western coasts by Scotti raiders, increased. Hit and run attacks were proving difficult to prevent. In Eboracum, the fortress garrison, now a fifth of its previous size, began to rent out areas of the fortress for civilian use. Blacksmiths and potters moved inside, and Augustus with his staff of butchers moved into the *principia* (head-quarters building) at the centre of the fort. With all those empty barracks going spare, many of the legionaries brought their families into the fortress, turning barrack-blocks into family chalets. The legionary fortress at Eboracum was quickly transformed into a fortified settlement of traders, craftsmen and military families.

On the Continent, Magnus Maximus took on the Western Emperor, Gratian, and won. Now, with Gratian's young half-brother as his junior partner (or co-emperor), Magnus set about establishing himself as a legitimate and competent Western Emperor. Andragathius was Magnus' ablest general.

> Andragathius obtained possession of the imperial chariot, and sent word to the Emperor that his consort was travelling towards his camp. Gratian, who was but recently married and youthful, as well as passionately attached to his wife, hastened incautiously across the river, and in his anxiety to meet her fell without forethought into the hands of Andragathius; he was seized, and, in a little while, put to death. He was in the twenty-fourth year of his age, and had reigned fifteen years.
>
> The Ecclesiastical History of
> Salaminius Hermias Sozomenus

That summer Gaius was spotted and identified as a veteran's son. Eligible for conscription, he was commanded to swear an oath to Magnus Maximus, new Emperor of the Western Empire, and then ordered to pack up his gear for the journey to Praesidium. The shore forts on both coasts were being strengthened to resist the sea raids of the barbarian tribes.

CHAPTER III
Training: 384 AD

There is nothing stabler nor more fortunate or admirable than a State which has copious supplies of soldiers who are well trained. For it is not fine raiment or stores of gold, silver and gems that bend our enemies to respect us; they are kept down solely by fear of our arms.

Vegetius 1.13

A new recruit into the legions needed to be trained. As in any army, then or now, this training served two purposes, to pass on skills and abilities that would later be needed in warfare, and also (more importantly) to indoctrinate the recruit. This military indoctrination came in the form of severe physical and mental stress designed to break down the soldier's identity and independence, replacing it with instinctive obedience and total loyalty to the legionary standards (the flags, images and symbols of the unit) that accompanied the troops into battle.

Gaius was the son of a soldier and he was very receptive to the methods used by the training officers. He embraced military life. Unwilling recruits, however, found the first few weeks to be much harder. Arduous marches along the Roman military roads were demanded of the recruits, 20 miles in five hours, or 24 miles at the 'fast step' if the commander was feeling cruel.[2] Other days, the recruits would be physically challenged: running, jumping, swimming, digging, digging and digging. Often, training camps would be dug out and used for overnight camping, before being abandoned the next day. Experts from the fort actually planned the camps, and the recruits dug out the earth, piled it into ramparts, cut out turfs and laid them like bricks onto the faces of the earthen walls. Relentless digging, coupled with continual marching, pushed the recruits to breaking point, and moulded them into warrior-pioneers – soldiers who were just as able to dig themselves a victory as they were to carve one out of the bodies of the enemy.

Severus proved to be Gaius' good companion during these first few weeks. They became united in their hatred of Ursinus the drillmaster (*campidoctor*), and of the legionary commander, the tribune Sextus Aemilianus. This tough and uncompromising commander had been hastily brought in by Maximus' new Duke of the Britains to reorganize the east coast defences. He found a garrison run down, demoralized and inefficient, a garrison that spent all its time in barracks and in the local settlements engaging in trade and private affairs.

Ursinus soon began teaching the recruits how to use the weapons of the legionary. The older soldiers were required to train in the morning, and were allowed the afternoons off. The new recruits, Gaius and Severus included, were at it all day long. They practised at the post with sword and shield, learning the correct strokes and the best locations on the human body to cause maximum damage. Later, javelins and weighted darts were thrown at the posts from a distance to build up muscles in the right arm and increase accuracy. Those recruits with an aptitude for the bow or the sling had to practise with those weapons to hit a straw target 180m away. In addition, some part of each day was given over to practice with spear and shield on the parade ground. The recruits were drilled with their entire cohort to march in line, to change direction, wheel and to 'march out' to double the frontage of the formation. These lessons in battle drill would prove crucial. Unless the soldiers fought together as a single fighting element, they were all doomed, no matter what their personal fighting skill.

Little is known of the internal divisions of units in the fourth century. A legion of only 1000 or so can no longer be subdivided into ten of the traditional 500-man cohorts, each made up of six centuries of 80 men each (despite the word 'century' meaning 100). However, the fourth-century legion was clearly still divided into smaller fighting and working units. The fourth-century military writer Vegetius refers to *centenarii* (commanders of 100) and *ducenarii* (commanders of 200) which gives some clue as to the fourth-century structure of the legion. He also conflates cohorts and centuries in this phrase: 'Within [camp] the first centuries, that is cohorts, pitch tents and set up the dragons and standards.' Later (Veg. 2.20) he explains how a legion is divided into 10 cohorts, and goes on to tells us how each cohort has its own dragon standard. This consisted of an openmouthed dragon's head, mounted on a pole, with a long tube of material attached to the back of the head. The breeze filled out the material like a modern windsock. Vegetius is a confusing source, since he discusses modern practice whilst comparing it to the Roman army of the past. His reference to dragon standards is clear however, and these were only used by infantry units in the Late Roman army. This would suggest that Vegetius was writing about the legions of his own day, and that they were divided into ten cohorts, each with its own dragon-standard.

For the purposes of this book, we will refer to the 100-man units as cohorts, although as in earlier periods this fighting unit may have been permanently under strength. We can speculate that the soldiers of the Praesidiensis were organised into 8-man *contubernia*, each commanded by a squad-leader (*caput contubernii*) who has the rank of *semissalis* (which means he can draw more rations than the other men in his squad). Ten squads lived and worked together as a cohort commanded by an officer of some status called a *centenarius*. An officer titled *ducenarius* may also have commanded troops in the fort, and reflecting earlier military practice we can postulate that Praesidium's 'commander of 200' was the officer in charge of a prestigious double-cohort that had cherry-picked the toughest veterans from the other units.[3] Although they did not normally command units, there were a number of other officers with other duties. The *draconarius* carried the dragon standard of the legion, with its long fabric tail that flapped in the wind. *Signifers* carried the battle-standards and also administered the men's pay. *Circitors* were tasked with checking the night-watches.

Unlike the legions of previous centuries, which fought hand-to-hand after discharging javelins into an enemy formation, the fourth-century legion had the capability to fight at a distance. It was the legion's goal to wear down or drive off an enemy unit by missile fire if at all possible. In addition, a greater defensive role, especially by the frontier legions, meant that missile weapons would prove much more useful than they had in earlier eras. To this end the recruits were introduced to the sling, bow, dart, javelin and throwing axe. Light troops would use some of these weapons to shoot over the main body of troops and hit the approaching foe. Such lightly armed missile troops were also used on scouting missions and long patrols. Troops might easily move from 'light' to 'heavy' infantry simply by putting on armour, and picking up a spear and shield. The legionary of the fourth century was rarely a specialist with one type of weapon.

The Sling

The sling was an ancient weapon that had been used by shepherds and mountain-folk for centuries. Most legionaries were given some basic training in the use of the sling because, although it was difficult to use accurately, it was cheap, portable and supplied by an unlimited source of ammunition (stones). A sling was no more than a pouch of leather connected to two leather cords at either end. Whipped over the head at great speed, a stone could be discharged with incredible force. Some slings were made of woven grass or animal hair, depending on the people making them and the materials available to them. Many tribal cultures, such as the mercenary slingers from the Balearic Islands, wove their slings, but a Roman legion with lots of cowhide available would find it easier to cut slings from leather. In fact a decorated leather sling pouch was found at the Vindolanda fort near Hadrian's Wall (figure 4).

The author has made a replica of the Vindolanda sling and become quite proficient in its use. The pouch is around 15cm long, and the two leather cords are 60cm long. One cord ends in a loop and fits over the index finger, the other cord ends in a knot which is pinched between thumb and forefinger. To release the stone during a sling, the knot is released and the stone flies toward the target. Two things become immediately clear when one begins to practice with the sling: it is a deadly weapon worthy of respect, but it takes a huge amount of practice to become even moderately proficient in its use. Slinging smooth pebbles out to 70 or 80 metres becomes fairly easy fairly quickly, but hitting a human-sized target at anything beyond 20m is difficult. For a cohort of slingers, accuracy would not have been a great concern. The objective for the unit as a whole was to cast their sling stones and simply hit the enemy formation, obviously this would be a large and relatively immobile target. Troops with minimal training would have been able to achieve this.

Difficulties arise when slinging at distance, in bad weather, or for accuracy. Contrary to a popular misconception, the sling is not whirled around the head at fantastic speed before being released. After only three revolutions the sling stone has already reached its maximum potential speed and further spinning just ruins the slinger's aim. Everything hangs on the timing of the release. In fact, through experimentation, the author has found that a single 'snap' motion provides a good deal of accuracy and power.

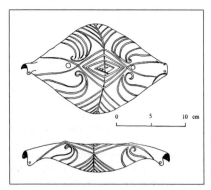

Figure 4. This large leather object has been interpreted as a sling pouch, and was found at Vindolanda. Lead sling bullets (glandes) were also discovered at the fort (after R. Birley).

They should also be accustomed to rotating the sling once only about the head, when the stone is discharged from it.

Vegetius,
Epitome of Military Science

The slinger can attempt one of three broad styles: overhead, over arm and under arm. Very likely, the trainer passed on the slinging method that he himself had first been taught. Slingers in the Roman army would also create their own bullets (*glandes*) of lead, of baked clay or even carved stone. Using smooth beach pebbles, the author noticed that it was difficult to increase accuracy because each stone was of a slightly different shape, a different weight and often a different density. Despite a consistent and methodical slinging style, the variations in the stones created variation in accuracy. Military slingers commonly melted lead into clay or stone moulds to create a reliable and consistent form of ammunition. Practicing with these *glandes* meant that a soldier could begin to improve his accuracy. Some moulds were simply sand trays with the impressions of spear butts or even thumbs in them! In addition to increased accuracy, the great density of lead meant that the sling bullets travelled faster and further and with much more power. Lead shot could easily match the range of a bow, and kill just as easily. Sling stones and bullets were invisible in flight, unlike arrows, and could not be dodged or easily defended against; in addition they were not affected by cross-winds as the fletchings on arrows were, although slinging in any kind of wind is difficult because the thongs tend to spin and tangle.

The fourth-century legions created a wholly new weapon that used the sling at its core. A 4ft staff had a sling knotted close to one of its ends, the other cord had a loop which slipped over the same end of the staff. The author has experimented with staff slings. With a stone in the pouch, the slinger holds the end of the staff with the sling dangling behind him. He then 'casts' it forward much the same way a fisherman casts a line from a rod. As the loaded sling reaches the apex of the curve the loose loop slides off the end of the staff and the stone flies forward with some momentum. At the point of release the stones are approximately 4m high up in the air. Staff slings are incredibly easy to use, without the difficult timing problems associated with the hand sling. A heavier weight of stone (or a shaped *glans*) can be shot from the staff sling, but with equal shot, the staff sling does not out-distance the venerable hand sling. What, then, could be gained from such a weapon? The larger and more deadly stones were useful in the East when attacking armoured war elephants, and equally useful when defending a city or fortress wall. A steady supply of stones resulted in the staff sling becoming almost hand-held artillery. The medieval trebuchet (a type of heavy single-arm catapult) used precisely the same mechanism to launch much heavier ammunition in a later era.

The Bow

Bows have a long history in warfare. The Romans realized early on the value of the eastern recurve bow, a bow that was manufactured using several materials to increase its flexibility, strength and inherent power. Traditionally wood, horn and animal sinew were used, the wood made up the core of the bow, with horn strips on the inner surface and sinew on the outer surface. The manufacture of these bows was a long and difficult process, but the bows produced were far superior to the single wood 'self-bows' used by the Germans, Gauls and Britons of the period. Often the ends or 'ears' of the bow were strengthened with bone 'laths' (figure 5), and the body of the bow was carefully covered with leather to protect it from moisture. Wet conditions could ruin a recurve bow, as could misuse. Leaving the bow stringed and ready for action ruins the springiness of the bow and reduces its power. Unlike the sling, specialist craftsmen were needed to make these complex weapons.

Arrows used by fourth-century archers had either socketed or tanged heads and varied in their shape. Some had three blades, some two, some were used for setting fires, some were 'bodkin' types that could punch through mail armour. All were held securely in cylindrical leather quivers slung over the archer's back. Thumb-rings of bronze, bone or leather were used by archers trained in eastern units, these rings eased the pressure on the thumb, which was used in the eastern archery tradition to pull back the string.

When used to the western method of drawing that uses the first three fingers, the thumb-ring release is very difficult and requires a great deal of strength in the right thumb.

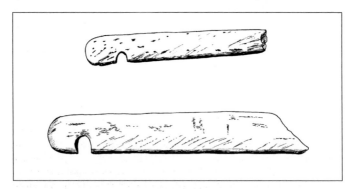

Figure 5. Bow laths, stiffeners of bone that protected the tips of Roman recurved bows. From the Chesters Museum.

The range of a bow is dependant on many factors, but a skilled archer can hit a human-sized target effectively at distances around 100m. Vegetius states that archers, like slingers, should practise their aim by shooting at a straw target 180m distant. Greater ranges are possible of course, and when fighting as a unit that is targeting an enemy formation, precision archery is not required. Instead, volleys can be shot high into the air over one's own troops to land onto the heads of the enemy force. Estimates and practical experiments have suggested that a skilled archer can achieve battlefield accuracy out to 200 or even 300m with some hope of target penetration.

The Plumbata

While most of the weapons of a fourth-century legion had been in common use for many centuries, the *plumbata* was a new and deadly invention. It was a lead-weighted throwing dart, a short arrow with a barbed head and an egg-shaped lead weight at the juncture of the iron head and wooden shaft. Several examples of *plumbata* heads have been found, and the length of the shaft has to be inferred from Vegetius' comment that legionaries could carry up to five of the darts inside their shields (plate 6). The author's reconstruction is 40cm long. There is no surviving account of how the *plumbatae* were discharged toward the enemy line. Were they tossed by hand? If so, was this an overhand (javelin-style) throw, an underhand throw, or a slingshot throw in the same way a modern discus is cast? Even more intriguingly, practical tests by the author have shown that these lead-weighted darts can even be throw from a leather sling, and even a staff-sling.

Vegetius also refers to the *plumbatae* as '*mattiobarbulus*', which is presumed to be an error, and should have originally read '*martiobarbalus*', meaning 'Mars-barb'. He also states that two Roman legions were renamed Martiobarbuli Iovani and Martiobarbuli Herculiani by the Emperors Diocletian and Maximian. This was because these units excelled at throwing the plumbatae and preferred it to all other weapons (presumably all other *missile* weapons). According to this writer, the darts were thrown both during the attack by charging troops, and defensively by rear-rank legionaries. The front rankers, presuming they carried the darts inside their shields, would be cast by hand and tests by the historical research group Comitatus have found that an underhand throw is by far the best method. The *plumbatae* can reach an impressive distance (easily exceeding 60m) and come down vertically directly onto the heads and shoulders of the enemy formation – truly Mars-barbs: lethal spikes of iron from the heavens. Rear ranks could use a leather sling to cast the *plumbatae*. Staff slings are also a possibility, but the use of a leather sling to cast a weighted dart is attested historically during the Roman conquest of Macedonia in the second century BC. The ancient writer Livy records that the Macedonians used the *'kestrosphendon'*, which seems to have been a traditional leather or woven sling, to cast a 35–40cm dart. Experiments by the author have shown that lead-weighted plumbatae cast in this way can reach distances of up to 100m, which would allow the rear-rankers of a fourth-century legion to sling darts well over the heads of their comrades.

The Javelin

For centuries, the *pilum*, a type of javelin with a long iron shank, had a distinguished history with the Roman army. Legionaries carried two of these deadly armour- and shield-piercing weapons and threw them at the enemy formation just prior to entering hand-to-hand combat. In the fourth century, the legions maintained their use of javelins, but a variation on the traditional *pilum* was now in use. The *spiculum* was a direct descendant, it had a shorter iron shank (only 30cm long instead of 60cm) but its barbed head of hardened steel still punched through shield and armour. As with the original pilum, the shank of the *spiculum*, mounted on the end of a wooden haft, was of soft iron and easily bent out of shape. This rendered it (and the shield, if it hit one) useless to the enemy. Not every legionary carried a *spiculum*, it may have been used by first-, second- or third-rank troops and could double easily as a spear. Modern replicas can be thrown with some accuracy out to 30m; it is a well-balanced weapon.

Other javelins, called *veruta*, were commonly carried by light troops, and may well have been carried into battle by the heavy infantry too. These were cheaply made javelins, no more than a 1m wood shaft tipped with a simple iron head (itself often no more than a triangle of iron hammered around the tip of the shaft and filed to a point). Some troops carried quivers of *veruta*, allowing them to keep up a barrage of javelins on the enemy force, or to pass the weapons along the line to their comrades. The javelin delivers a more powerful punch than the arrow or slingstone, but because of its size is in much shorter supply on the battlefield. Accounts tell of javelins being used by the light infantry in a skirmishing role to harass an enemy formation, as well as by heavy (armoured) infantry just before they close with the enemy line. Tests with replica *veruta* have shown them to be unbalanced and accuracy is questionable at distances in excess of 20m.

The Throwing Axe

The axe was a barbarian weapon, introduced into the legions by a great influx of recruits from the German and Gothic tribes. Of particular military significance was the *francisca*, a short-handled throwing axe with a heavy, curved blade (plate 3). A Germanic tribe called the Franks was associated with this weapon; either they were renowned for using the axe, or alternatively, they gave their name *to* the axe. Other tribes also used the throwing axe in combat. In some legions, axes like the *francisca* would outnumber swords. As well as being more familiar to poor barbarian recruits, the axe proved to be a handy camp tool and could also be used as a sidearm in close-quarter fighting.

The throwing axe was not a precision weapon, and was best employed in a mass volley prior to the charge. Reconstructions of *francisca* cannot be thrown far, although once they have hit the ground they can tumble some distance, possibly into the legs of an enemy battle-line. The axe is a great shield-smasher, and even if it hits an armoured opponent, it matters not whether the blade or the wooden handle strikes first – the concussive effect of the heavy weapon will be enough to knock the man over.

The Crossbow

Although the hand-held crossbow is popularly associated with the Medieval period, the Late Roman legions may also have employed it as a weapon of war, and known it as an *arcuballista* (plate 30). They certainly were aware of its potential as an accurate missile weapon, and parts of the crossbow mechanism have survived in the ground. A Pictish rock-carving records the fact that these barbarians were also aware of the weapon, presumably from Roman origins. Vegetius records its use by Roman soldiers,[4] and the Late Roman historian Ammianus Marcellinus reports that the Emperor Julian was accompanied on a journey by an escort of *ballistarii*.[5] It seems ridiculous to suppose that this meant his bodyguard consisted of bolt-shooting artillerymen and some historians have suggested that these *ballistarii* were in fact *arcuballistarii*, or crossbowmen. The *arcuballista* is a portable and easy to use weapon, though dreadfully under-powered in comparison with recurve bows of the day, it requires less training to use, but is remarkably accurate at shorter ranges. The *arcuballista* is perhaps useful as a sniper's weapon, advantageous in a siege where one would not want to expose oneself to enemy missiles. Bodyguards may also find the crossbow useful; it is less encumbering than a recurve bow and can be held cocked, ready for immediate use.

Much of Gaius' missile practice took place out on the parade ground, a levelled area just outside the west gate of the fort. A raised platform had been constructed overlooking the area and the unit commander, Sextus Aemilianus, occasionally sat there to imperiously oversee the training of recruits. An indoor archery and javelin range had stood inside the fort for many years, it allowed the troops to practice in the worst winter weathers. Aemilianus had it converted into a riding hall for his horses. The tribune loved horses. It meant that in snow or driving hail, Severus, Gaius and the other shivering recruits would have to fight the numbing pain and hit the targets. Only when they had achieved the required score did Ursinus allow them inside to eat, rest and warm their frozen bodies.

Training in drill and weapon skills, coupled with long training marches onto the Moors or along the cliff top paths, lasted into spring of AD 384. Gradually, the wrath of the drillmaster lessened and the recruits settled into fortress life as legionaries – albeit new, untried and untested legionaries. Peace on the east coast of Britain did not last long in these dark and worrisome days, however. One evening in mid-April, as the sun set the heavens ablaze with crimson clouds and an orange sky, the beacon up on Flamborough Head burst into life. Gaius had not seen it lit before. The thick column of black smoke rose vertically in the still air, and even from the fort next to the beach, all of the garrison could see the flames flickering at the top of the tall beacon tower on the cliff-top. Severus was in a panic, no-one could convince him that barbarian raiders were not about to sail into the harbour any minute. Gaius got some sense out of Ursinus, despite the panic erupting throughout the fort. The beacon was lit because three of the northern lights had been lit. The raiders (whoever they were) had reached the coast several days' march north of Praesidium. The threat to this fort was not great.

All through the night and into the next day the legion was on alert. Civilians living outside the fort grew agitated and nervous. One of the new recruits tried to escape across the fields. Sextus Aemilianus had him stoned to death when the sun rose. The next evening every eye in the garrison was on the beacon tower on the headland, not just those of the sentries. Sure enough, it flickered into life as folk were drawing into their homes for their evening meal. A galloper arrived at the fortress gates within the hour to pass on the dire news. Only the two signal stations north of Praesidium had burst into life this time. The threat was closer. Day dawned and as the garrison broke for lunch, a rider came in from the north, sweating and dusty. His news was unwanted. Two hundred Pictish raiders had landed only one day's march north, below the station guarding Two Bays. These Picts had gone inland on stolen horses to raid and pillage, leaving only a light picket at the boats. Two Bays was 20 miles (32 km) further north along the coastal path. Aemilianus ordered a strong force to march toward Two Bays, he hoped it would catch the Pictish sentries unawares, burn the boats and be ready to trap the returning raiders, arms filled with booty. Severus was chosen to accompany this hastily assembled detachment. Gaius was staying behind to guard the fort. He cursed his luck.

Over 400 legionaries left Praesidium to march northwards. Night fell and Gaius watched the beacon on the headland burst into life once more. The enemy were still at Two Bays. It burned steadily all night. Gaius was on sentry duty in the early morning. He watched the dawn rays catch the white cliffs, and he saw the smoky column snake into the pale blue sky; out to sea he could see the white sails of boats. Twelve sails, twelve Pictish boats. War curachs, stretched-hide boats, each holding twenty barbarian warriors. The alarm horns sounded, trumpets blared and the garrison was shaken out of its sleep. Civilians in the settlement outside the walls ran screaming into the fort, whilst the remaining officers organised the ill-trained soldiers to defend it. Within the hour the boats were beached. The Picts, savage and garishly clad, assaulted the walls of the fort with a fervour.

As archers fired a barrage of arrows at the oncoming raiders, Gaius prepared a handful of *plumbatae* and another of javelins. He waited for the command to throw. Gaius readied a lead-weighted dart behind the parapet; he could not throw it underarm, battlefield style, because the wall in front of him would get in the way. Instead he threw as trained, over arm. His *plumbatae* went wild. The Picts were screaming. Some were shooting back with wooden self bows. A legionary near Gaius was flung back off the wall. The barbarians had lots of ropes as well as burning firebrands. With the ropes the Picts tossed up iron hooks to grapple the parapets, some hooked defenders and dragged them over, flailing, into the ditch. Gaius threw a *spiculum* at a stationary Pict and hit him in the face with the barbed tip. Clutching the shaft of the javelin with desperate fingers, his target also rolled down into the ditch.

For two hours the raiders assaulted the walls whilst others of their number ransacked the civilian settlement nearby. The recruits and younger legionaries proved that they had certainly learnt from the drillmaster. Many Picts were killed by javelin, *plumbata*, arrow or heavy thrown stone. At the sight of a reinforcing unit marching into sight (the entire garrison of forty legionaries from the signal station on the headland), the Picts abandoned the walls and ditches of the fort and fled back to their boats.

The battle was over. The Picts had sailed down the coast and around the headland from Two Bays in the night, using the beacon fires to guide them. No-one knew why they had chosen to strike at Praesidium. It may have been its central role in organising the east coast defences. Perhaps an even larger force was poised to sail south should the knock-out attack succeed. But it did not…

Training picked up again in the days that followed the raid. Armour and shields were handed out for the route marches. Gaius began to reel from the amount of equipment he needed to carry and maintain (and of course replace if he lost or damaged it). Ursinus continued to drill the recruits on the parade ground, now with more emphasis on the sword and shield. They trained with double-weighted wooden swords and wicker shields against both posts, and against one another. They also trained (at first slowly and cautiously) with sharp swords.

The Sword

Since earliest times, the sword had been the weapon of choice for the Roman legions. They had fought Hannibal, Boudicca and Spartacus with the *gladius*, a razor-sharp short sword designed for stabbing attacks into the belly and chest of a foe. Sometime in the second century, however, the longer cavalry sword, the *spatha*, replaced the short *gladius* as the primary weapon of the foot soldier. The *gladius* measured on average 40-50cm while the *spatha* were commonly 65-70cm long. It is thought that a change in fighting style was the main reason for the change in sword. The *gladius* seems suited to fighting at close quarters from behind the traditional curved rectangular shield, while the longer *spatha* was better used when fighting with a large oval shield. The *spatha* gave the legionary the reach he needed to get around this oval shield.

A legionary's sword was fundamental to his role as an infantryman. It was his primary killing weapon, used to stab and thrust, as before, but also capable of slashing and hacking at the head and shoulders of a fleeing soldier.

> ...they learned to strike not with the edge, but with the point. For the Romans not only easily beat those fighting with the edge, but even made mock of them, as a cut, whatever its force, seldom kills, because the vitals are protected by both armour and bones. But a stab driven two inches in is fatal; for necessarily whatever goes in penetrates the vitals. Secondly, while a cut is being delivered the right arm and flank are exposed, whereas a stab is inflicted with the body remaining covered, and the enemy is wounded before he realises it.
>
> Vegetius Book 1:12

Spatha were not crude mass-produced weapons, they were carefully wrought swords, often with pattern-welded blades. These blades were formed from several iron bars, all of differing carbon content, that were twisted into a screw shape and then hammered and folded repeatedly. To this strong, yet flexible core, hardened steel cutting edges were welded. The blades are strong and beautiful, with long straight sides and sharp points. The hilts and pommels were crafted from wood, horn or bone – all organic materials. In earlier centuries, the legionary sword hung on the soldier's right side, but in the fourth century, soldiers wore their swords on the left, traditionally the preserve of centurions and senior officers. Swords sat in a scabbard of wood, sheathed in leather. To protect the tip of the scabbard from knocks, a metal or bone 'chape' was fixed to the scabbard tip; to allow the scabbard to be slung from the shoulder or the waist, a bracket of iron, bronze or bone (a scabbard 'slide') was fitted close to the top. Through it a leather belt was wound, and this allowed the legionary to wear the sword around his waist, or from his shoulder, as he preferred.

In man-to-man combat the sword was used to stab into the body of a foe, but when engaging a shielded target the long *spatha* could be used to reach over the shield to strike the head or neck, the shoulders, the sword arm, or the left leg (which usually led) and was easily visible below the shield.

The Spear

In the fourth century the spear, or *lancea*, was an important factor in legionary warfare. The legions had adopted the oval shield, the long *spatha* sword and the long spear. Traditionally, they threw iron-shanked javelins (*pila*) at their enemy, but by the fourth century, many Roman legionaries carried long spears into battle and waged spear and shield warfare with their foes. The length of these *lancea* is unknown for certain, but may have ranged between 2–2.7m. (plate 4). It is still not known today, however, exactly what proportion of soldiers in a unit carried spears. Was it all of them? Was it just the first rank or first two ranks? Many still carried the *spiculum* (the fourth-century version of the *pilum*) so the *lancea* was probably not a universal weapon. There may even have been a mix of *lancea* and *spicula*, since the *spiculum* made a reasonably good short spear, and could be thrown at the enemy when the time came. Spearheads were often long and leaf shaped, designed to penetrate deeply, cut muscle and rend internal organs with their long cutting blades. Each spear shaft terminated in a ferrule, a sharp iron spike, that was used to plant the spear in the ground during rest periods but also to spear defenceless or wounded foes that were being trampled underfoot. Spear shafts may have been decorated in the Late Roman period with spirals of colour running along them.

Popular with armies for centuries, the spear, used in formation, proved exceptionally efficient. Static units of infantrymen with shields and spears bristling outwards like the spikes of a sea urchin were of great defensive value on their own, even without the legionaries doing anything at all! Cavalry find a wall of spears and shields very intimidating, and infantry units were wary of advancing on Roman spearmen, unless they had long spears themselves with which to reach the Roman foe. That is the great advantage of the spear over other weapons: it has great defensive value and if used in conjunction with others is able to keep an attacker well beyond arm's length. Spears can be used over-arm to stab down onto a foe, over his shield, but to do this the spear must be held near to the midpoint and is greatly foreshortened. In addition to losing the great advantage of the spear – its length – attacking over arm presents a spearman's right arm, armpit and right chest to the attacker. Better, is the under arm spear thrust. The spear is held closer to the butt, which tucks under the forearm. Held like this the spear is stabbed powerfully forward into an enemy without exposing oneself to attack. It also allows better control of the spear shaft for raking aside an enemy spear, or for parrying the spear thrust of a foe.

Reconstructions of spear and shield fighting methods have shown that the spear is effective when used in a dense formation, but is ungainly and disadvantaged when used in open skirmishing warfare. Of course, any modern reconstruction cannot do justice to the power and lethality of these weapons. Any form of weapon re-enactment is bound by strict safety rules, but it is clear that the most vulnerable targets open to a spear-wielding legionary are the face and shins of an enemy warrior – exactly those areas of the body strictly off-limits as target areas in modern battle re-enactments.

The author participated in an experiment to recreate two legionary battle-lines coming into contact. Prior to the shield-walls slamming together, the (blunted) spear-points slid off of the shield boards and everyone involved had to keep their heads down to avoid getting a spear-point in the face. One participant was unlucky enough to receive a very minor cut to the cheek. Spear-points also slid down towards the shins and feet, though with much less danger of serious injury.

The Shield

Mention has been made of the shield during the discussions of sword and spear. Shields have been used by pre-industrial societies since the start of warfare. Their value in hand-to-hand combat is immense and by far eclipses the role played by body armour. The most common type of shield attested in wall paintings and sculpture for the fourth century is circular or oval, and large. Some seem to be dished, rather than flat.

A number of well-preserved Roman shields were discovered at the site of Dura Europus in modern-day Syria (dated to the mid-third century), and these have provided us with fascinating details about Roman shield construction. Broad oval shields were in the majority, and they measured between 107 and 118cm in length, and between 92 and 97cm in width. Although the use of plywood was well known to the Romans, most of the Dura shields were manufactured with planks of poplar wood, 8–12mm thick (figure 6). Two hand holes were cut in the centre, and the space between provided a handgrip, often reinforced with an iron bar. Holes for the stitching on of a rawhide or leather rim were discovered around the outside edges of the shields. In the centre of each shield would be an iron or bronze boss, a dome of metal that protected the hand of the shield-bearer.

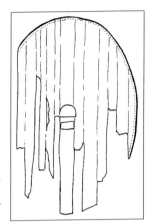

Figure **6**. Surviving shield board from Dura Europus, showing planked design, cut-outs that form both hand-holds and handgrip and stitch holes around the perimeter (after S. James).

Each shield was faced with leather or with linen, which both strengthened the shield and allowed it to be painted. Various shield designs are represented on the fourth-century document called the *Notitia Dignitatum* which gives historians a guide to the shield designs of the period. Paints were not as vivid and as hard-wearing as modern acrylic paints, however. Experiments by the re-enactment group Cohors Quinta Gallorum, operating from the Roman fort at South Shields, have shown that shields can be painted using paint made with an egg base. The yolk gives a slight gloss, but is slightly soft, whilst the 'glair' gives a harder finish, but is more brittle. Glair is made from egg-white which has been whipped to froth and allowed to stand, or strained through a cloth or a sponge. It was found that a mixture of the two works well. How often a soldier was able to repaint his shield is unknown; on campaign, such touching up might prove difficult, but a legionary like Gaius in garrison would no doubt have the time and materials to repaint his shield. Gaius, like other soldiers, also painted on his name and his unit for identification purposes. He most likely painted the inside of his shield any colour he desired, and he may have copied patterns he liked, or even painted a Christian *chi-rho* monogram inside his shield (plate 1).

Shields made the army. Without a shield, a Roman soldier is simply a walking target. Unlike the sword fights of Hollywood movies, hand-to-hand fights did not often turn into 'steel-on-steel' combats with swords clanging on sword with lunges and parries. These weapons, as experience has shown, do not take kindly to such treatment. A shield was the only real defence. As a unit the legionaries could, at an order, lock their large oval shields together to create a defensible barrier from which they could launch spear attacks and repel an enemy charge. This tactic was particularly successful against cavalry. With the *foulkon* manoeuvre, the shields of an entire unit were used to create a shield wall behind which the frontline crouched; the second and third lines lifted up their shields to create a 'roof' that was proof against hostile missile fire (plate 32). Finally, the unit could manoeuvre close to an enemy or a city wall under siege using a tactic called a '*testudo*' (plate 34). Much like a *foulkon*, the shields were used to box in the legionaries, but this formation gave the unit the ability to move, albeit slowly, and could advance toward a hostile city wall without suffering casualties from skirmishers.

Shield training was invaluable for the new recruit, in particular he was expected to use the shield in conjunction with his comrades *en masse*. The shield itself was a tool of war, used to push back the enemy and force a collapse of the enemy battle-line. To this end, the Late Roman army practised a unique form of training activity, whereby a group of soldiers with shields occupied some point, and tried with all their might to remain there in formation whilst other recruits charged them with a shield wall of their own. This game of 'pushing and shoving' would later prove invaluable on the battlefield.

Helmets

If one item of equipment marks out the Late Roman infantryman from his earlier forebears, it is his helmet. The financial and military crisis that almost brought the Roman empire crashing down in the middle of the third century was averted by the extreme measures put in place by Diocletian (AD 284–305). One effect of his reforms was a radical change in weaponry and equipment. The traditional Roman helmets were replaced with much simpler and cheaper forms. Rather than being manufactured as a single one-piece bowl, 'ridge' helmets were now composed of several iron pieces attached together by a ridged strip riveted in place to connect together the metal plates. The simplest of these was made of a bipartite bowl connected by a central ridge. Cheek-plates and a single back-plate were not attached to the helmet with elaborate hinges as they had been in previous centuries, but simple sewn on. This most straightforward of helmet designs is typified by finds from Intercisa in Hungary (figure 7). More than a dozen examples were found there. Similar helmets have been found at Worms, Trier, Augst and Augsburg-Pfersee.

Two helmets discovered at Augsberg-Pfersee were coated with a silver sheathing, and there is some evidence that a number of the Intercisa examples may have been just as elaborately decorated. Such decoration may not have stopped there. Written accounts as well as carved depictions indicate that many helmets were crested. Indeed one famous example from Intercisa has an integral iron crest running down its centre-line. Another, from Augst, has three slots cut into the central ridge, presumably to take a crest box, that will have held either horsehair, or feathers. The author has made such a modification to an Intercisa replica, cutting a single slot into the top of the helmet. The crest box was decorated with over thirty black crow feathers. From beneath the box, a single metal plate was attached which passed snugly through the slot in the top of the Intercisa helm. The portion of the plate that passed into the helmet had been cut into three strips, which were folded out against the inside of the helmet, fitting the crest box firmly in place (figure 8).

Some of the Intercisa-type helmets were also decorated with embossed 'eyes' or 'crosses', the meaning of which is not known.

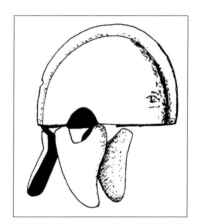

Figure 7. Intercisa helmet (after Bishop).

Figure 8. Possible method of attaching a crest box to a Late Roman ridge helmet. 1. Augst-type helmet with a single slot cut into the helmet crest. 2. Wooden crest box holding horsehair, with a metal plate protruding. It is cut into three equal sections. 3. Detail showing how the metal plate, once inserted into the slot, is opened out to lay flat along the inside of the helmet dome.

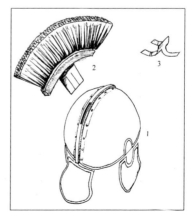

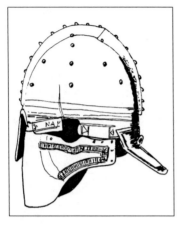

Figure 9. Berkasovo helmet
(after Bishop).

More complex versions of the ridge helm were also constructed for the legions, although the surviving examples differ from one another in details of design. Two helmets were discovered at Berkasovo, in Serbia, both with decorative sheathing and very large cheek-pieces as well as a T-shaped nose guard riveted to the inside rim that looks more Viking than Roman! Unlike the cheek- and back-plates of the Intercisa designs, those of the Berkasovo helmets were attached with buckles (figure 9). The most elaborately decorated Berkasovo helmet is studded with glass paste gems, and must have belonged to a wealthy officer.[6] The bowl of this ornamented helmet was constructed from four sections, rather than two.

Another helmet with four-piece bowl construction was discovered at Concesti, in Romania, and other examples were found at Burgh Castle, in England and Deurne in the Netherlands. All vary in the amount of applied decoration, in the arrangement of rivets and in the shape of cheek- and neck-guards. These more enclosed and ornamented helmets are generally believed to have been worn by cavalry troopers, although it is likely that the infantry also wore helmets such as this when they could get them.[7]

The ridge helmet was accompanied in Late Roman armouries by the *spangenhelm*, which was formed of a multi-piece segmented bowl. It was an Eastern design adopted (if the carvings on the Arch of Galerius can be trusted) by some of the legions en masse by AD 310. The most famous of these *spangenhelm* designs is from Dar al-Madinah, in Egypt (figure 10). Six iron plates are attached to six iron bands, and the whole design was surmounted by a disc riveted to the top of the bowl. Other *spangenhelm* designs vary the number of plates and bands, and feature variations in the style of cheek and neck guards. Some designs feature a nasal guard.

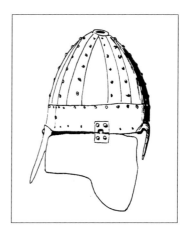

Figure **10**. Dar al-Madinah helmet
(after Bishop).

Any or all of these helmet types could have been worn by legionaries based in fourth-century Britain. Compared to helmet designs from the early imperial period, they are cheap, mass-produced items churned out in their thousands by the state arms factories (*fabricae*) (figure 11). They symbolise an empire on the back-foot, forced to arm and armour the increasing number of soldiers recruited to swell the ranks of the fourth-century legions. Those helmets that boasted silver coatings may well have had such embellishments applied during the life of the item – a soldier could have grabbed some booty on the battlefield or had a decent pay bonus from the Emperor, and used the cash to have his helmet silvered.

Unlike the earlier helmets, which are shown slung on a cord around the neck while on the march, the ridge and *spangenhelms* were not capable of being transported in this way. Rather, they were carried in leather bags fitted with drawstrings. These goat- or calf-skin bags kept the helmets dry and free from rust. If most helmets had some form of precious-metal plating, then the carry-bags would protect that also. While the helmet sat in the bag the soldier would wear his *pilleus*, or Pannonian cap, a pillbox-shaped hat that may well have served as a comfortable helmet liner. The author has worn such a hat and it has provided excellent padding for an Intercisa-style helmet. On particularly gruelling marches or drill exercises in the summer, the soft-wool *pilleus* also soaks up a prodigious amount of sweat.

One final type of head protection must be mentioned: the ringmail coif, a flexible hood of iron rings that is traditionally associated with medieval knights. Wall paintings from Dura Europus and an illustration in the Vergilius Vaticanus manuscript clearly show that some Roman soldiers had adopted coifs as early as the mid-third century (figure 12).

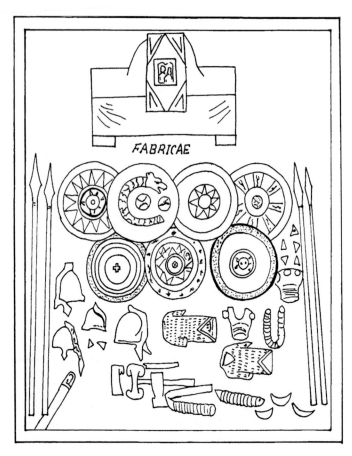

Figure **11**. Taken from the *Notitia Dignitatum*, insignia of the Magistri Officiorum, showing their responsibility for the arms factories (*fabricae*) that supplied the legions of the west (after K.R. Dixon).

Figure **12**. Soldiers depicted in the *Vergilius Vaticanus* manuscript. They wear ringmail coats complete with coifs that cover the head (after Bishop).

This form of head protection requires padding, and unlike the medieval coif, was worn without a helmet to cover it. It is likely that the coif came to the legions via the heavily armoured cavalry warriors ('cataphracts') of the East.

Armour

The shield can be described as a piece of mobile armour and is by far the most useful and versatile method of defence any ancient soldier could take with him onto the battlefield. Not only does it shield part of the body, it can be used to intercept incoming blows and can also be used as a weapon in itself. The helmet is the next essential piece of armour. It is essential on two counts: the head is vulnerable since the soldier must look out from behind his shield to move and fight; secondly, the head is, of course, extremely fragile, despite the existence of the skull, and even a minor trauma here can incapacitate or kill the unfortunate legionary. With a shield and a helmet a soldier in the ancient world has an excellent chance of defending himself.

Body armour provides an additional level of personal protection, but it is a last-ditch defence against the glancing blows that have passed the all-important shield. No ancient soldier would dare to rely on the dead-weight of metal armour hanging off his body to protect it from extreme trauma and deep penetrative wounds. This fact is crucial to understanding where armour was worn, and what from it was made.

In the Late Roman period, body armour came in two main forms: *lorica hamata* (known today as ringmail or, more popularly, chainmail), and *lorica squamata* (known today either as scale armour, 'locked' scale, or lamellar).

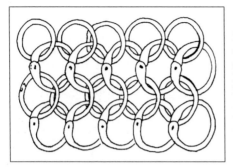

Figure 13. Ringmail from Thorsbjerg showing clearly the Roman method of linking rings to one another; rows of closed, welded rings alternate with rows of rings riveted together (after Engelhardt).

Lorica hamata was fashioned from small iron rings, with each ring passing through two other rings directly above and below it. Roman mail armour was made up of rows of solid rings, alternating with rows of rings that have their ends riveted together. This time-consuming method of manufacture created an incredibly strong 'net' of iron rings that was extremely difficult to force open with fast-moving arrowheads or powerfully thrust spear-points (figure 13). Ringmail was certainly able to prevent deep cuts from slashing blades, as well as the penetration of spears and arrows; but the massive trauma inflicted by a powerful blow during an adrenaline-fuelled battle would easily pass through a thin layer of metal rings. A solid strike from a *spatha*, or a spear, could easily break ribs and crack collar-bones, whether ringmail was worn or not. Consequently, a padded garment was worn beneath the armour. This *subarmalis* can sometimes be seen peeking out from beneath armour on wall-paintings and in mosaics of the period, but no physical examples have survived. Typically, the *subarmalis* is constructed from linen (those depicted are white, which often denotes the use of undyed linen), either a score or more layers glued together, or two layers with wool packed between them and then quilted. Both create a viable 'dead' space behind the ringmail which provides that vital protection from blunt trauma.

Ringmail is prone to rusting, and must be dried quickly and effectively if exposed to rain. The movement of the rings rubbing against one another will prevent the most serious rusting, but in damp conditions the armour will turn brown very easily. This layer of fine rust will stain the *subarmalis* or any tunic that the soldier wears beneath it.

Contrary to popular opinion, although heavy, this form of armour is very flexible. While ringmail shirts from the earlier imperial period were short-sleeved and waist-length, by the fourth century the shirts often reached to the mid-thigh and down to the elbow or even wrist. Such shirts, containing many more rings in their makeup, were even heavier!

Mail shirts found at Caerleon in Wales, South Shields in England, Buch, Künzing and Bertoldsheim in Germany, and Dura Europus in Syria show a remarkable uniformity in the size of the iron rings used, with an empire-wide standard of 7mm external diameter and 1mm thickness. A number of these mail coats were found rolled up by their former owners. Just as helmets were transported in waterproof leather bags, there is evidence that ringmail was rolled up, stored and carried in a cylindrical leather case.[8]

Lorica squamata was made up of small metal plates that were sewn onto a linen or leather backing. The plates were often bronze or brass, but iron scales are also known. Each scale was punctured with pairs of holes that enabled the manufacturer to sew the scales both to the backing fabric, to their neighbours and to a horizontal linen thread. Earlier scale was only sewn to a horizontal thread, and resembled 'fish scale'. The leather backing also acted as an additional *subarmalis*, although a suit of padding was still required, particularly because the locked scale could not extend below the waist. Finds of scale from the third century are as common as rings from *lorica hamata,* and the representational evidence in the fourth century suggests that both ringmail and scale were equally popular with the legions. Bronze scale looks impressive and is not as badly affected by damp. In addition, the armour is easy to wear and much lighter than an equivalent-sized shirt of ringmail. Because the shirt is made rigid by the scales, it must have a full-length opening to allow the wearer to put it on. Once on, the scale shirt is fastened up with buckles. Most modern re-creations place this vulnerable opening at the side, under the arm, where the seam cannot be exploited by an enemy thrust. Integral arms cannot be made into a suit of scale armour due to the inflexibility of the design, but sleeves of scale can be attached with buckles and straps most successfully.

Lorica squamata does have its drawbacks, which explains the historical survival of ringmail and scale together in the same army, the same legions, perhaps even in the same squads. On a practical level, threads can break when they get caught, scales can come off and gaps can appear in the armour. Where ringmail is durable and tough, yet prone to damp and rust, scale is light and comfortable, yet needs regular maintenance.

Locked scale armour was inflexible. With each plate wired to the backing and to its neighbours, there was no movement. The author has discovered that modern examples of locked scale ride up against the wearer's throat when a climb is attempted. In addition, the scales do not expand or contract like the rings of a *hamata* shirt, and this makes climbing uphill very difficult; when a deep breath is required, the scale refuses to expand and one can feel restricted and short of breath. The answer of course is to loosen the straps, but at the expense of opening up a split in the side of the scale suit.

A final form of body armour had always been utilised by the Roman legions to some extent over the previous centuries: it was leg armour, commonly known as greaves (*ocrea*). In the earlier imperial period it seems the centurions wore a set of bronze or iron greaves and these were often decorated. By AD 100, and possibly earlier, leg protection was becoming popular amongst other ranks. In the third century soldiers are shown on wall-paintings at Dura Europus wearing iron greaves, and a fine example of around the same date has been preserved from Künzing in Germany. Although there are no pictorial representations of greaves surviving from the fourth century, Maurice in the Strategikon recommends that front-rank legionaries wear greaves, either of iron or wood. The Strategikon dates from the late 500s, and it is extremely likely that greaves continued in use from the third century through the fourth and into the fifth. Iron greaves used by the Roman army protected the shins, from ankle to knee. They were folded around the front and sides of the lower leg, and attached with straps of leather. Greaves were essential for the front-rank soldiers. Their shields were not big enough to protect shins unless the order was given for the frontline to kneel and ground its shields.

The author has manufactured iron greaves based on the Künzing model and found that even a fairly thin iron sheet can still protect the shins adequately from moderate trauma. After being cut to shape, the greave is bent down its centre giving a line of strength that faces forward. The greave is then gently and repeatedly bent to form a comfortable fit around the lower leg. Both upper and lower edges are 'turned' in order to prevent the edge of the greave digging into the skin. Padding is essential, and thick leg wraps or a padded layer of cloth wrapped or tied around the lower leg, serves this purpose well.

The wooden greaves mentioned in the *Strategikon* are unlikely to have been fashioned in a single piece. More likely, they were made to a 'splint' pattern, similar to the iron strip-type greaves found at Valsgärde in Sweden and dated to the seventh century. These strips of hardwood were most likely curved and shaped and attached closely to one another by leather straps.

CHAPTER IV

Perks of the Job: 385–387 AD

To pacify the army and to explain the reason why its supplies were
held up, [the praetorian prefect] was obliged to go in person to visit
the troops, whose surliness was increased by shortage of food and
who in any case are traditionally rough and brutal in their behaviour
to civil functionaries.

Ammianus Marcellinus 14.10

The end of August in AD 385 was a time of plenty. The military store-
houses (*horrea*) were bursting with grain and the unit was busy preparing
for one of the three *stipendia*, the legionary pay-days that were traditionally marked with ceremonies, parades and inspections. Both Gaius
and Severus spent time in the evening polishing metalwork, sharpening
blades, and oiling leather straps, shield covers, bags and belts. Veterans
took out their best tunics and cloaks, reserved for just such an occasion
while the younger men had to make do with their (hopefully) cleaner
spare tunic. Fraying tunics needed mending, cloaks and trousers had to be
washed. Ribbons were passed around all of the barrack rooms and tied to
spear-heads and helmets. Fresh horse hair or bird feathers were also used
to decorate the helmet crests. This was an exciting time to get noticed and

to make your mark on the parade ground. It was one of the few times that the legion would come together in one place, when those men on detached duty would all return to the fort to collect their pay.

Legionary Pay

The *stipendium* had nearly always been paid, as military custom demanded, in three instalments, probably on 1 January, 1 May and 1 September and had always been a grand occasion. For the soldiers of the Legio Praesidiensis this still held true, although the payout was hardly a fortune. The last time this annual wage (*stipendium*) had been increased was a century-and-a-half ago despite rampant inflation across the empire! Historians argue about the exact sum of money paid out, but it is unlikely to have been more than 1800 *denarii*.[9] To give some idea of the paltry sum that the *stipendium* had become, the price of a common tunic around AD 100 was 3 *denarii* (according to a surviving tablet from Vindolanda[10]). The Edict of Diocletion dating from AD 301, however, sets the price of a woman's third quality dalmatic tunic at 3000 *denarii*, almost twice the annual *stipendium* of a legionary soldier!

On the morning of 1 September, the eight-man squads formed up outside their barrack blocks. Marching behind the file-leader (*caput contubernii*) they left the fort through the western gate and formed up on the parade ground in their assigned positions. The legion looked magnificent, summer sun glinting from polished ridge helmets and long spear-heads, the breeze animating ribbons, banners and nodding horse-hair crests. The file-leaders, the experienced veterans, stood in the front rank. The officers, like Ursinus, a *centenarius*, commanding perhaps 100 men, eyed their men sternly. A *ducenarius*, one of the senior officers that probably commanded 200 men, paced up and down expectantly. At the tribunal sat Aemilianus, surrounded by his aides and secretaries. Tables had been set up, piled high with sacks and chests. Tablets of wax and of wood were in hand to record all payments. But in reality, today was more about the parade and the inspection rather than the money.

Gaius could see the crowds gathered along the perimeter of the drill field. They had come out from the settlement to watch husbands, brothers and friends. There would be drill practice, battle manoeuvres, salutes to Magnus Maximus, to the *Dux*, to Aemilianus, pledges of loyalty to the imperial family and, of course, an inspection. On such a day there might even be decorations and promotions – perhaps on days like this the old-timers would step out of the ranks and receive the *honesta missio* (honourable discharge) that followed twenty years' military service. To qualify for full privileges the veteran would need to serve at least twenty-four years and receive an *emerita missio*.

Of course, the Late Roman soldier did not risk life and limb each year simply for the price of a third-rate tunic. The *stipendium* was an established tradition, but in reality the bulk of the soldier's pay came in the form of gifts (called donatives) and rations of food and clothing (*annonae*). Donatives had been a long standing part of the imperial military system. To ensure the loyalty of the troops, many emperors had, since the time of Claudius, offered them large sums of money. These payments often occurred on the emperor's accession to the throne and then at five-yearly intervals. Of course, in this period there were usually two co-emperors in the West and two more in the East increasing the number of possible donatives... In AD 360 the Emperor Julian awarded a donative of five gold coins (*solidi*) and one pound of silver (roughly equal to four more *solidii*) to his loyal troops, which represents a fairly typical amount for a donative. The five-yearly (or 'quinquennial') donative seems to have been around five *solidii*. Obviously, these were neither regular nor reliable payments.

The most important aspect of the soldier's pay was the *annonae*, a ration which varied with rank and position. Foot soldiers like Gaius and Severus received a single yearly ration, whilst those of *semissalis* rank (the file leaders and other junior officers such as standard-bearers and aides) received one-and-a-half years' ration. Ursinus and the other *centenarii* received two-and-a-half, whilst the more senior *ducenarii* received three-and-a-half. Every soldier, whatever his rank, collected the rations due to him from the storehouse piecemeal as he needed them throughout the year. Grain, olive oil, wine and both cured and fresh meat were the common daily foodstuffs of Roman soldiers everywhere, but here in Britannia the imported wine was often replaced with wheat beer (*cervesa*) and the imported oil replaced with animal fat. Here were the essentials of life! It is likely that vegetables were also part of the *annonae*. Radishes, beans, beetroot, and lentils appear on the Vindolanda tablets from northern Britain, but leeks, cabbages, carrots, peas, onions, shallots, turnips, parsnips, celery and asparagus were all grown in the British provinces during the Roman period. Evidence for the consumption of eggs, cheese, honey, oysters, nuts, fish, native fruits and milk are also found on forts throughout the province.

In AD 445 the Emperor Valentinian III put a value on the *annonae* (as the rations were dispensed in the North African provinces, at least). It was calculated that one *annona* was worth four *solidii* per annum, which gives us some idea of its worth to the soldier in Britannia, especially when compared to the donative 'bribes' of the emperors.

To the modern eye, a life in the legions of the Late Roman army may not seem very attractive, but for a hungry tenant farmer without prospects, the army provided good food on a regular basis, safety, camaraderie and excellent medical facilities. Of course, promotion and the potential wealth that went with it was also a significant draw.

It was December at Praesidium, the sea was an iron grey, washing white foam onto the seaweed-strewn beach. Most seabirds had migrated away, only herring gulls, oyster catchers and sanderlings could be still seen. Gaius was beach-combing with Athulf, the squad's *caput contubernii* or file-leader across the chalk shingle. All manner of useful materials could be found, such as pieces of jet, small semi-precious stones that could be polished, bird-feathers, flints for fire-starting, and flat stones suitable for sharpening blades. There were two men of *semissalis* rank in the eight-man squad, one senior (the file-leader) and one junior (the file-closer). Athulf was the file-leader, in command of the eight men, the mule and the two barrack-rooms that they all shared. He had to keep them going, get them organised, chastise them, tutor them and give them their marching orders. Athulf was of Frankish blood. The Franks were a barbarian tribe that had been defeated and settled in parts of Gaul. Many Franks like Athulf had joined the legions, becoming part of the civilised world, so much a part that they would fight against their own folk to defend it. He was an intense, moody man to whom the squad rarely talked.

Gaius asked him plainly, why had he not drawn any rations from the granary recently? Christmas was approaching and the soldiers traditionally held feasts on 20 December. It was an old pagan festival, the Saturnalia, but the soldiers at Praesidium had stubbornly stuck to that date when celebrating the birth of the Christ.

'Because I'm clever,' answered Athulf. 'I go hungry, borrow a little, get by, then I go to the storehouse after Christmas, when there's nothing left. I ask for my *annona*, as much as I've managed to save up – and of course the quartermaster cannot supply me. By law he must, or he must commute the rations to gold coin. You know how hard it is for us legionaries to get hold of coin these days. I'll have a pouchful of coins to do with as I will after the Christian festival …'

This was bending the rules rather than corruption. Coin could be saved, it could be used to purchase slaves or be lent out in order to earn interest, it could be used as a deposit on a loan or to make the kind of purchase that simply could not be bartered for with rations of food. Gold coin (and only gold – the silver coinage always fell victim to inflation) was often preferable to rations. It lasted longer of course, and for a *semissalis*, and even more so for a *centenarius*, *ducenarius* or staff officer, who all received extra rations in lieu of pay, coin could be saved. Bread, bacon, oil and cheese could not.

Gaius asked another question. Why was it that the quartermaster (the *praefectus castrorum*) was unable to supply Athulf with his rations? There must be a big surplus – their squad was two men short, in fact there were only a dozen squads that *weren't* missing a man or two. And yet Sextus Aemilianus was refusing to accept any further recruits till the summer. Why?

'Everyone plays the game, Gaius, from different ends and with different means. Aemilianus sends off his papers to Eboracum. And the papers say we are a full-strength unit. One-thousand two-hundred biscuit-eaters, fighting fit, eager to kill the Saxon and the Pict. We know there are maybe one-thousand legionaries here, if that. The tribune is claiming rations for dead men. He doesn't bring in replacements, he pockets the *annonae* for himself. And much of that surplus his men sell in the town for gold coin.'

'Boots and Straps'

In AD 386, the soldiers' pay also came in the form of clothing. During the more prosperous periods, the legionary was paid wholly in coin and had rations and clothing deducted as expenses. For the Late Roman army of the fourth century, inflation proved a wild and unpredictable beast and rather than trust the vicissitudes of the runaway economic system, the emperors favoured the allocation of essentials such as food and clothing directly to the men in lieu of pay.

A surviving Egyptian papyrus records deductions from the *stipendium* of a first-century legionary. It records all deductions in the local Eastern currency. The deductions include 10 drachmas for hay (used as bedding perhaps), 80 drachmas for food, 12 drachmas for 'boots and straps', and 145½ drachmas for clothing. The Roman army considered each of these essential enough that no choice in their procurement was given to the soldier. He *had* to have them. Little evidence of this type survives into the fourth century, but there is more than a fair chance that the military commanders in AD 386 still considered food, clothing, boots and hay to be just as essential for the fighting man. It's not known if the Late Roman clothing ration was issued three times a year, like the *stipendium*.

We've already looked at rations – but what about clothing and the enigmatic 'boots and straps'? A law of Emperor Valens put the cost of clothing a new recruit at 6 *solidii*. A military cloak was reported to have cost 1 *solidi* in AD 396, and so the legionary clothing ration can only have provided the essentials which were: a tunic (*dalmatica*), an under-tunic (*subucula*), cloak (*sagum*), Pannonian hat and 'boots and straps' (as that Egyptian papyrus refers to them). The straps may have been socks (*udones*), or leg-wraps (*fascia*). Several items seem to be missing. Trousers (*bracae*) were never essential for the Roman soldier, even in the Late Empire when they were particularly fashionable, a man could still be seen in public wearing only a tunic. Soldiers in Britannia may have purchased *bracae* separately however, since the climate certainly encourages their use! The military belt is not mentioned in any surviving monetary accounts. Yet the belt (*balteus*) was incredibly important to the Roman soldier in every age. Since coinage was so hard to come by in the fourth century, the state had to provide the essentials, and a military belt was certainly essential. Even out of armour and in 'civilian' attire, the military belt set the soldier apart from the crowd and told others of his status. The military belts also incorporated a large amount of ornate metalwork, and it is hard to imagine a fresh recruit being left to acquire one on his own.

Clothing was certainly produced by state-run factories in the Western Empire, but these workshops may have focussed more on the demands of the high-profile mobile army, the *comitatensis*, rather than frontier units like the Praesidiensis. Some commanders were introducing clothing allowances in cash at this time, giving the men a fixed value of coin to give them the freedom to purchase local clothing themselves. The motivation behind this decision may simply have been the growing difficulty in organising and operating a state-run clothing ration – shipping cloaks, blankets and tunics hundreds of miles to the more remote forts.

Reliance on local manufacture was a realistic option for the frontier forces, who did not move around like the *comitatensis*. For troops of the Legio Praesidiensis based at the coastal fort, their clothes and other items of equipment will have, in the main, come from a store / commissary within the fort, or attached to it. There would be a great deal of local flavour in the weaves, the colours and the designs of the various garments. The tailors will have won some kind of military contract to supply the army and they may have been local (based in the town outside the fort) or they may have been more centrally based (in Eboracum or Cataractonium). This would allow them to supply the garrisons of several forts simultaneously.

Roman soldiers in the fourth century, whether stationed in Britannia or Egypt, Syria or Illyricum wore the same style and type of clothes. This was less of a uniform, as we know it today, and more of a common military fashion. Even the emperors themselves adopted this fashion, not as uniforms denoting actual status within the military machine (as male members of the British royal family, such as Prince Phillip and Prince Harry, do today) but as Fidel Castro or Saddam Hussein – an appeal to the common soldier. This empire-wide fashion took the form of a decorated long-sleeved tunic, an under-tunic, trousers (*bracae*), a wide military belt, enclosed marching boots, a pill-box hat and a long rectangular army cloak (plate 35). This fashion is represented in mosaics found at the Villa Armerina in Sicily, in illuminated manuscripts of the fifth and sixth centuries as well as a number of wall paintings. As with all historical fashions, the clothing of a fourth-century legionary is a product of its age. Stepping inside those clothes certainly helps one to step into the past. The author has studied surviving fourth- and fifth-century examples as well as pictorial representations to manufacture a complete set of fourth-century soldier's clothing.

The Tunic

For the Roman, a tunic was the essential piece of attire. In the first and second centuries tunics were either T-shaped or square, but always baggy and short-sleeved or sleeveless. By the third century, a new style of tunic called the *dalmatica* had become very fashionable amongst the soldiers who introduced it into Roman society. This was barbarian-style costume, favoured by the numerous German recruits into the legions and popularised by some of the earlier emperors who wanted to 'curry favour' with the army. The *dalmatic* tunic had long sleeves which tapered to the wrist. It was often white or off-white and was invariably elaborately decorated. In the fourth century, this decoration followed a certain style. Cuffs were always decorated with two coloured bands, and a pair of decorated stripes (*clavi*) ran from the neckline down both the chest and the back. The fashion also included decorated circles (*orbiculi*) that were located at the corners of the hem (front and back), and two much larger *orbiculi* on each shoulder (plate 36). The tunics of soldiers, noblemen, children and the poor were all decorated in this way. There were variations, of course, but Gaius and his comrades would have worn tunics of this style. Remarkably, all of the decoration was woven into the tunic on the loom and not added later as embroidery. Because of its value, however, when a tunic wore out, the *clavi* and *orbiculi* were routinely cut out and stitched onto a new, plain tunic – thus saving money. This recycling of expensive materials is attested in the archaeological record. Decoration varied; a simpler tunic might have very narrow *clavi* and small *orbiculi*, featuring a simple repeated geometric pattern. At the other end of the scale the *clavi* and *orbiculi* could be extremely wide with intricate geometric motifs. Such tunics were a mark of status.

Most of the tunics recovered are of wool manufacture, although linen tunics are also known. This matches the illustrations in paintings, manuscripts and mosaics, where an off-white tunic seems most common – an unbleached or undyed wool tunic will appear to be an off-white colour. The natural colours of the sheep often determined the colours of clothing for the poor. White, off-white, tan and brown predominate. Most decorative elements were a shade of purple, but others were known. There were red, green, blue, yellow and orange tunics, with decorative elements woven in yellow, white, black, brown, red or green, but these dyes all pushed up the price of a tunic.

A tunic was long: unbelted it often fell below the knees. Once a belt had been fastened, the tunic could be pulled up and over to make it more manageable. In practice, this creates a very baggy top, but some illustrations depict tunics whose over folds completely obscure the wearer's waist belt.

An under-tunic (*subucula*) was not essential, but is often seen in mosaics of the period, peeking from under the tunic at the cuffs and at the neck. It was invariably white, which suggests it was of linen manufacture – linen is very comfortable to wear on the skin. Of course, an under-tunic was greatly valued in the cooler climate of Britannia as an extra layer. In cold weather it was usual to wear more than one tunic, and a poor man might be forced to wear all the tunics that he owned.

The Leggings

The barbarian fashion of northern Europe not only introduced the legions to the long-sleeved *dalmatica*, but also to the *bracae* – the long trousers. Celtic and Germanic tribesmen had worn *bracae* for centuries, and traditionally the Romans had scorned their use as effete and uncultured. The adoption of barbarian-style clothing in the third century changed all that. Throughout the empire in the late fourth century, long trousers were routinely worn with long-sleeved decorated tunics. These *bracae* were quite tight-fitting and made of wool, and it is quite probable that they were all made with integral feet that served as a sock. One contemporary wall-painting shows a pair of *bracae* with belt loops and belt being carried by a slave (figure 14). We do not know if all trousers had belt loops. Barbarian *bracae* were kept up by rolling over the hem at the waist and stitching it to create a tunnel through which a cord-tie could be fed. *Bracae* may have been made by tailoring woollen cloth or by sprang-work, a method of knotting fabric which has some similarities to knitting. Sprang trousers can be made close-fitting yet still allow legs to bend, but cloth *bracae* must be made in a looser fit if the feet are to get through. For centuries, leg-wrappings (*fascia*) had been worn by Romans who needed some form of leg protection, either from the cold weather or from nettles, brambles and the muck of the fields. Often, these wraps were simply rectangles of woollen cloth wrapped around the lower leg and fixed with ties (figure 15). Farmers, the infirm, travellers and huntsmen are habitually depicted wearing this type of clothing in wall paintings. The emperors began to wear them too. Augustus, often ill and always feeling the cold, wore *fascia*, and two centuries later Emperor Alexander Severus wore them as a fashionable item. In the fourth century, the Roman soldier may have worn these rectangles of cloth to protect his expensive *bracae* from vegetation and mud. Even more likely in the fourth century, however, are the long strips of cloth commonly depicted on the mosaics of the Villa Armerina on Sicily and in a manuscript depicting the crucifixion from the Biblioteca Laurenziana, Florence. In the Great Hunt Mosaic, famous for its depiction of wonderfully decorated fourth-century tunics, many of the hunters are wearing strips of cloth wound around their lower legs (figure 15). The British Army called these articles of clothing 'puttees' – the Romans also

Figure **14**. Man carrying footed trousers, showing both the belt and the integral belt loops. From a tomb painting at Silistra, Bulgaria (after Croom).

termed them *fascia*. In practical experiments, the long-strip *fascia* need to be bound tightly, first wrapping around the ankle several times before circling the lower leg. If each time one of the ends passes the front of the leg the fabric is folded over, the final result certainly resembles the bindings of those on The Great Hunt. After wrapping several times tightly below the knee they can be tied off. On an ascent of England's highest mountain, Scafell Pike, in winter, the *fascia* proved their worth. While crossing a bog called the Great Moss, the author went up to his knees in mud without a spot touching his *bracae*. Later they were easily washed out and dried. After the author marched many miles through forest underbrush, heather and thorns, he also began to appreciate the protection that the *fascia* offered.

Spring 386. Winter was a distant memory and the spring of AD 386 promised to be fruitful. Lambing season had begun early and cattle could be moved out onto the pastures, for the grass had begun to grow again. Many of the legionaries owned land outside the walls and grew wheat or barley and cultivated vegetables such as turnips, carrots, cabbage and onions. Of course the military commanders new that better weather meant that the tribes beyond the frontier could begin raiding once again. Spies had reported a good deal of activity amongst the Picts of the far north. The

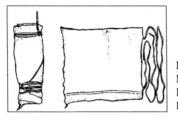

Figure 15. Leg-wrap from Søgaards Mose, shown wrapped around the leg, and also unwrapped (after Van Driel-Murray).

governors of the British provinces looked to the *dux britanniarum* for a strategy. There would be little direction from the newly installed Emperor. Magnus Maximus was ruling the western half of the empire from Trier. Theodosius, ruling in the East was the stronger partner and a threat to the British usurper, but he was too preoccupied with military affairs there to move against Maximus. The veteran British commander had his sights set on Rome, and on eliminating Gratian's younger brother, Valentinian III, not on the growing Pictish threat behind him.

At midday lunch, whilst the men sat on the river bank and unwrapped cooked ham and cheese bread, talk went about of the galloper that had arrived from Eboracum. It was said that the Duke of the Britains, Caelius,[11] was planning a tour of the east-coast defences, and that he would begin with Praesidium. Athulf was grumbling, he predicted a lot of pressure from Ursinus and the other officers, extra work duties and perhaps some covering up of bad practices. Severus worried because he had sold all of his javelins to a legionary in one of the other cohorts and would be called to account. Severus worried about everything, though. Marcus Gavius was laughing. This man was the file closer, a *semissalis*. No-one liked old Gavius; he was a living skeleton, his face sharp as an axe and he was as argumentative as he was thin, but he could march further and carry twice as much as any man in the entire legion. Ursinus was heard to say that Gavius was so thin none of the enemy could ever hit him with their swords – that nothing could kill him. Marcus Gavius wryly commented that the Dux would at last find out all of Aemilianus' dirty secrets and then force him to fall on his own sword. He laughed loudly and everyone turned away.

Two girls from the *vicus* had been sent across by their mothers with a couple of jugs of wheat beer, and Gaius was more interested in Modesta, the pretty blonde, than talk of the imminent inspection from headquarters. She obviously liked Gaius, and after the two girls had gone there was much joking at Gaius' expense.

In the days leading up to the inspection, the clothing ration arrived early – at Aemilianus' request. The ration had arrived by boat and the *centenarii* marched to the east gate with a working party to carry their allotment back to the barrack blocks. There was always much excitement and apprehension, there were plenty of new clothes in the ration, but also some recycled pieces, and some items that other units did not want. Outside the barrack block, Athulf's squad lined up and each man received one cloak, one tunic, a pair of leg wraps and a pair of *bracae*. Gaius was not amused with his tunic; it was made to fit a giant. Severus was equally dismayed with his, which had on the chest a stain that looked unpleasantly like an old blood splash. With only two days until the inspection, both men had to urgently find solutions to their problems. Severus visited the fuller in the vicus, and despite his slaves treading good-quality urine into the garment, the stain stuck fast. All Severus could do was reverse the tunic and hide the stain, for the most part, with his cloak.

Gaius had a more difficult task. The oversized tunic was richly decorated with *clavi* and *orbiculi* in deep purple, black and blue. He carefully unpicked the stitching and removed this decoration, selling it in the vicus for 2 *solidii*.[12] The plain tunic he bartered for a sheath-knife with a soldier in the next barrack block who was built like an ox. The 2 *solidii* enabled Gaius to purchase a tunic of his size with some simple decoration. It didn't really reflect the fact that he was a legionary with three years' service under his belt, but it fit him well enough and was clean and unpatched. This was the reality of the clothing ration. No-one quite seemed to get what they wanted, but with a little ingenuity the soldiers at Praesidium could come to a satisfactory arrangement.

The Cloak and Brooch

Cloaks were an essential item of male Roman attire, from emperors down to swineherds. The cloak was at once an overcoat and jacket, and an expression of modesty (much as hats were in the nineteenth century). Dining cloaks were commonly worn at dinner parties. Soldiers had favoured a thick rectangular cloak called the *sagum* for centuries, and such was its association with the army that it became a symbol of war. The most commonly depicted colours of the military cloak in wall paintings are various shades of browns (particularly yellow-browns) and red. Many historians believe that the figures wearing red cloaks are officers.

In the fourth century, cloaks were sometimes decorated, although not as lavishly as the tunics. Fringed cloaks were popular, as were cloaks that had been woven with two *orbiculi* in their bottom corners (figure 17). A wall painting from Silistra, Bulgaria, shows a man carrying a cloak (with brooch still fastened) that is decorated with a pair of swastikas – a fairly ubiquitous religious symbol in the ancient world. More lavish cloaks for command officers and members of the imperial household were of patterned cloth. Alternatively, they wore pure white cloaks that had a *tablion*, an angled square of coloured cloth, set halfway down the front edge of the cloak.

Above left: Figure **16**. Decorated cloak, worn by a hunter on the Piazza Armerina mosaic, Sicily. It is fringed and has two *orbiculi* woven into the fabric.

Above right: Figure **17**. Man with a cloak ready to wear; it is interesting to note that the crossbow brooch has been left fastened. From a tomb wall-painting, Silistra, Bulgaria (after A. Croom).

From a practical stand-point, the military cloak had many uses for the Roman soldier on campaign. Out in bad weather, a thick cloak is essential. More than likely the wool fabric still retained its natural oils to provide a degree of waterproofing. Even without it, in the author's experience, a thick cloak is good against high winds, biting cold and rain. The long *sagum* can also be pulled up to create a hood if needed. Of course, the uses that the soldier could put a cloak to do not stop there, which is echoed in the modern infantryman's poncho of the US Army, which can be used as an improvised shelter, a tarpaulin or a rain garment. Modern experiments have found that the *sagum* makes an excellent blanket, it can serve as a groundsheet and can even be tied to another *sagum* to make up a tent canvas. The earlier Roman writer Tacitus recorded the use of cloaks as shields, rolled around the left arm of legionaries when they were surprised by rebels at night. He also relates how some of the Roman auxiliary troops had even used their cloaks as makeshift sails! There are other uses too: four men can hold each corner and carry a wounded comrade in an improvised stretcher, and rolled up and slung over the shoulder the *sagum* can be transformed into a 'blanket-roll' to carry extra clothing and small items of equipment. More details of how the fourth-century soldier may have used his equipment on the march is discussed in Chapter 6.

A cloak requires a brooch to fasten it, and this brooch was always worn on the right shoulder (to allow freedom of movement for the right arm). From the Silistra wall painting, we know that brooches could be fastened permanently to cloaks. They are common archaeological finds at military sites across the empire, testifying to their tendency to come undone and fall off. Crossbow brooches were most fashionable in the fourth century, they were cast mainly in bronze and could be plated with silver or gold (figure 18). A number of examples of gold crossbow brooches have even been discovered bearing inscriptions that suggest they might have been gifts from an emperor to a trusted officer. We know from representations that the crossbow brooch was always worn in a specific way, with the 'cross' part of the 'crossbow' facing the ground, the long body of the brooch standing up on top of the shoulder. The brooch marked the soldier out, it was a symbol of the power that he represented, and it was a brooch and a badge favoured by all members of the imperial bureaucracy.

There were two other brooch styles utilised by British troops: the first, the disc brooch, was slowly eclipsed by the crossbow brooch; the second, the penannular brooch, was a peculiarly north-western brooch type. It had existed prior to the Roman invasions, and would survive the Romans to be worn by Saxons and Vikings. The penannular brooch was a 'broken circle' with a pin that could slide along the ring. It was an ingenious design: the pin was folded back and pierced the cloak, the ring was then brought over and the end of the pin passed through the gap in the ring. Once there, the ring was slid around to lock the end of the pin against it. This brooch seems far more sturdy and reliable than the early Roman fibula or the fourth-century crossbow brooch. It is no wonder the design lasted a thousand years with only cosmetic changes (figure 19).

Legionaries in previous centuries also wore a type of cloak sometimes called a *paenula*, a hooded cloak. This item of clothing was intended for outdoor wear; it was favoured by travellers, soldiers and anyone working outdoors for any time in bad weather. Generally, the cape was semi-circular, included a hood, and was usually stitched from the neck down across the chest. Some were long, others just covered the head and shoulders. It is unclear whether soldiers in the fourth century wore these hooded capes, but Romano-British civilians certainly did. There are a host of names associated with the cloaks, from *paenula* to *byrrus*, *caracallus* to *cucullus*, but these names cannot be matched up with specific styles of cape. It may be they refer to the same garment just as jacket, coat, waterproof, raincoat and overcoat may all be terms that apply to the same twenty-first-century garment.

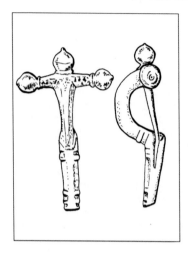

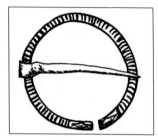

Left: Figure **18**. Crossbow brooch from St. Paul's, Lincoln (after E. Wilson).

Above: Figure **19**. Penannular brooch from the fourth century (after Laing).

The British troops would certainly have heard the terms '*byrrus Britannicus*' and '*cucullus*', since both terms are evidenced in the written record. Practical trials of a long, hooded cloak in torrential downpours confirm its usefulness in bad weather. Thick woollen cloth, together with an ankle-length design, make the cape virtually wind-proof and able to protect against prolonged rain. Carried on the march in case of heavy rain, the author also found another use for the thick cape: as a sleeping bag. The ankle-length style can be wrapped around the body, the hood can be pulled over the face, and the soldier can sleep snugly even on a frosty winter's night. However, the Edict of Diocletion does mention much thinner hooded cloaks – perhaps thinner materials (such as goatskin), different lengths, or cloak shapes are an explanation for the numerous names for this type of garment.

The Belt

Civilians across the empire belted their tunics using simple cords or thin leather straps. Some may have had buckles, but these will have been unadorned. In contrast, the soldier and (in the bureaucratically dominated fourth century) the majority of civil servants wore an impressive leather belt (*balteus*), heavily ornamented with metal fittings. These belts were badges of rank that went together with the crossbow brooch to mark out the wearer as a government official, a soldier, tax collector or other member of that oppressive military and administrative system that continually exploited the lower classes. For the soldier the belt was important:

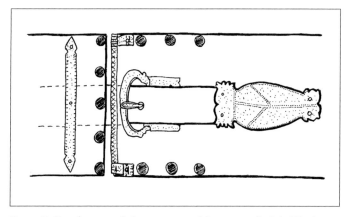

Figure **20**. Fourth-century belt, reconstructed from grave finds in Winchester (after K.R. Dixon).

it meant he could retain his status even when dressed in civilian garb and without his distinctive arms and armour. Units that performed dishonourably in battle might be punished by standing in some visible place around the fort wearing their tunic unbelted; although this might not seem too severe, it obviously meant a great deal to the soldiers. Such was the power of the *balteus*. By Gaius' time the leather belts had reached extreme proportions, some were as wide as 10cm and so required rectangles of bronze rivetted on to keep the belt flat and stiff (figure 20). There is also evidence that belts might be made up of two layers of leather, stitched together and sandwiching a third layer of linen between them. The emphasis was on a big, wide, thick belt that was impossible to ignore!

The metal fittings could be incredibly elaborate. One of the most famous finds of belt parts in Britain comes from Dorchester-on-Thames. It contained a buckle, a strap-end (a tapered bronze plate that stopped the belt end from fraying), nine stiffeners (around 8cm long, indicating the width of this particular belt), two terminal bars for each end of the *balteus* and four suspension rings. These are bronze rings that would hang from the belt and allow equipment to be carried from the belt. Such a system is used by most modern armies today. What did the soldier hang from these equipment loops? Perhaps a pouch, a knife, keys, a whetstone, a bronze toilet set, perhaps even a sword if two suspension rings were used in conjunction.

Although the belts were impressively wide, the strap that fed through the buckle was obviously very narrow, and it seems, very long – at times being looped up, tucked into the belt over the hip and being left to dangle on the soldier's thigh, the metal strap end swinging as the legionary walked. Belts depicted on wall-paintings are either brown (denoting the natural leather) or red (denoting a belt that has been painted). A painted *balteus* is impressive; baldrics, sword scabbards and belts may all have been painted by the legionary.

The Duke of the Britains arrived at Praesidium with his cavalry. Trumpets were sounded and from within the fort Ursinus' cohort filed out of the south gate (*porta principalis sinistra*) to form up as an honour guard. The south gate had been chosen, for the usually busy west gate (*porta praetoria*) was fronted by the civilian settlement. The *Dux* did not want to buy willow baskets and fish on his way to visit the tribune Sextus! The Praesidiensis looked well turned-out, more impressive even than on any of the payday parades, thought Gaius. Everyone wore their best cloaks and tunics, all the ribbons were out once again, along with crests of horsehair and feathers. As the cortege trotted between the two columns of flanking guards, the foot-soldiers gave up a shout while simultaneously raising their spears in salute: '*salutate*!' Again the men roared, '*salutate*!' One of the horses in the party reared nervously.

It was a good chance for Gaius to admire the clothing of Caelius, the *dux*, and his entourage. The great commander himself wore a pure white tunic, richly patterned with thick *clavi* woven with gold and silver thread. Eagle designs in purple decorated each *orbiculi*, which were also picked out in silver thread. His cloak was of deep crimson and it had a *tablion* of black. His enclosed boots were painted red and looked unused. All of the fittings on his belt, as well as his brooch and his sword scabbard shone with gold. Caelius wore a heavy silver-plated helmet, encrusted with gemstones. Around his neck he wore a golden torc, and a heavy gold ring on his finger. Rather than wear leg-bindings over his *bracae*, the *Dux* wore elaborately decorated shin-guards (*ocrea*) of beaten bronze with designs picked out in silver.

The cavalry troop were also well presented. Scale armour was polished, helmets silver-plated, cloaks of white with black *tablions* fluttered in the breeze. Tunics were red or purple or blue, and again they did not spare the decoration. Many of the riders wore tight-fitting *bracae* of fine white wool. Their spear-shafts were multicoloured, painted in a wonderful spiralling pattern and their round shields bore the *chi-rho* symbol adopted by the *Dux* for his bodyguard.

With kittiwakes wheeling noisily above their heads the legionaries turned and filed in through the south gate behind the Duke's cavalry. Gaius watched his fellows as they reached the barrack block and the order '*demitto!*' was given. Everyone relaxed and shrugged off shields and baldrics, They looked like poor soldiers, frontier troops at the limit of civilisation in comparison to the unbridled wealth and prosperity of Caelius' men.

'Are the field armies made up of soldiers like that?' he asked.

'They get the best of everything,' answered Athulf, 'if you want the best clothing and equipment you should have joined the *comitatensis*. First in line for everything. Out here, on the edge of the frontier – you make do. But they'll expect us to march just as hard and fight just as well as the fancy field armies. Just on less pay, with less food and in cheaper clothing.'

The Boots

In armies throughout the ages, the marching boot has been a prized possession. Weapons will only be needed in times of war, but the boot is needed every single day. Command sent the soldier into awful terrain on a regular basis, for long periods of time, often to cover very large distances. Earlier legionaries wore the *caligae*, open sandal-like boots that had thick soles held together with hobnails. From the late first century onwards, the army began to equip itself with *calcei*, an enclosed boot more often used by civilian workers. This transition may reflect the fact that more recruits were coming from the northern frontiers, where enclosed boots are of great benefit, or it might reflect changes in the supply system, with legions turning to civilian sources for their footwear.

Whatever the reason, *calcei* were ubiquitous in the British provinces. At Vindolanda, the wet conditions have preserved many examples of Roman footwear, civilian and military, adult and child. A great proportion (of all types) have hobnails hammered into the soles, a technique which binds the thick soles strongly together, which reduces wear and tear, and which gives an excellent grip akin to wearing modern football boots!

Each *calcei* was made up of three major parts: an insole and an outer sole as well as one large upper. The flexible leather upper was curved around and then whip-stitched to the insole (figure 22). After this, the outer sole was placed onto the bottom of the boot and hobnails were then hammered into the outer sole and bent over to bind the three pieces of leather together (figure 23). Individual *calcei* have been found that are held together with more than a hundred hobnails! The upper part of each boot is brought together and stitched up the front and again up the heel. There are other stages, too, such as building up a heel with extra layers of leather *between the soles* (no Roman boot has an exterior heel), and inserting internal toe and heel strengtheners.

The author has made a pair of *calcei* and walked tens of miles across country in them. Much was learnt about boot construction in the field as the *calcei* began to deteriorate, the weaknesses in construction quickly became apparent. The biggest problem with Roman footwear was discovered prior to a 10-mile march along Hadrian's Wall. The campsite used by the author (and a number of walking companions from the historical research group Comitatus) was extremely boggy and by the morning of the walk, everyone's boots had become extremely waterlogged.

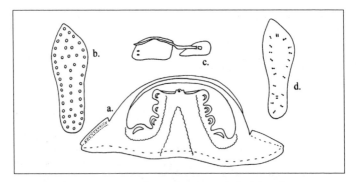

Figure **21**. Component parts of an enclosed boot (calcei) found at Zwammerdam, Netherlands. (a) The upper complete with integral laces, sheepskin reinforcement around the eyelets and heel area, and the 'lasting' margin allowing the upper to be stitched loosely to the insole (d). The leather parts (c) are heel and sole supports that are sandwiched between the insole (d) and the outer sole (b) (after van Driel-Murray).

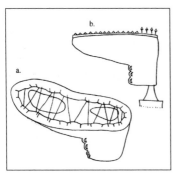

Figure 22. Construction of the enclosed boot. Below, (a) shows how the upper is loosely whipped to the insole, the leather supports are in place; (b) shows the outer sole being nailed onto the shoe, the hobnails driving through outer sole, the lasting margin, supports and insole to secure all parts of the boots firmly in place. In the fourth century some outer soles were sewn on, rather than nailed.

During the initial climb up to the highest part of the Wall, the outer sole came completely away from the boot. Water allows the leather to stretch and expand. The holes that held the hobnails had widened, and the nails had slipped out of the inner sole. The mistake was obvious: the shanks of the hobnails had not been long enough and they had simply been hammered into the triple layers of sole leather. The authentic remedy was to use nails with longer shanks that could be hammered through the sole leather and then 'clinched over' (the shanks hammered flat on the inside of the boot). Ideally, this process should be conducted while the boot leather is wet. As it dries, it pulls tight and firmly grips the shanks of the hobnails.

Wearing Roman marching boots day after day in rough terrain made the author aware of other problems too. Hobnails can come out, a situation which often occurs when negotiating rocks and boulders. Waterlogged leather is weak. When wet boots are caked in mud the extra weight on the bottom of the boot can create tears in the leather upper. Less of a problem when travelling across country is the effect that hobnailed boots have on smooth paved surfaces. The Roman marching boot is lethal on smooth surfaces, slipping easily and landing the over-burdened legionary on his back! This might seem amusing, but history suggests that more than one Roman foot-soldier has been killed by his boots. The Jewish chronicler Josephus, writing about the Roman siege of Jerusalem in AD 70, recounted the death of a centurion called Julianus who had seen his soldiers putting up a poor defence, and who had sprung forward to charge into the mass of Jewish rebels single-handed. He killed many and chased the rest to a corner of the inner court of the Temple. There was a reason that Roman roads were surfaced with gravel and not flagstones, for: 'he was wearing the ordinary military boots studded with masses of sharp nails, and as he ran across the pavement he slipped and fell flat on his back, his armour clanging so loudly that the runaways turned to look.' His men were too terrified to go to the rescue, and so: 'the Jews crowded round him and aimed blows from all directions with their spears and swords … Even then as he lay he stabbed many with his sword … but at last, when all his limbs were slashed and no one dared come to his aid, he ceased to struggle.'

Authentic boots keep the feet dry in most situations, but peat bogs, river crossings and flooded ground all soak through the *calcei*. Attempts at waterproofing have been mixed. Neat's foot oil, nut oil, or olive oil can be rubbed into the leather and if soaked in heavily can deny the space to the unwanted water. Melted lard or melted beeswax can have the same effect. It seems, however, that the best way to deal with waterlogged boots is to ensure they are well made and well 'clinched'. Walking in dry conditions for a day, and sleeping with the boots on will generally give body heat time to dry them out. No legionary valuing his skin would ever have been caught around the evening campfire with his wet boots drying over the flames! Besides getting a roasting from the *centenarius*, savage barbarians like the Picts, Scotti or Saxons (or even treacherous local rebels) are likely to ambush the Roman patrol while they relax around the campfire. And from a practical stand-point, fire-drying leather boots makes them brittle and prone to cracking, at which point the oil comes in very useful to add suppleness and flexibility back to the *calcei*.

A fine experiment was conducted by a group of students from the University of Regensburg in 2004. For a full month the men marched with a full complement of third-century arms, armour and equipment from

Regensburg in Bavaria, Germany to Trent in northern Italy, a distance of over 500km! The group, which was attempting to recreate a deployment of soldiers from the Legio III Italica, was able to road-test ten pairs of *calcei*. Instead of suffering from continual water-logging, the students encountered other problems. Road-walking drove the clinched nails painfully up into the foot, and these had to be occasionally beaten back down. The hard road surfaces also rapidly wore down the hobnails, some of which fell out, while others wore down so that only the shanks remained, still stuck into the sole (plate 15). Interestingly, the students discovered that the wear and tear on hobnails and boots varied with the 'aggressiveness' of the walker, his body weight and the amount of equipment he carried, as well as the pattern of the hobnails on the sole of the boots.

Detailed information on how many hobnails fell out, when, and where during the 500km march was collected by Florian Himmler. He deduced that the maximum number of nails replaced on one shoe during individual repairs was 8, although 2–5 was far more common. The Vindolanda tablets record the purchase of equally small amounts of nails, probably for repairs.[13] It is also interesting to note that the historian Tacitus records that in the first century, the early legionaries received 'nail money' with which to buy replacement hobnails, and this bonus seems to have been in addition to the *stipendium*.[14]

The warm southerly breezes of the summer also brought fresh news of Magnus Maximus' bid for the imperial throne. The soldiers' favourite had ridden across the Alps at the head of a great army to seize Rome and to deny Gratian's surviving son, Valentinian III, access to the throne of the Western Empire. It was a move that succeeded! When Sextus Aemilianus announced Magnus' exploits to the troops assembled on the field, they gave a great roar of approval. He was *their* emperor, a general who had fought the Picts, protected the British provinces, pushed back the barbarians and treated the British legions well. And of course there were loved ones with him even now, fathers, brothers, uncles, sons ... they had crossed the Alps. They were far from home. They had taken Italy itself. There were two emperors now, of equal power and resolve: Magnus Maximus in the Roman heartland of Italy, and Theodosius (the son of Magnus' old commanding officer) in the East.

> [Maximus] was watching and intriguing for the imperial rule in such a way that it might appear as if he had acquired the Roman government by law, and not by force.
>
> Salaminius Hermias Sozomenus

Was this the new order?

CHAPTER V

The Fort and Work: 388–390 AD

> Army officers take their cue from the behaviour of the supreme com-
> mander, copying his strictness or indulging in lengthy mess-dinners.
> By the same token the ordinary soldier either does his duty conscien-
> tiously or gets out of hand.
>
> Tacitus, *The Histories* 2.68

There were officially eight men in Gaius' *contubernium* or 'tent-group'.[15] Athulf was of *semissalis* rank and commanded, assisted by the skeleton-like Marcus Gavius the second *semissalis*. The squad also consisted of Gaius and Severus, who had both joined up in the summer of AD 383, and who were now soldiers of some experience. Two other men, Brocchus and Cassius, were members of the *contubernium*, both had ten years' service under their belt. That left two men short. One, Tetricus, had broken his leg during the winter whilst the squad were shifting some stonework – he had sickened and died of the fever in the fort's hospital. The second, Sabinus, had been a casualty of the Pictish raid back in AD 384 and had never been replaced. The men of the *contubernium* had found out later that the tribune had left Sabinus on the rolls and had doctored the paperwork to make it seem as if the man were still part of the garrison. In black humour, when

61

challenged by a junior officer about some missing equipment or poorly executed job, they would reply 'Sabinus has it!' or 'Sabinus did it!', much to the officer's obvious annoyance.

These five other men had proven to be Gaius' new family. They were an incredibly close-knit group that had to rely on one another to survive the rigors of military life. The tough pressures of routine and discipline forced the legionaries together to share hardships and pleasures alike. This did not mean that they were the best of friends. Athulf was still distant; Marcus Gavius was hated by all; Severus was a depressing pessimist; Brocchus was always impeccably dressed, styling himself as a ladies' man, which aroused the jealousy of the others; and Cassius of Calleva was chided for 'not pulling his weight' in the squad. Gaius could only guess what the other members of the squad thought of *him*. All but Brocchus and Athulf were local-born, raised in Britannia. Athulf was a German, and Brocchus had been recruited on the banks of the River Danube.

On campaign, the *contubernium* was to share a single tent. In practice this meant that it was responsible for the tent as well as all of the equipment that the eight men would need to live and work away from the fort. Wagons were detailed to carry the heavy tents on campaign, and in addition each squad could load the rest of its equipment onto a mule provided for that purpose.

A more detailed look at life on the march is presented in Chapter 6. Within the fort the *contubernium* still played a fundamental part of legionary life.

The Fort Buildings

The fort of Praesidium has never been found, but it is likely to have resembled other Roman forts built for auxiliary troops in the reign of Emperor Vespasian (AD 69–79) during the conquest of northern Britain. It will have been laid out to the standard 'playing card' shape: a rectangle perhaps 200m long and 130m wide, with rounded corners. The defences consisted of three ditches and a high stone wall backed by a turf rampart. The ditches had a V-shaped section, which would have made it difficult for an enemy force to cross. The stone walls were broken by double-span gates, with one set in each of the four walls. Although it is difficult to calculate, the walls may have been a little over 4m high, with a walkway along the top. Each of the gateways was fortified with two imposing towers, and towers also stood at each corner of the fort (figure 23).

The buildings within the walls were laid out to a regular street plan. There were two roads in particular that formed the focus of the plan, the *via principalis* which connected the gateways on the long walls, and the *via praetoria* which led from the main gate (*porta praetoria*) to the headquarters building which lay on the other side of the *via principalis*.

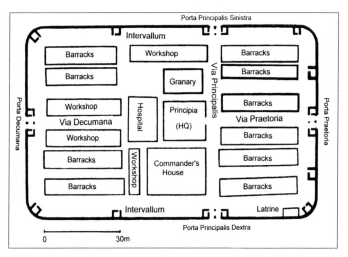

Figure **23**. Plan of an auxiliary fort built to accommodate 1,000 troops. Based on Housesteads fort, Northumberland.

A third road connected the gateway called the *porta decumana* to the central range of buildings. Other buildings and roads fitted into this basic layout. There were granaries, barracks, workshops, stables (if required), a hospital, a house for the commanding officer and various minor buildings perhaps including latrines, offices and store sheds.

The barrack blocks that housed the legionaries played a fundamental part in their lives. Each block had originally been built to house around 80 men and consisted of a long, narrow range of rooms that ended in a suite of rooms for the officer commanding those men. This arrangement mimicked the layout of the legion's tents whilst on campaign. The *contubernium* would erect its tent in line with all the others of the unit, the commander (in the earlier period, a centurion) had his tent pitched at the end of that line. In this way, a Roman marching camp was well organised. Inside the fort the same arrangement was followed, except that instead of a tent the squad was allocated a pair of rooms, one behind the other and linked by a doorway. The first, which opened onto a colonnade and often faced another barrack block across a street, seems to have been used as an equipment store and perhaps a common room. Another possibility is that the front room was used exclusively by the squad leader (*caput contubernii*). Sleeping quarters were in the back room. The rooms were originally small, a little over 2m square, and there has been some speculation that bunk beds were used to cram the eight men into this room (plate 12).

A huge number of earlier first- and second-century forts were remodelled in some way during the fourth century. Barracks were often altered, although it is difficult to understand the complex changes going on. Rooms could be knocked through, other fort buildings could be converted into military accommodation or a barrack block could be totally demolished to be replaced with a line of smaller, separate dwellings divided by narrow alleys. Too little is known about the manpower that the different officer grades commanded, and about the way in which soldiers were quartered in the forts of the Late Empire to be more specific. It is *probable* that the *centenarius* commanded 80 men (in theory) that were organised in ten eight-man squads. It is *probable* that he lived in the old centurion's quarters of Praesidium and that some or most of his men lived in the barrack block adjacent. Perhaps the ten squads were all accommodated in the remodelled barracks, or perhaps some of the squads had rooms up inside the towers or gateways of the fort. Some are likely to have been posted out to the watchtowers and signal stations that proliferated in the local area. In this era of drastically reduced unit strengths, there may sometimes been as few as 50, 40 or even 30 men in the cohort, and it is easy to see how an officer might reduce the number of squads in his century to compensate. It is no use maintaining 10 squads if each has only 3 men; it would make more sense to amalgamate the *contubernia* to produce five squads, each with six men. This kind of reorganisation may well explain some of the remodelling that can be observed in barrack block layouts throughout this period. Falling manpower called for a rethink.

Whatever the arrangements were, life in the barracks must have been fairly cramped. Part of the fort's headquarters building seems to have often served as a central weapons store (*armamentarium*) with its own officer (*custodes armorum*) but these armouries are unlikely to have held all of a soldier's equipment, concentrating instead on collective kit and on armour and weapon repairs.[16] In some cases, helmets and even spears have been inscribed by the owner, indicating personal possession. Was it hung from pegs? Stacked on shelves? Placed in chests or pushed under the beds? In all probability, all of these. In this room, the troops could clean and repair kit, apply oil or paint and polish helmets and swords. The lack of a central dining hall implies that squads ate in their barracks, and some front rooms were indeed provided with hearths for cooking. It seems likely that a *contubernium* prepared its own food and ate together, either sat on stools or on their bunks, or outside under the colonnade. Indeed the space between the long blocks may have resembled either a miniature parade ground, swept and cleaned and inspected daily by the *centenarius*. Or it could have resembled a Mediterranean street café, with tables and chairs along the colonnade filled with off-duty legionaries playing dice or board-games, cooking, eating, drinking, talking and arguing, shouting down to other *contubernia* or over the street to members of the cohort across the way. Unfortunately, we have no way of knowing.

Ursinus would have had his quarters in the spacious rooms at the end of the block, not just sleeping and living accommodation, but also offices, a lavatory and rooms for servants and for family. These apartments would have been nicely furnished, and decorated with wall-paintings.

A figure like the tribune Sextus Aemilianus would not live 'in barracks'. The commander resided in a splendid Roman house that sat next to the headquarters' building, close to the centre of the fort. In the huge legionary fortresses, such as the Sixth Legion's base at Eboracum, this commander's house (*praetorium*) was itself a magnificent palace, with courtyards, dining rooms, mosaic-floored corridors and a multitude of rooms (plate 16). Of course, the tribune commanding a small force on the very edge of empire did not have a palace, but he certainly had one of the most lavishly decorated and well-appointed houses in the area. This was a Roman house for a man of rank. The *praetorium* at Praesidium will have had a central courtyard, under-floor heating, a *triclinium* or dining room (plate 19), and the luxury of a private bath-house. That these *praetoria* had three distinct entrances at the front of the building tells us a great deal about the nature of the tribune's visitors. The first entrance was for servants and slaves. The second and central entrance was for distinguished visitors; it led directly through a cloakroom into the courtyard and on towards the *triclinium*. The third entrance was reserved for military officials and may have been the busiest of the doorways. This often had an external waiting room, and led into a reception room. The *praetorium* was a tranquil haven of civilian pleasures amongst the harsh discipline of military life within the fort. One wonders what martial sounds its inhabitants might have heard whilst relaxing in the courtyard amongst flowers and fish ponds; the screams of drill-masters, the tramp of hobnailed boots, the baritone chant of legionaries being drilled outside their barrack blocks, perhaps even the clang and clatter of tools being used in the workshops.

The nerve-centre of every fort in the Roman military system was the headquarters building (*principia*). It lay at the very centre of the fort, and the main street (the *via praetoria*) led from the main gate (the *porta praetoria*) directly to this important administrative building. It was the fort's office, its command centre, and strong-room. Since it was the first stop for any visitor to the fort the entrance to the *principia* was architecturally impressive. This entrance opened out into a high-walled, colonnaded courtyard paved with flagstones. A well was often located in a corner of the courtyard, and there is some evidence (such as at Housesteads and Künzing) that the rooms arranged around this courtyard stored weaponry, equipment and armour. In the far wall, opposite the gateway was a doorway into a large cross hall. The hall, or *basilica*, was the beating heart of every fort. This lofty hall had two sets of columns running down its length. It may be that the hall served as an assembly point for the unit. A tribunal, or raised stone platform, sat at one end that enabled the commanding officer to review small units of troops or to provide briefings to officers. Here the tribune could dispense justice, dispense important orders and present awards to heroic individuals.

Directly across the middle of the hall stood the doorway into the shrine of the standards (*sacellum* or *aedes*). Either side of the shrine were a pair of offices. One pair was used by the clerks, led by an officer called the *cornicularius*. A huge amount of paperwork would have been processed by these men, logging everything from sick-leave to hobnail payouts, the height of new recruits and daily duty rosters. The other pair of offices was traditionally used by the regimental standard bearers (*signiferi*) who were responsible not only for the military standards of the entire legion, but also for the pay and the savings of the troops. The shrine itself had, in pagan times, housed the standards of the unit, and in AD 390 the standards would still have been held in this very sacred space. It is not known whether Christian iconography was ever kept within the shrine during this era. In fact, a remarkably small number of Christian artefacts have been found on military sites in Britain. Underneath the shrine, a stone-lined cellar held the unit's pay chests. This was the preserve of the commander's most trusted officials.

Every fort had granaries (*horrea*), but more properly they were store-houses, since they were used to store all manner of foodstuffs (plate 40). Evidence at a number of sites has shown that these buildings were not merely barns filled with sacks of grain. They were carefully defended from any attack by being placed close to the centre of the fort. This speeded the allocation of rations, but more importantly it protected the building from fire-arrows shot over the walls by a besieging enemy. Each granary was massively built, with buttresses that helped support a wide roof that was designed to keep rainwater well away from the immediate vicinity of the building. Damp would quickly spoil any dry food held in storage. Further reducing the effects of damp, granaries were raised up on pillars to allow air to circulate. Some of these sturdy buildings had a stone platform at the front entrance which served as a loading bay for supply wagons. Within the storehouse, grain may have been stored in sacks or barrels, or, more likely, in wooden bins – with each unit within the fort allocated their own grain bin.

Every Roman fort has a number of long buildings often with an indeterminate use. It is likely (on the evidence of finds) that these buildings were workshops (*fabricae*), providing the troops with the material support they needed to operate. All manner of craft activities would be practised here, from carpentry to metalwork, boot-manufacture to leatherwork. While large-scale production was carried out on the Continent within state-run factories, the small fort workshops probably produced minor goods and repaired damaged military equipment.

An extraordinary feature of the huge legionary fortresses across the empire was the existence of a military hospital (*valetudinarium*), usually sited close to the centre of the military enclosure. In only a few instances so far have hospitals been positively identified in the smaller auxiliary forts. This building and its trained staff gave wounded troops a much improved chance of survival. It also served to provide care for those soldiers suffering illness or disease, or those unfortunates who were recovering from surgery. Roman medicine was extremely advanced in comparison to many contemporary cultures, and surgery was certainly performed at these hospitals. Depending on the size of the fort or the medical demands placed on it, the *valetudinarium* could either take the form of a courtyard building, or of a barrack block. In the latter case, the hospital might have one large ward, or be divided up into smaller rooms that could accommodate half a dozen patients at one time.

Lesser buildings would certainly exist alongside these more important structures. Wells, water tanks and communal latrines were very necessary amenities that no fort could do without. There might also be a bread oven built into the earthen rampart on the inner face of the fortress wall. These ovens would be used on some sort of rota basis by the different units in the fort. The separate *contubernia* usually received grain rations, not baked bread, and they would have had to grind the grain, make the dough and have it baked at the fort's ovens before it could be turned into a meal. Military bread stamps have been discovered, perhaps evidence that bread was marked by the cohort for which it was being baked. Stabling may also have been provided for the horses of the officer class, and perhaps for working animals used on a daily basis (mules, donkeys and ponies). The fourth-century garrison at Praesidium was an infantry legion, but by the early fifth century it seems a cavalry unit had moved in. A Roman cavalry regiment would of course need a huge amount of stabling, its workshops would produce and repair riding tack, and space within the *horrea* would need to take into account winter fodder for the horses.

Gaius and the men were resting in woodland, just off the road that headed south. It was unbearably hot, but the western sky was black with a mountain of cloud. There would be rain soon and the squad wanted to be under cover when it arrived. They ate what little food they had with them, sharing out the rations – a nearby stream provided drinking water. This was a well-trodden patrol route. The *contubernium* had been ordered to march south until it reached the post-house (*mansio*), the men would sleep over there and then march back. The duty rosters often arranged for there to be a 'check-in' point on the patrols; too many of the men were finding somewhere cosy where they could sit out the day and get drunk. Of course, Athulf and the men simply paid the *mansio* owner in various military foodstuffs once a week (butter, smoked cheese, smoked had-dock); he vouched for their arrival every other day, while they rested over in the woods a few miles from the fort. It beat a 40-mile walk.

This day, however, it would be impossible to avoid trouble. Hearing the sound of hoof-beats on the road made the squad sit up in alarm. When the horse seemed to stop close by, the men gathered up their gear and quietly filed toward the road. They found there a military messenger slumped over his saddle, the horse stood motionless on the road, a legionary arrow shaft protruded from one of the man's thighs. Gaius and the men under-stood the situation. This messenger from the south had been ambushed by the same army deserters that they were supposed to be looking for. After giving what aid they could, the squad marched back to Praesidium leading the horse with its unconscious rider.

As the sun set, the squad trudged through the open southern gateway of the fort. The road ran through two arched gateways, both flanked by iron-bound oak gates. The gate-house itself was only two stories high, with an open walkway above the gates, and two roofed towers at either side. Fires had been lit. Sentries leaned over and asked for the passwords. Gavius shouted the reply of the day to the lads standing on duty in the gloom. They were admitted into the fort. Burning torches illuminated the walls, and across the fort lights were springing into life. Just behind the gateway, up against the wall a dozen soldiers were sat drinking around the two bread ovens buried deep into the turf rampart, waiting for their turn to bake bread. The tired infantrymen then passed between a barrack block and a workshop. Soldiers were outside their quarters, some cook-ing dinner on makeshift hearths, others were hanging off the veranda. Clothing was still hanging from lines, drying in the summer heat. A friend called out to Cassius, but was waved away.

Passing between more barracks and the front of the granary, the squad arrived at the *principia*, the fort's headquarters. It was here they checked-in. Other legionaries were filing out of the courtyard, having made their report, ready for food and bed. Guards allowed Athulf's men into the dimly lit courtyard, and there the duty officer signed them off. This man was a well-educated soldier, lucky enough to be assigned to the headquar-ters. He had his men help the wounded messenger of his horse, and within minutes the courier was on his way to the *valetudinarium* with the officer in close attendance.

'What's all that about?' asked Gaius.

Athulf shrugged. They would find out in the morning.

At sun-up all the members of the squad were dressed and ready, a long-time habit, the body waking at the same time every morning. Severus fried bacon on their little hearth and Gaius passed around fresh bread from a basket that hung from a rafter. They cleaned up the bacon fat with the bread. It wasn't a lot, but it was enough to start the day. Slaves had been around to fill up the water buckets, bowls were washed out and fresh water was drunk. Ursinus the *centenarius* swaggered out of his quarters and called the men to order. They marched solemnly to the *principia* and lined up within the cross-hall ready for an address by the commander. It was a tight fit; the unit was pressed in, men shoulder to shoulder.

Sextus Aemilianus looked tired and drawn. The news was not good. Magnus Maximus had failed to hold the throne of the Western Empire. Theodosius, the Eastern Emperor, had finally moved against him with a massive army, filled with Goths, Huns and other barbarians. The battle had been fought in northern Italy, with Maximus' army finally giving way. The general who had become an emperor fled to the city of Aquileia but had been treacherously handed over to Theodosius and then beheaded. His son, Victor, was also tracked down and executed.

The hall echoed with murmurs. The legionaries knew men who had marched south with Maximus. Where were they? They knew officers and wealthy British noblemen who had supported Maximus and urged him on to claim the throne for himself. What would happen to them? And of course everyone grumbled: what does this mean for *us*?

Of course Sextus Aemilianus could not answer these questions, and so the troops were marched out of the shaded hall by the screaming *centenarii* and were assigned their regular duties.

The Soldiering Life

The Roman soldier spent very little of his time actually on the battlefield. In fact a legionary might easily spend his entire career without once seeing action in a big battle. Skirmishes, police actions, riots, rebellions and raids were all too common, however, and no doubt every legionary had to face these once or twice in his career. Day-in, day-out, the real concerns of the legionary were focused, not on the death or glory of pitched battle, but on sentry duty, local patrols, customs searches, loading and unloading grain, foraging for firewood … and on making money. In the fourth century, everyone, from the tribune in command down to the newest recruit, was on the take. Everyone wanted to make some extra cash, to try and stay above the rising tide of inflation.

Amazingly, the duty roster for a Roman century was discovered in Egypt, and although dated to the late first century, gives an excellent idea of the daily routine of our Late Roman soldiers while in garrison. According to the surviving roster, soldiers seem to have been allocated their tasks individually, rather than by *contubernium* or cohort. Some of the duties lasted one day, others two or more and all of the obvious garrison tasks are listed. Sentry duty at the headquarters building, the gatehouses, the towers and on the ramparts all appear on the roster as does 'latrines', which can only mean cleaning out the communal fort toilets. Likewise, assignment to the bath-house probably meant assisting with its maintenance and operation, rather than enjoying its luxuries. There were several men assigned to road patrol, one to street cleaning and another to the lines or side streets of the camp. There is no explicit duty connected with the fort storehouse, which would be expected considering its key role in the daily life of the legion. There is, however, a duty that has been translated as 'camp market duty' which might well refer to work in the stores. Assignments also refer to 'stretchers' (the fort hospital?), to artillery, to standards (guarding or polishing?), to drainage (no doubt cleaning!) and to escort duty with centurions and senior officers. A common assignment is called 'in century' which might have meant serving as available manpower for the centurion. Boot duty is also common, and might refer to repairing the unit's footwear, but is more likely to have meant that the soldier served an officer as 'bootman' or servant for the day. The most intriguing of the tasks is 'plain clothes' a duty to which Marcus Antonius Crispus is assigned on 4 October. We know that legionaries sometimes served as crowd control or as an *ad hoc* police force, and we also have literary evidence that they could be sent into the streets in civilian attire, armed with a dagger or a concealed club to be ready for civil disturbance. Was M. Antonius Crispus working undercover in this way?

The roster, written on papyrus, may have recorded details of Legio III Cyrenaica, which was stationed in Egypt at the time. Although useful, is there any evidence relevant for life in a small fort in a wet and windy corner of northern Britain? With the recovery and conservation of the Vindolanda tablets, a number of tasks assigned to the frontier troops at the Vindolanda fort close to Hadrian's Wall have been recorded. Not as thorough and detailed as the Egyptian roster, the tablets still add an extra dimension to the working lives of Roman soldiers in garrison.

There is a request for a centurion, Vocontius, to bring wagons to transport building stone,[17] and a troop report that informs us that 46 men were on secondment to the governor of the province as guards, 9 had been sent to Gaul with a centurion, and 11 more soldiers were in Eboracum to collect the unit's pay.[18] Another tablet, dated 24 April, lists some of the trades to which the skilled soldiers were assigned (probably outside the fort at the small industrial town of Coria, modern-day Corbridge).[19] A huge number of these regular soldiers, 343 out of a total of around 750, were involved in trades away from the fort. The list includes plasterers, builders, sawmen (probably workers in the timber yard), shoemakers, lead workers and kiln -operators.

Another strength report, this time recording the troop levels of a frontier garrison in Moesia, on the Danube frontier, gives us a number of new duties to add to those already discussed.[20] It is easy to imagine the legionaries at Praesidium being assigned these types of missions:

In Gaul to get clothing
Likewise to get grain
Across the [river] to get horses …
At Castra in garrison
In Dardania at the mines …
At Piroboridava in garrison
At Buridava in garrison
Across the Danube on an expedition …
Likewise across to defend the grain supply
Likewise scouting with the centurion …
At the grain ships …
At headquarters with the clerks
To the Haemus Mountains to bring cattle
On guard over draft animals …

We can see that the life of a legionary in garrison was filled with far more than simply walking the fortress ramparts. In addition to the crafts already mentioned, there is evidence for armourers, weaponsmiths, bow-makers, boat-builders, glass-fitters, bronze-smiths, blacksmiths, carpenters, roofers, stonemasons, woodcutters, butchers, hunters, charcoal burners and millers. And if the army depended on a resource, then the army often controlled that resource. Lead mining, iron smelting, quarrying and tile manufacture had all been carried out by the legions in the past. Agriculture, however, was one essential activity that had traditionally been left to the civilians within the province. But in the Late Empire even this resource began to be martialled by the legions. *Limitanei* soldiers, like those of the Praesidiensis, were settled and rooted to that part of the frontier that they defended. It seems that many troops had farmland outside the fort walls and grew their own crops. However, it is not known whether the food produced in this way belonged to the unit as a whole, or to the individual soldiers who owned the fields.

As the only force legally sanctioned to carry weapons, the soldiers were often used to police the province (and to enforce the collection of taxes). Local folk routinely petitioned military officers for justice of some kind when they could not get redress from the traditional urban or tribal system. Often, these petitions wanted redress against thieves, and many complained of being physically assaulted. Tribunes commanding small frontier forts like Praesidium will no doubt have received many such petitions, as did any junior officers who were stationed in remote fortlets or on some industrial site away from the fort. As well as responding to pleas, the military officers of a province would always be ready to administer out imperial justice. Individuals might be arrested by soldiers and then brought to trial, and any punishments deemed necessary might be meted out. Executions, beatings and punitive attacks on villages or communities were all routine aspects of the imperial justice system, and were most probably familiar to every soldier.

One great draw the legions had (even the glamourless *limitanei*) was their ability to protect the recruit from army abuses on the civilian population. In the fourth century, the civilians saw the army not as a proud defending force, a brave legion of local boys fighting for the homeland; they invariably saw them as predators, a gang of government-sanctioned thieves and marauders. Roman units needed rations and took a hefty slice of the grain harvest directly. When demanding goods for the state, however, as taxes in kind or as military requisitions, there are instances recorded of soldiers taking more than they were due – often at swordpoint, or after administering a good beating.

An unnamed merchant petitioned the commanding officer of the fort at Vindolanda, and his plea is recorded on one of the tablets:

> …he punished me all the more until I should declare my goods to be worthless or pour them down the drain. As befits an honest man I implore your majesty not to allow me, an innocent man, to have been beaten with rods and … I have complained to the *beneficiarius* and the rest of the centurions of his unit, I accordingly implore your mercifulness not to allow me, a man from overseas and an innocent one … to be bloodied by rods as if I had in some way committed crimes.[21]

Cerialis, the *dux* responsible for the defence of the Libyan provinces, actually profited from his troops' terrorisation of the populace. He extorted gold coin from the city authorities that garrisoned his legions, and then moved them on to a new city, where his extortion would begin again.[22] While being housed by families within the city, soldiers were known to demand firewood, meals, oil and other 'extras' from their unwilling hosts. It is no exaggeration to say that the inhabitants of the frontier provinces were often more afraid of the Roman military than they were of the enemy. In fairness to the men of the Praesidiensis, many of the abuses are recorded as having being carried out by the rootless soldiers of the *comitatenses*, the mobile armies that had no forts and that were quartered within the cities alongside the civilians, from whom they took what they needed. Troops of the *limitanei* were much more self sufficient. Indeed, although the local populace would undoubtedly have suffered at their hands from time to time, the troops of the frontier legions could sometimes find themselves being exploited by an unscrupulous and avaricious officer class. These men found themselves isolated on a frontier fort, with little opportunity to make appeals to a higher authority.

A common form of exploitation was the seizure of men's rations, which the clever commander could commute to gold coin. Officers were awarded large *annonae*, much more than they or their households could readily consume, and so ways were found to commute the food rations to coin. It was Athulf's scam, but on a much larger scale. Perhaps inevitably, these officers looked around for some way to increase this illegal income. Stealing the garrison's food to turn into even more ready coin seems to have been popular in the fourth and fifth centuries (at least with the officers involved!). The *Codex Theodosius* actually declared it legal in AD 406 for a commander to seize seven days' rations from every man every year – and turn those rations into gold coin.[23] Thirty-six years later, a new law decreed that the highest-ranking military officers of a province (the *dux*, his *princeps* and the fort commanders under him) could appropriate one-twelfth of the troops' *annonae*, presumably to transform into gold coin. How the *limitanei* soldiers felt about losing a month's ration of grain, oil, beer, bacon and vegetables is unknown. In the fourth century, the exploitation of the frontier units occurred piecemeal, but by the early fifth century the exploitation had obviously become institutionalised.

There were other ways the troops could be exploited by their commanders as just another source of revenue. The sixth-century writer Procopius documented the abuses of a *praetorian prefect* called John, and on one occasion he skimmed the profits from the bakeries, ordering them to bake the soldier's hardtack (*buccellatum*) only once, instead of twice as was customary. He pocketed the profit, but the bread quickly fouled and the men on campaign fell ill – some even died.[24]

We know that troops at Praesidium were entitled to leave; this was a privilege long enjoyed by the legions. Of course it had always been a system that could be exploited by the officers. In the fourth century only the very highest ranking military commanders (a count, a duke or the *magister militum*) had the authority to grant leave to a soldier, but it seems unit commanders like Sextus Aemilianus were often tempted to bypass the official channels and issue passes themselves. This enabled them to extort money from their own soldiers in return for leave to which they were already entitled. The imperial authorities resorted to draconian measures to curb this practice, at one point introducing the death penalty for tribunes and other officers who exploited their men in this way. After AD 352, however, the death penalty was replaced in favour of a fine of 5lbs of gold.[25]

It is not known how long a soldier could go on leave, or how far he could travel. A number of the Vindolanda tablets deal with requests and they show the formulaic nature of these requests for leave. Unfortunately, they are not very informative: '…I ask … that you consider me a worthy person to whom to grant leave at Ulucium.'[26] We do not know the whereabouts of Ulucium. Coria (modern-day Corbridge) is also mentioned in one of the requests, it was a small town and supply base one full day's walk from Vindolanda. Given the time, a soldier granted leave could travel much farther afield, possibly even out of the province.

It seems to have been common for soldiers of the *limitanei* to take up jobs 'on the side'. The static nature of these frontier forces meant that there was ample opportunity to take up a trade, and to establish a network of customers. Others farmed their own land near the fort, or worked the land of powerful land-owners in the neighbourhood. In the mid-400s, the Emperor Leo demanded that imperial troops should not become involved in commerce, herd animals or farm the land; they should instead devote themselves fully to serving the state. The *Codex Justinianus* explicitly orders dismissal for any soldier found to be engaging in private business without his commander's permission.[27]

It was difficult to stop these men supplementing their meagre income, however. One soldier, garrisoned in the north of Egypt, spent much of his time weaving baskets, and he only turned up for the roll-call in the evening.

Obviously, a unit's military efficiency is going to suffer in comparison with an army that drilled with arms and conducted route marches and exercises all day long. A soldier's commitment to his legion and to its aims and objectives will be split. Making money, running a business and turning a profit will most likely occupy the thoughts of these 'part-time' warriors. Fourth-century frontier forts like Praesidium began to resemble fortified communities and the soldiers manning them looked more and more like part-time militias: civilians trained and equipped to fight if trouble broke out, but otherwise leading a peaceful and productive life raising crops, children and animals and engaging in crafts and trades. This appearance was deceptive however; it seems the frontier forces were on the whole well equipped, well trained and regularly drilled. When mobilised they could take part in serious fighting, sometimes in concert with the elite field armies. More than one *limitanei* unit was actually assimilated into the field army, the *comitatensis*, becoming, in Roman military parlance, a *pseudo-comitatensis*. It is difficult to imagine a force of armed peasants enjoying such a privilege.

Gaius joined the legion with a useful trade. There were many subsidiary occupations within the Roman army, and luckily for Gaius, butchery was one of them. As a butcher he would be quickly promoted to that class of soldiers called *immunis* (immune from fatigues) and would thereby avoid many of the more onerous camp tasks (sentry and latrine duty for example!). Unfortunately, Severus was a farmer and the only talent of his that the army recognised was his ability to dig for hours on end. Severus' continually gloomy mood was not improved by regular stints cleaning out blocked drains, digging weeds out of the fort ditches, and pacing the wall-walks on guard duty.

Athulf was a bow-maker and repairer (*acuarius*). Brocchus was a plasterer, a busy job on a fort that required almost every stone wall to be rendered with a smooth plaster surface. Lazy Cassius had no trade, despite living ten years under the legionary standards. Gavius had once been a cook for a wealthy landowner, but the squad flatly refused to let him prepare their food. Instead, Severus made do with the home-cooking skills he had been taught on the farmstead. He prepared simple but filling meals that the entire squad enjoyed.

What did they eat? The author has prepared a number of dishes that are likely to have been eaten by soldiers at Praesidium. These meals are very different from the dried trail rations discussed in Chapter 6, but they are also much changed from the elaborate recipe suggestions of the Roman cookbook titled *Apicius*. The authors of *Apicius* wrote a great deal on Roman cookery and much can be learned from their cooking methods and from their choice of ingredients. However, the recipes were compiled for the use of the wealthy houses of the Italian cities, which means that advice must all be balanced with Praesidium's location (the remote northern province of Britain) and by its class of diner (relatively poor soldiers). These factors alter the availability of ingredients as well as the level of the meal's sophistication and complexity.

Although it would bring us immeasurably closer to the men of the legions, no surviving fortress menu exists – nor is it likely ever to have existed. In trying to create a list of typical barrack-room meals, we need to consider the foodstuffs and the cooking facilities available to the common soldier in Britannia. Most of Severus' ingredients would be sourced locally, there would be shipments of olive oil, wine, lentils, dates, figs and raisins coming across from the Continent, but these cost money. It is doubtful that these luxuries would have been seen very often by the men of the *contubernium*. The commanding officer at Vindolanda certainly enjoyed some of these imported goods.

Beef was the preferred meat of Roman troops in Britain, and pork was also popular where pigs were raised. Troops depended on pig fat (lard) as part of their marching rations. Olive oil would have been available to those wealthy enough to buy it, but for the soldier in barracks, food would be cooked with lard. Troops further north on Hadrian's Wall also ate a great deal of mutton – the landscape there is ideal for sheep grazing. Geese and hens were also eaten in Roman Britain. Meat would not have been eaten every day, though. It was certainly a luxury for most Romans.

Diocletian's Edict of AD 301 provides prices with which we can compare the value of meat with that of vegetables. Twelve *denarii* could purchase a pound of pork or good quality fish. In contrast, the same sum of money could buy nearly three pounds of beans or barley. To put those prices in context, a baker could expect to earn 50 *denarii* in a day, a farmer around half that sum. At these prices, grains and vegetables would naturally feed the vast majority of the Roman population. It wasn't meat but bread that formed the staple food of the legions and vegetables often formed an accompaniment. It seems that the army awarded the bread ration to its soldiers in the form of wheat grains, rather than fresh bread. Each *contubernium* will have owned a small millstone and a member of the squad (who and when, we do not know) would grind the squad's grain ration into flour.[28] Bread ovens were built into the turf rampart on the inside of fort walls and they were used on a daily basis by those soldiers trained as bakers.[29] Descriptions of some of the staples and cooking procedures follow.

Pulmentum (Wheat Porridge, Soldier's Porridge, or Gruel): The food of the working man across the empire, *pulmentum* was the ancestor of modern Italian polenta. Water is brought to the boil and wheat flour added slowly, beaten in with a wooden spoon. The *pulmentum* is stirred continuously for at least half an hour after which it will begin to separate from the sides of the pot and from the spoon. Once this thick consistency is achieved the dish is ready to eat. It looks unappetising and is bland in taste, and it is likely that the legionaries would liven it up with honey, a few vegetables or cheese.

Army Camp Bread (*Panis militaris castrensis*): This wholemeal bread was baked and eaten on a daily basis by the legionaries. A little salt was added to the flour in a mixing bowl (*mortarium*). Warm water was then added along with leaven (a piece of old and fermenting dough) and mixed well until a dough was formed. A small piece of the mixture is kept to one side for use in future. The dough would then be thoroughly kneaded and then left to rise until the *contubernium's* turn came up to use the bread oven. There is evidence that some loaves were sprinkled with poppy, celery or coriander seeds, all mixed with egg to make them stick. Within the spacious domed oven, a large fire was lit and left to burn until it had reduced to ashes. These would be raked out and loaves for as many *contubernia* as possible slid in. The door was blocked up and the bread left to cook simply from the residual heat within the clay dome. One can just imagine the scene surrounding the bread ovens, bakers sat waiting, chatting with one another, assistants shovelling ashes into buckets, sweeping up while the new batch was baking. Firewood stacked up ready under a wooden lean-to to keep it dry. A bread known as *panis militaris mundus* (quality army bread) was also baked and this was probably a finer, lighter loaf for the officers. The loaves were probably circular. Those baked at Pompeii (and discovered, carbonised, inside the oven of the baker Modestus) were divided into eight portions before baking. Away from the fort, the Romans enjoyed many other types of bread, with ingredients varying from cheese to milk, honey, celery, bran, pepper and so on. A little like the modern pizza, there seems to have been few ingredients the Romans couldn't add to their bread.

Creamed Wheat (*Granea Triticea*): Similar to *pulmentum*, this dish involves boiling wheat flakes in water for ten minutes. Milk is then added slowly and simmered for a further ten minutes, which creates a thick cream. Creamed wheat is quite bland, cream or honey makes the dish more palatable.

Barley Soup *(Hordeum)*: Barley was not well thought of by Roman soldiers, at least when it replaced the wheat ration. Barley has very little protein, and almost no gluten. It makes poor loaves that were ordinarily fed to slaves. Legions in disgrace had their wheat ration replaced with barley as a punishment – the Roman equivalent of 'bread and water'.[30] The author can testify to the bread's heavy and earthy taste. However, barley has other uses, it makes a tasty soup that was well known to the Romans. The physician Galen recommended that pearl barley be soaked overnight and then put into a pot with a little chopped leek and dill, as well as white wine vinegar. Water is added and brought to the boil, thereafter it is simmered for an hour, with salt added before serving. The olive oil that Galen suggests as an ingredient may not be available to Severus or the other *contubernia* cooks at Praesidium. This is a tasty and filling meal.

Pea Soup: This Roman recipe is less of a soup and more of a 'mush', the dried peas are soaked overnight then boiled in water until tender. Once soft they are drained and then pounded in a *mortaria* to create a smooth paste. To flavour the peas, fish sauce (*garum*), a little wine, white wine vinegar and honey can all be added. Boiled egg yolks can also be added to the mixture, as can pepper and ginger (if available to the *contubernium* cook). These mushy peas are delicious and an able accompaniment to fresh bread.

Dandelion: The dandelion plant native to Britain must have been consumed by the troops. The bright yellow flower heads can be steeped to make a drink (they can also be used to create a yellow dye), the leaves are rich and tasty, and the bulb, once baked, can be ground to make flour.

Nettle Puree (*Urticae*): Nettles are a ubiquitous plant found throughout Britain, useful not only for making cord, but also for eating. The tops of young nettles are boiled briskly until tender, then drained and chopped. Dandelion, thistle and watercress leaves could also be added to the pot. Butter and salt are added to the cooked leaves which are reheated and then served.

Celtic Beans (*Faba Integra*): The Celtic bean was a slightly smaller native version of the broad bean, and the Roman legions had a recipe for this vegetable. Water is boiled in a pot along with meat or vegetable stock. The beans are added to the water, along with a spoonful of olive oil if available, and then left to simmer until tender. Once cooked, leave the beans to stand a while in the sauce.

Carrots (*Pastinacae*): The carrot introduced into Britain by Rome was small and pale, white rather than bright orange in colour. The Roman writer Anthimus provides guidance on cooking carrots and parsnips. The carrots (or parsnips) are chopped and then boiled briskly in a little water until tender. They are then transferred to a pan and fried in lard. Pepper, cumin, coriander or salt can all be added at this stage to flavour the vegetables.

Lentil Stew (*Lenticula*): Dried lentils could be transported easily in large storage amphora. The British legions may have eaten lentils, their *commilitos* (army comrades) in southern Europe certainly did. In fact, lentils probably formed a large part of the standard legionary diet, after wheat grain. Lentils will have been on the Praesidium menu, but to what extent we may never know – they certainly appear on one of the Vindolanda tablets. To cook *lenticula*, an onion is fried with lard in a pot until brown. Water is then added, along with a decent measure of red wine and the lentils. Aniseed, cumin and dill can be added at this point (if available to the cook). The dish is simmered until the lentils are tender, at which point the meal is served. There should be little liquid, the lentils are eaten with fingers (as are most Roman meals) or scooped up with bread. This is a substantial and delicious meal. A variation of this dish involves spicing up the lentils with sumach (or lemon), olive oil, red wine vinegar and ground coriander seeds.

Fried Liver (*Ficatum Porcinum*): This dish, and the four that follow, represent the fact that common soldiers may not always have been presented with beef steak just because beef was being handed out by the quartermaster. Every part of an animal was eaten or used in the ancient world, and it would have been a lucky *contubernium* that received beef rations week after week in the form of steak cuts. More often than not, 'meat' rations would have come as less appetising (to the modern palate) cuts of meat: kidney, heart, tongue, liver, brain, stomach-lining, testicles, oxtail, and so on. In the Western world, we often forgo the consumption of these animal parts. Two thousand years ago (just as in many parts of the Third World today), meat was far too valuable a commodity to throw out, never mind which part of the animal it came from. No doubt the *centenarii*, *ducenarii* and the family of the tribune ate well on beef steaks, while the offal was cut up for the hungry men of the *contubernia*.

The term *'ficatum'* refers to a liver fattened up on figs, which modern pigs will certainly not have been brought up on! Anthimus, a sixth-century Byzantine Greek who wrote the treatise *De observatione ciborum* (On the observance of foods), describes pork livers barbecued over charcoal, after basting with olive oil or lard. Both salt and ground coriander seeds are recommended as effective seasonings to *ficatum porcinum*. British soldiers could easily barbecue livers with salt and lard over their barrack-room hearths.

Grilled Ox Tails: The ox tails are divided into pieces at the joints and placed in the pot with meat stock. After simmering for a couple of hours the meat is drained and cooled. Once cold, each ox tail is dipped in beaten egg and then rolled in breadcrumbs. They are then grilled until brown and then served.

Marrow Bones: Butchery remains from Tanner Row in York (Roman Eboracum)[31] show that cattle bones were extensively smashed in order to retrieve the marrow. The bones are cut into two-inch pieces and capped with a flour and water dough. Once sealed, the bones are cooked in salted water for a couple of hours. At this point the bones are removed and served with bread – the marrow is easily removed with a knife or the pointed end of the Roman spoon. Well-cooked marrow is mild tasting with a consistency equivalent to butter.

Julian Pottage: Wheat grains are soaked overnight and then boiled in a pot. Lard is added and the wheat is cooked until soft. Meanwhile brains (of ox, sheep or pig) and a little chopped meat are mixed in a *mortarium*. They are cooked in a pot with lard, and if available, wine, garum, fennel seed, pepper and lovage are added along with some stock. As the dish beings to boil add it to the wheat, mixing it steadily until the consistency of thick soup is reached. The pottage is ready to be served.

Myma: This dish throws everything together and uses meat off-cuts, mashed offal, intestines and blood. It is probably more representative of a soldier's meat dish than barbecued steaks! An onion is sliced and fried in lard in a cooking pot, the meat is added and is seasoned with salt, vinegar and white wine. Thyme and savory are placed on top of the dish, along with slices of goat's cheese. The *myma* is then left to simmer for an hour or so. As with most of these dishes, the *myma* is spooned into a bowl and eaten with fingers and bread.

Beef Casserole (*Carnes Vaccinae*): This is a better-quality meat dish. Beef steak is cubed and then fried in lard with an onion. Once browned, the cook adds coarsely chopped celery, leek and fennel along with red wine vinegar and red wine. Water tops up the cook-pot and the stew is left to simmer for an hour or two. Half an hour before serving, *sapa* (reduced grape juice), pepper, honey, and the herbs pennyroyal, spikenard and cost-mary can be added to the stew. *Carnes Vaccinae* is served with bread and vegetables. Like many classic Roman dishes it combines sweet flavours (grape juice and honey) with sour (vinegar), this combination delighted the Roman palate and once acquired is a satisfying and aromatic taste.

Meat Pieces *à la Apicius*: A variety of meats can be used with this dish, either beef steaks, pork chops or mutton. The meat is put over hot char-coal, either on an iron grill, or threaded onto green sticks (kebab style), where it is cooked until tender. Whilst the meat is over the coals, pepper, lovage, cyperus and cumin is pounded in a *mortarium* (the same squad *mortarium* used to grind the wheat ration). The *mortarium* served as both a food blender and a mixing bowl, grinding up herbs and spices for most of the soldier's meals. *Garum* (fermented fish sauce) was added to the mixing bowl along with *passum* (a sweet, white cooking wine). The next stage is to transfer the meat across to a frying pan where it is cooked with the sauce. Apicius recommends serving the meat portions without the sauce, but no soldier would waste such a delicious flavouring, and it is easily soaked up with fresh bread.

Beef Patties: Beef, finely chopped and then ground within the *mortarium*, is mixed with other ingredients ground up in the bowl: pine kernels, peppercorns, mustard seed and juniper berries. To finish off, a healthy dash of *garum* is added. *Garum* was imported from fish processing centres on the Continent, bottled in *amphorae* and shipped to Britain. It was the tomato ketchup of its day and featured in many Roman recipes, also as a dipping sauce for the table. The pungent brew was created by allowing fish guts to slowly ferment in the sun. Liquids running off were filtered and bottled, graded according to strength of flavour. There was a variety of fish sauce grades, from *muria* and *garum* to *liquamen*. Certainly an acquired taste, Roman fish sauce adds a surprising depth and 'meat' to a dish. The ground beef mixture, once moistened with *garum*, is divided into small patties which are then fried in a little lard.

Fronto's Chicken (*Pullum Frontinianum*): This is an Apician dish that can be adapted for use by the *contubernium* cook. Rather than cook a whole chicken, the soldier can take chicken thighs, drumsticks and wings and fry them in a mixture of fish sauce and lard. Once the meat is sealed it is placed in a pot to cook for another hour. The sauce used to cover the meat is made up of stock with a dash of fish sauce. Add ground aniseed, savoury, coriander and some chopped chives. White wine can be added to the pot also. Served with bread, *pullum frontinianum* is a delicious meal and very easy to eat.

Boiled Crab: Crab remains have been found in York, indicating that this creature was eaten in this part of Britannia Secunda. The crabs are very likely to have originated in Gabranticorum Bay (Bridlington Bay – the site of Praesidium) and were certainly on the menu inside the fort. The following two recipes also use ingredients taken from the waters of the bay. Bread is used to block any holes in the fresh crab's shell, it is then dropped into boiling, salted water and cooked for 15 minutes. When it has cooled sufficiently, the claws are removed and the flesh is removed from the shell. The gills, stomach and green parts are discarded. Both dark and white crab meat can be enjoyed with a small loaf of buttered bread.

Boiled Mussels: Mussels are abundant on the rocks of Bridlington Bay, as are limpets (which were also eaten, but certainly do not taste as good). Mussels are first cleaned and any that are open are discarded. They are then heated in a frying pan, whilst covered with a damp cloth, and shaken vigorously for a few minutes until the shells open. Once open, the mussel flesh is removed from the shells and the beards removed. The cook can either serve the mussels whole with a sauce of *passum*, honey, *garum*, pepper and celery seed, or they can be pounded up in a mortar and added to

freshly cooked lentils that were cooked with onion, pepper, cumin, coriander, mint, rue, honey, *garum* and *defructum* (reduced cooking wine).

Fish Soup: Haddock was plentiful in the Mare Germanicum (North Sea)
and one is needed for this recipe. The trimmings and head of any large
fish are cleaned and put into a pot along with the haddock. Cold salted
water is added and then brought to the boil. After 40 minutes or so, the
liquid is strained and then mixed with a paste made up of milk and flour.
This paste thickens the fish stock. The soup is brought to the boil before
serving.

The *contubernium* cook had very limited cooking facilities, probably no
more than a small hearth inside the first of the squad's two barrack rooms.
We can suppose that he cooked on charcoal rather than firewood, but he
had no oven with which to bake. He was limited to the type of stove-top
cookery that was practised throughout the Roman world and that was
perfectly illustrated by the tiny kitchens of the town houses in Pompeii. A
simple iron grill sits over charcoal, and all cooking is done here. The soldier
would have used some kind of cooking pot and a pan. With those two utensils he could cook most dishes for the squad. Civilians used heavy-duty clay
pots, but these were of course, prone to breakage, especially in the mobile
world of the legionary soldier. His cooking equipment will doubtless have
served him equally well on the march as in the barracks. Experiments conducted by the author have found that clay pots need to be slowly warmed
by the fire before they can be put to any useful task. The impatient cook
risks cracking open the pot as it heats up too quickly. For this reason it is
likely that Severus used a bronze or iron cooking pot (*situla*). Examples
have been found on the site of many Roman forts,[32] and although expensive
compared to a clay cook-pot, the bronze *situla* will not crack over a fire and
can therefore produce cooked food quickly; it is lighter than pottery and
therefore easier to carry on the march; and it is much more robust.

Most of the pottery used by soldiers of the Praesidiensis was Crambeck
ware (figure 24). This pottery type dominated the north-east of Britannia
throughout the fourth century and was manufactured in Derventio
(Malton). It came in a variety of different colours, from orange-red to
white and white-yellow, although the most popular form of Crambeck
ware had a grey colour. Open dishes often had a conical cross-section and
distinctive flanged rims, while Crambeck cooking jars were made with
integral handles.

Patera were deep-bowled pans that turn up archaeologically in military
contexts. They were flat bottomed with high sides and a handle. *Patera*
made excellent general purpose cooking pans. An intriguing style of frying pan with a folding handle (*sartago*) is sometimes found; this was emi-
nently suited to the military life. It could be folded up to fit inside the kit
bag and carried on the march, its flat iron bottom allowed not just food to

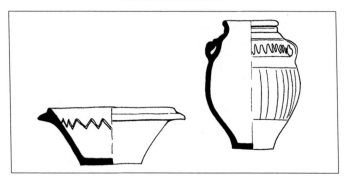

Figure **24**. Pottery from the fourth century Crambeck kilns at Malton, North Yorkshire. Left: A flanged bowl. Right: A cordoned cooking pot (after Lyne and Jeffires, and Corder).

be fried, but also flat unleavened bread to be baked over a fire (plate 27).

Soldiers coming in from duties around the fort to eat the food served out by Severus would have offered him an empty bowl. Every man had a bowl, and he more than likely scored his name on the underside. He probably owned a wooden spoon too – the typical Roman fashion was for spoons with pointed ends, since forks were rare. This prong could be used to spear portions of meat or even pull seafood out of its shell. By far the most common eating implement was the hand. Food was eaten with fingers where possible, but of course bread was always on hand to mop up sauce and to shovel up lentils or vegetables. Soldiers all had knives with them as multi-purpose tools, and at meal time the knife was used to cut up meat and bread (plate 5). As already discussed, soldiers probably sat on stools or on their beds to eat. If the weather was kind they might even sit out on the veranda to eat. Whatever eating times were observed in the Late Roman army are now unknown to us, but in earlier days there were set mealtimes. Josephus in *The Jewish War* describes how 'They do not have supper or breakfast just when they fancy at their individual discretion, but all together. Times for sleep, guard-duty, and reveille are announced by trumpet-calls, and nothing whatever is done without orders.'[33]

November AD 388. A week of heavy rain and occasional windstorms had damaged several parts of the fort. One of the barrack blocks had flooded, two of the bread ovens had collapsed and part of the turf rampart on the inner face of the fort wall had slipped, bringing mud down into the stables. All of this had to be rectified, and the *centenarii* were not waiting for the weather to change. Gangs of soldiers were organised to repair the damage in the pouring rain.

At the end of the week, an important official arrived from Eboracum. Latinus came from the emperor himself. He was a notary, an imperial secretary, charged with carrying orders and messages to officers of the state – and reporting back directly to the Emperor. Latinus was an extension of the Emperor Theodosius' pleasure or wrath. And in late AD 388, he had nothing but wrath for this hateful little province and its rebellious soldiers, so impudent that they would set up their general as emperor. Latinus arrived swathed in a large hooded cloak, his rank denoted by the wide military belt and gold crossbow brooch that he wore. He was accompanied by a dozen attendants. All were magnificently clothed. They were accommodated within the *praetorium* – Sextus Aemilianus had guest quarters, and his slaves attended to the needs of the imperial notary and his staff.

In the morning after roll-call, all the cohorts were ordered to report to the cross-hall in the *principia*. Shoulder to shoulder they faced the raised dais from where Latinus was to address the troops. Steam rose from the rain-soaked troops, roof-tiles rattled in the wind. The commander looked nervous – which put the troops and officers on edge.

'Our Lord Imperator Flavius Theodosius the Ever Victorious Dutiful and Fortunate Caesar Augustus wishes it to be known that the traitor Magnus Maximus has been executed as a criminal. His son, Victor, and all of the traitor's associates have likewise been dealt with. It has come to the attention of my Lord that certain elements of the garrison in Eboracum actively supported the traitor. Many of those disloyal and treacherous ingrates now serve in forts throughout the province of Britannia Secunda. My job is to find these conspirators and bring them to justice, lest they elevate another criminal to challenge Our Lord Imperator Flavius Theodosius.'

He was met with stony silence. In the days that followed it seemed as if Latinus had come to Praesidium to root out a whole batch of suspects. Gaius was given the dubious honour of butchering a wild boar for a feast held at the commander's house. He had to prepare the carcass in the kitchens while under the watchful eye of Aemilianus' cook. Everything had to be perfect. Gaius would help bring the cooked pig out on a platter, and watch as the beast was cut open and to the surprise of Latinus and the other guests, thrushes would fly out of the opening. Nets had been readied and the thrushes were to be caught and then quickly cooked over charcoal – to the delight of the assembled diners.

Would such extravagances make an impression on the cynical Latinus? Would the festivities remove Sextus Aemilianus from fear of suspicion? At midnight, the esteemed imperial visitor presented his own entertainments. Thirteen men were marched into the mosaic-floored dining room under guard. There stood two of the legion's *centenarii*, the *ducenarius* and ten rankers, including Athulf. All looked bewildered, as if shaken from their beds. Gaius stood to the rear of the dining room watching with a sick stomach. Latinus, half boasting and half threatening, read out the charges against the men. They had led the treacherous insurrection, they had recruited plotters, they had spoken evil of his August Majesty, they had consulted astrologers and divined the fall of Theodosius from the pattern of the stars in the sky. Both *centenarii* and the *ducenarius*, men of wealth and rank, were to be shackled and bound for execution at dawn.

Gaius gripped the handle of the knife he held. Athulf was his mess-mate, mentor, friend and confidant. He had guided Gaius through those first years and made a soldier out of him. Difficult to talk to, difficult to reach, Athulf had been something that Gaius could aspire to – a man of trust and integrity. A leader by virtue of his wisdom and his honesty. Latinus then read out the punishment for the ranking soldiers. They were all to be shackled and bound for transportation to the iron quarries south of the great river. There they would spend their lives, serving Rome as slaves.

The ten men were roughly pushed back out of the door. Athulf looked straight at Gaius. They would never see one another again.

At dawn the legion was again assembled, this time on the grassy parade ground outside the fort walls. Latinus sat with Aemilianus at the tribunal to observe the executions. All three men were marched out, barefoot, without their military belts or cloaks, extravagantly embroidered tunics hanging loose. One by one they were beheaded by one of Latinus' slaves. Ursinus, the *centenarius*, watched the proceedings with a pale face, he had known the victims as close friends for over a decade. Gaius (angry but subdued) and Severus (quaking with fear) were watching in line with their mess-mates. The repulsive Marcus Gavius was now squad leader! He had chosen Brocchus to be his second. This Latinus had brought misery by the bucket-full to the fort of Praesidium!

Across from Gaius was a motley group of recruits, all in their thirties, bearded, well-fed – unlikely soldiers. All looked sick to their stomachs, watching the executions with awe and repulsion. Gavius laughed quietly. He said those men were all *centenarii* from the mighty fortress at Eboracum. All were plotters and traitors. They had lost their fine clothes, slaves, social rank, heated baths and private houses to become raw recruits in Legio Praesidiensis. Worse than dead, these educated, elevated and privileged officers were now common soldiers, sleeping eight to a room, eligible for night watches, latrine duties and ditch digging. And the *centenarius'* rod would fall so much more heavily on their backs...

Gaius counted himself lucky. Severus was by his side, Ursinus was still in charge, even Sextus Aemilianus had managed to stay clear of guilt – unless those public executions had been aimed at cowing him into submission... What became of their comrades? Legionaries of the Sixth Legion that had marched proudly out of Eboracum's gateway five long years ago. They had bound themselves to the cause of Magnus Maximus, but that cause had foundered.

It is unlikely they ever returned to Britain. Sending detachments (*vexillationes*) of much larger units to hotspots had always been an alternative to redeploying an entire legion (with all the chaos that would create). Often these detached *vexillationes* never returned, and in the fourth century they were actually reorganised as separate military entities in their own right. This explains why the famous military register, the *Notitia Dignitatum*, records several units with similar names – some of them originated from the same parent legion and never returned. And so it is that an army of Roman soldiers that supported a rebel general, now dead, would find itself renamed and redeployed and considered lucky that its soldiers hadn't been executed as an example to future usurpers. One possibility suggested by the *Notitia Dignitatum* is that the weary legionaries from Eboracum ended their days at the Egyptian fort of Coptos, by the River Nile. There they patrolled the dry and dusty caravan route that led out to the Red Sea.[34]

Off Duty

Almost every Roman fort had developed its *vicus*, or civilian settlement, over the years. These had begun as shanty towns that were the dwellings of the army's camp followers, the merchants and prostitutes, the soldier's families and the wine-sellers that habitually followed the unit from one posting to another. Over time these temporary settlements became something more formal, often built in stone with a degree of order that suggests the army itself may have had some part to play in their planning or construction. An established *vicus* did a little more than just house the camp followers, however. Although it could provide much needed services for the soldiers within the fort, it was often a thriving community in its own right that may even have appointed its own magistrates. A *vicus* was usually of modest size, often no more than a single paved road leading directly to one of the gateways of the fort. Strip-houses, long and thin, were laid out either side of this main street, and the ends of the houses on the street front became shops or stalls or entrances. Traders clamoured for space on this street-front, hence the construction of long, thin buildings. Everyone wanted to attract the custom of the soldiers.

There were undoubtedly many soldiers who took up residence in the *vici* with their wives and families (Roman soldiers had been free to marry for almost two hundred years). From here they could carry out trades, serving not just the local community, but soldiers in the fort and perhaps even other fort garrisons or nearby settlements. However, by the end of the fourth century, the civilian population throughout the British provinces felt exposed and under constant threat. Many *vici* were abandoned after AD 370 and some historians believe that the civilians moved, with all their belongings, families and slaves, inside the fort walls. This would, in effect, turn those forts into well-fortified villages.[35]

Any surviving *vicus* in the north of Britain, such as the one that we can postulate for Praesidium, may have boasted the services of a jet-worker, potter, baker, blacksmith, leather-worker, cobbler, tailor, grocer, bone-worker, basket-weaver, bronzesmith and butcher, as well as experts in a number of other crafts. These men provided goods that the soldiers needed and that the army either could not supply, or supplied in limited quantities. This trade in locally manufactured items meant that the army unit had become an integral part of the local economy, and its diet and equipment would have reflected that. A similar situation developed during the 1960s when US troops were stationed in South Vietnam. Initially issued with regulation field uniforms and equipment, the American soldiers soon began to replace damaged or inferior kit with local South Vietnamese versions. Camouflage uniforms were in short supply but they could be purchased from or modified by local tailors, while pilots had custom holsters and gun-belts made up for them by Vietnamese leatherworkers. The popular and comfortable broad-brimmed bush-hat could be bought from local shops in a variety of simple styles and even customized insignia patches could be purchased from local tailors. The most popular piece of locally made kit was the South Vietnamese Army (ARVN) rucksack, which was roomier and easier to use than the US Army version. Armies throughout the centuries have been trading with the locals to acquire suitable clothing and equipment.[36]

Vici across the empire also provided weary soldiers with services of every kind, including drinking dens, tavernas, bath-houses, brothels and shrines. Celtic beer (*cervesa*) was popular in the drinking establishments, imported wines will have also been on the menu. Bar snacks would be served with the drinks, everything from honey cakes to beef patties, cheeses, sausages, bread, chicken, fried fish, dried fruits, herb purees (*mixtura*),.and even fried pasta (*lagana*). If a brothel existed in the settlement it might easily be associated with the tavern, in the Roman world many inns and taverns had rooms upstairs for the entertainment of lonely travellers (or soldiers).

Bath-houses were a luxury that no Roman could do without. Many were built in the British provinces on villa estates, in the big cities like Eboracum or Londinium, in or adjacent to forts, and also within *vici*. Baths that catered to the inhabitants of the *vicus* would almost certainly attract the custom of the soldier off-duty. Here he could refresh himself in the plunge bath of the cold-room (*frigidarium*) before stepping with friends into the dry room (*laconium*). He would finish off with a spell in the warm steam room (*tepidarium*) and then the hot steam room (*caldarium*). These bath-houses, with their under-floor heating and running water, were much more than bathing pools, they provided a social centre to the settlement, however small. It was here that business was done, friends met and relaxed, deals were made, and money lost and won in dice games (or on the outcome of various Roman board-games). As in the taverns, snacks were always on hand to feed the hungry bathers. The *vicus* at Praesidium will certainly have had a public bath-house. A growing trend in the late fourth century, however, was for public buildings like the bath house to become neglected, abandoned or demolished. Most probably this was due to a lack of skilled labour. If a fire broke out, or a section collapsed, the building would not be rebuilt but either be left to rot or stripped of useful building materials. It seems that the highly skilled Roman builders that had been so prevalent in the British provinces only fifty years earlier were now in very short supply. If the bath-house at Praesidium still operated, then its bathers could consider themselves very lucky indeed.

In the autumn of AD 389, when the beech trees in the woods were spindly and bare and the grey sky threatened rain, Gaius arranged to meet Modestus in the *vicus* bath-house. Modestus was an older man, a long-serving veteran of Legio Praesidiensis, with three daughters. It had been Modesta, his eldest who had caught Gaius' eye. The two had courted, and now the professional soldier was ready to settle down with a local wife. He had 'followed the standards' for six years. Only five weeks previously, on 1 September, the soldiers in line at the pay-parade had been anxiously awaiting their donative. It was the quinquennial anniversary of Emperor Theodosius' accession to the throne, and the troops were expecting a fat donative in gold. They were not disappointed.

Now Gaius sat in the bath's *laconium* and drank wine with Modestus, gold and silver clanking heavily in his money pouch. The old veteran couldn't supply a dowry, but a deal was struck, and at a discount price Gaius bought up the old man's leather-supply business, lock, stock and barrel. The men shook hands, the deal was made, and Gaius married his pretty red-haired bride in the spring of AD 390. The couple looked forward to a happy future, with a secure income from the fort, supplemented by a trade in tanned leather hides imported into the *vicus*. With the business came contacts in Eboracum, two slaves, a wagon and ox and all of Modestus' current stock. However, warehousing would be a problem that Gaius would need to take care of himself. He planned to move the business into the fort. There was plenty of space, since equipment and food was now stored centrally and transported by wagon as and when needed. Like many other soldiers, Gaius could rent space in the granary from the commanding officer. This he would use for his leather import business. He shared the granary (now a warehouse-cum-workshop) with a bone-worker, bronze-caster and jewellery maker – all soldiers working part-time to supplement their income. Many of these crafts had been adopted from their veteran fathers who had tried to make a living in the *vicus* (remember that the son of a veteran had to serve in the legions). One veteran's legacy to his son was his amber-carving business, another veteran handed on his business making hobnailed boots and shoes. With soldiers taking up money-making activities like these while still in-service, it seemed only natural that they should bring those trades inside the fort walls. And so the vicus began to decline.

The fact that serving soldiers had the afternoons off, coupled with a severe lack of ready coin, naturally resulted in the growth of trades and crafts amongst serving legionaries. Once these trades became established within the fort, the *vicus* outside that had traditionally supplied these services, began to dwindle. If, when, and how a soldier's family moved into the fort with him, we cannot know. Many forts from earlier Roman times show definite remodelling of their internal buildings in the late fourth century. Principia fall out of use, granaries sometimes change their function, bath-houses are built and of course, barrack-blocks are rebuilt. It seems as if the garrison of the fort is slowly replacing the established community, both military and civilian, for the area around the fort.

CHAPTER VI

On The March: 391–394 AD

> We learned that for a distance of seventy miles over the arid plain we
> should find no water that was not salty and stinking, and nothing to
> eat but… bitter herbs. All the receptacles we had with us were filled
> with fresh water, and food of a sort, however unwholesome, was
> provided by slaughtering camels and baggage animals.
>
> Ammianus Marcellinus 25.7

It was AD 391 and the new-found leather trade established by Gaius and
his wife Modesta seemed to be quite lucrative. True, there were far fewer
customers than there had been ten years ago, forts were being depleted,
and garrisons had followed Maximus across the sea to Gaul. With the
soldiers went the families and the traders and craftsman who had made
their livings supplying those soldiers.

Tanned hides were purchased in Eboracum by Gaius' slaves and loaded
onto the ox-cart for the journey to Praesidium. Three days later they
arrived at the fort and were admitted. The hides were stored in a rented
space within one of the fort's old granaries. Gaius checked the leather himself and kept the accounts. The slaves slept in bunks with the stock, but
during the day one attended Modesta whilst the other saw to the varied
duties required of Gaius around camp. This slave would clean equipment,
prepare food, muck out the ox, fetch and carry messages regarding the sale
of the leather hides, and make preparations for the trip back to Eboracum.

Everyone needed good tanned leather. Boot-makers relied on the leather trade, and the leatherworkers in (and out of) the fort used the material to make belts, tents, bags, pouches, scabbards, shield-covers, waterskins, and knife-sheaths amongst many other things.

Reports had come in from outposts and from the garrisons of neighbouring forts that the enemy was abroad once more. Raids and sporadic attacks had continued in the years following Magnus Maximus' departure, but the greatly feared mass attack of Picts and Saxons had not, mercifully, occurred.[37] Pictish raids were on the increase along the east coast, and there were increasing reports of barbarian ships penetrating inland up the larger rivers. The garrison at Praesidium played a crucial part in spotting these Pictish raiders, in preventing their escape, and in reporting their unwelcome presence to the Duke of the Britains at his headquarters in Eboracum.

Looking for Trouble - the *Limitanei*

It had been the first Christian Emperor, Constantine the Great, who had split the Roman military forces into the *limitanei* (the frontier armies) and the *comitatenses* (field armies).[38] Prior to AD 311 the legions had struggled to carry out both tasks simultaneously, at once guarding the frontiers against hostile tribes, and sending large amounts of men rapidly across the empire to deal with an invasion, to join a military expedition abroad, or to defend the Emperor against an usurper. Once established in a region, a legion was difficult to remove without upsetting the peace and order of the surrounding area. The division of the armies into frontier troops and field troops was aimed at solving this problem.

Naturally, the *comitatenses* received the best recruits, the better pay and most of the glory, while the humbler *limitanei* soldiers earned a lesser wage, fought fewer battles and saw far less of the world. The two parts of the army needed one another, however. The border forces were a suitable deterrent against hostile attacks by barbarian tribes, and they were also able to provide headquarters with a warning of enemy activity. Unable to cope with all but the smallest of incursions, the *limitanei* bought valuable time for the field army as it marched rapidly to deal with the threat.

The four British provinces (Britannia Prima, Britannia Secunda, Flavia Caesariensis and Maxima Caesariensis) all lay within a frontier zone, surrounded on three sides by hostile barbarian cultures. Certainly right up until the last few years of the fourth century, every Roman unit stationed within Britain was a member of the *limitanei*. There was no elite field army poised in the centre of Britain to dash to the defence of the border garrisons. The frontier troops were expected to deal with any threat that emerged, Their forts were arranged in-depth, providing a heavily militarised zone from Hadrian's Wall down to the Pennines and into Wales. A *dux* commanded all of the *limitanei* troops in the frontier zone.[39] The Duke of the Britains probably had his permanent headquarters at Eboracum (York), but will have spent considerable time at the other forts in his command, especially Deva (Chester). There were high-placed professional officers like him throughout the empire. The *Notitia Dignitatum* records a Dux Thebaidos, Dux Syriae et Eufratensis Syriae, Dux Moesiae, Dux Pannoniae Primae et Norici Ripensis, and so on. Clearly they operated across more than one province, establishing a regional command that could muster the border troops.

Since the battles fought by the frontier soldiers were on a much smaller scale than those waged by the elite field armies, their exploits were rarely documented. Indeed, Ammianus Marcellenus admitted at the beginning of his history that he had left out several minor conflicts 'because their results led to nothing worthwhile and because it is not fitting to spin out a history with insignificant details'. The skirmishes and battles, ambushes and cross-border raids of the Legio Praesidiensis will no doubt have been dismissed by Ammianus as some of those 'insignificant details'. Counter-insurgency, then as now, lacked the glory of an epic battle ending in absolute victory.

The dukes were responsible to their regional commander, a high-ranking general called the *magister militum*. Below the dukes were the garrison commanders, the prefects and the tribunes, the men like Sextus Aemilianus who had served in one of the elite 'staff college' units and learned the art of war there, before being given command of a frontier fort. Although the mobile field troops were billeted inside the big cities, frontier soldiers like Gaius and Severus were garrisoned inside the forts that Rome had built to protect the empire over two centuries ago. Many of these earlier forts had recently had their defences extensively improved to suit the fourth-century style of war-making, while others were entirely new constructions. They were tough and heavily fortified. The Saxon Shore Forts on the south coast of Britain were of this new type of fort, designed to withstand a siege with massive towers and platforms for artillery. The rest of the forts in the British provinces remained little changed – the Duke seems to have been satisfied with their much older style of defensive capabilities.

The headquarters of the unit was stationed at the fort named in the *Notitia Dignitatum* associated with it, but many of the unit's soldiers would actually be deployed to outposts: forts, fortlets, watchtowers and signal-stations strung out across the unit's zone of control. A number of forts are known to have been occupied in the late fourth century that do not appear in the *Notitia*. We can infer that soldiers from nearby units were garrisoned inside them. Troops from Legio Praesidiensis will have been widely dispersed, occupying the fortified stone-built signal stations on the east coast cliffs. They may also have manned smaller wooden watchtowers now lost, and perhaps a chain of similar stone or wooden signal stations south along the shores of Holderness.

In trying to determine what daily life was like for members of the garrison at Praesidium, it is helpful to look at the mission assigned by the Duke to the troops. Why were they there? What was their role? The soldiers did not sit inside barracks all day waiting for battle, nor were they asked to fight every day.

An anonymous sixth-century writer describes the function of a *limitanei* fort:

> [they] are used for several purposes: first, to observe the approach of the enemy; second, to receive deserters from the enemy; third, to hold back any fugitives from our own side. The fourth is to facilitate assembly for raids against outlying enemy territories. These are undertaken not so much for plunder as for finding out what the enemy can do and what plans they are making against us.[40]

Key to understanding the role of these frontier forts is the reference to 'observing the enemy' and also to 'assembling for raids into enemy territory'. But why the mention of deserters? Surely desertion to the ranks of the enemy (or the arrival or barbarian recruits) could not have been so great a problem that one of the missions of a fort was to act as a deterrent to it? Although hard to imagine today with nations waging war on other nations, the difference between 'them and us' was far less in many parts of the Late Roman Empire. The army recruited huge numbers of barbarians (in the west especially Alemanni, Franks and Burgundi), not only in ones and twos but also wholesale – entire tribes or clans brought into the empire and into the army. Obviously, it was advantageous to the Roman frontier forces to accept new 'recruits' who wanted to swap life in the tribes for life in the legions – possibly alongside fellow countrymen. It was the frontier fort that acted as a recruiting centre for these barbarian malcontents.

Perhaps almost as common was the legionary deserter. Roman military discipline was legendary, and although the severity of some punishments had lessened in the late fourth century due to manpower shortages, the individual legionary could still expect to be severely punished for misconduct. Many deserters would have been soldiers who were desperate to avoid their punishment. Others may have chafed under the iron discipline and found the benefits of Roman life (including pay, rations, pension and so forth) little compensation for life in the fort. Flitting back to the tribe was an easy option if that is where they had come from and they might just take friends with them, and perhaps even rumours of imminent plans or weaknesses in the frontier.[41]

The flow of traffic into and out of the empire was essentially controlled by the forces of the *limitanei*. In most cases movement was unrestricted, but there were some controls in place where security was especially at risk.

The export of weapons and gold to the barbarians was strictly prohibited, and it seems that the tribes had limits set on their trading activities within the empire. The frontier troops were most effective out on patrol, checking for legionary deserters, apprehending spies or known malcontents and searching wagons and pack-animals for illegal goods. The highest importance must have been attached to intercepting and preventing large groups of barbarians crossing the border. In Britain that would mean Picts, Attacotti and perhaps Scotti crossing Hadrian's Wall or landing on the Welsh coast and pushing into the settled areas unchecked. This unregulated movement of peoples across the frontier was always frowned upon by the Roman state and dealt with most efficiently.

The *limitanei* certainly waged war, even crossing the frontier to take the fight into enemy territory, carrying out reprisals or pre-emptive strikes. This was their *raison d'être*, this was the reason they were so well trained and were so well equipped. Patrols could detect the presence of large barbarian groups and report back to the parent unit. This unit would then march to intercept the enemy force; of course, there was an upper limit on the enemy unit size that a 500- or 1000-man unit could successfully engage. According to the historian Hugh Elton there are no recorded barbarian incursions numbering less than 400 men in the fourth century,[42] implying that the *limitanei* effectively dealt with those smaller groups without them appearing in the written record. We should remember what Ammianus Marcellinus said about spinning out a history of 'insignificant details', although he does commend the frontier forces stationed on the Danube with the following words:

> [the Emperor Julian] strengthened … the frontier fortifications, and took particular care that the troops posted along the Danube, of whose watchfulness and energy in the face of barbarian attacks he heard good reports, should not lack either arms and clothing or pay and food.[43]

This certainly sounds as if the Danubian frontier garrisons were able to provide excellent intelligence regarding the raids of barbarian Goths, and indeed confront them vigorously.

The true role of a *limitanei* fort, however, was to stand guard on the frontier, to watch for trouble brewing in barbarian lands, and to control any movement of peoples and goods across that frontier. The siting of most forts at convenient crossing points, on rivers and trade routes enabled the unit to monitor local traffic and to pick up rumours from travellers of tribal politics, cultural changes, and the arrival of new groups beyond the Roman frontier. Constant infantry or cavalry patrols out into the countryside on both sides of the borders and into local villages also provided the fort commander with reliable intelligence. The familiarity of the patrolling troops with the geographic region around the fort would also prove a valuable asset in times of war. The garrison commander would have sent the most valuable or urgent information to the *dux*, and at times this was passed up to the *magister militum* and even to the emperor. One tablet at Vindolanda, a fort on the northern frontier of Britannia Secunda, actually records part of a report on the local tribes and it seems likely this was written not for the Dux Britanniarum, but for the commander's replacement: '…the Britons are unprotected by armour. There are very many cavalry. The cavalry do not use swords nor do the wretched Britons mount in order to throw javelins.'[44]

Scouting the Seas

It was AD 392. During the late spring and summer there were always ships riding at anchor in Gabranticorum Bay, some were the long, oared galleys of the Roman fleet, but most were the tubby merchant ships decorated with swan-necked figureheads (plate 38). Ocelus Headland (modern-day Flamborough Head) stuck out into the Mare Germanicum like an ominous white wall, and ships trying to sail around it had to time their passage well. Sudden and savage squalls could dash a vessel onto the hidden reefs that ranged all along the treacherous headland. As a consequence, ships often sat at anchor for a few hours in the Bay, waiting for the weather to clear. When dark storms loomed, captains pulled their boats up onto the wide golden beach of the bay and spent the night there, camping on the sands.

The nearest Roman naval base lay in the shelter of the mighty River Tinea (River Tyne)[45] many miles to the north, but warships regularly pulled up onto the shore beneath Praesidium. Squadrons of fast patrol galleys were deployed all along the east coast and moved steadily from one anchorage to the next, taking on water and food, waiting out bad weather if need be, collecting reports of enemy activity from the local commanders, then setting sail and moving off once again.

Modesta had just thrown a pottery cheese press at Gaius that had smashed against the wall behind him. It was their first big argument, and Gaius was not going to hang around. His bag was packed, slung over his shoulder, and he stood in the doorway of the family house in the *vicus*. Modesta was enraged that, so soon, she would have to run the leather-import business and manage the slaves on her own. Gaius had volunteered to take ship up to Arbeia, a fort way up north along the coast, without consulting her! Why had he been so rash? A naval squadron had arrived yesterday afternoon, but almost half of the men were deathly sick, poisoned by cheaply made hardtack rations issued by their corrupt fleet commander. The squadron commander was desperate for manpower to continue his voyage north, he had important imperial officers on board who he had to transport to Arbeia. There they would first check provisions and supplies, and then begin an inspection of the Wall forts. He had begged Sextus Aemilianus for men, for volunteers, and Gaius along with Severus and many other legionaries, had offered to man the oars. Thinking that the promise of adventure and an up-front cash payment of one gold *solidus* per man would be adequate compensation, they had jumped at the chance to serve with the fleet.

For years, Gaius had watched local fishermen launching their boats into the pounding surf, and those boats were made up of waterproof ox-skins, held in shape by a strong willow framework. They were coracles. The *Diomedes*, the Roman warship that Gaius and Severus were assigned to was huge in comparison: fifteen oars to a side and a main mast that was ready to unfurl a massive white sail at an order. A shelter at the stern provided some protection for the captain and his passengers, but by no means could it be considered luxury accommodation. The boat was blue, timbers coated in blue wax, although the sail was white. The crew that remained were all dressed in blue tunics and grey trousers and they were a surly, unfriendly lot. As the ship got underway Gaius' mind reeled. This 20m of wood was his home for the next week or two, open to rain and wind, without an open fire or a dry bed. Severus quickly paled – sea sickness gripped him and would not let go. Gaius was luckier, he kept busy, he talked to the sailors as they checked the lines that kept the sail taut. The breeze was brisk and the ship made good time, speeding past Ocelus Headland and on to Two Bays where the signal station stood majestically on the cliff-top. Here the squadron disembarked for the night, leaving the ships in the care of the sailors. The officers and the volunteers from Praesidium climbed the path to the small square watchtower that sat on the cliff-top.

Centenarius Brigionus, cloaked and smiling, welcomed the men. Gaius, Severus and the other legionaries were led through the main gate and into the square courtyard. There, a five-storey tower stood, silhouetted against the stars. While the officers retired to the third floor for wine and good food, the common soldiers bunked with the tower-guards on the first floor. Of course there was a great deal of beer drinking and dice rolling. A good time was had by all, although Severus needed a decent night's sleep far more than he needed entertainment or food.

In the morning, the squadron pushed off again, the blue galleys spreading their sails to catch the breeze. They beached again in a river mouth, and again, a day later, in Dunum Bay where seals lay on wide beaches in the sun. The next morning, the captain promised that they would sight Arbeia by nightfall, and as the sun sank to the horizon, they spotted the fort atop the hill. Severus was first off the ship.

The *Diomedes* had tied up at a wharf that was jammed with merchant ships. Amphorae, sacks and boxes were piled across the quayside and workmen were rushing to get the cargoes inside the warehouses before dark. Beyond the buildings on the quay, a road climbed the hill to the fort of Arbeia. To his right, Gaius could make out a squadron of sleek warships, like the *Diomedes*, pulled up onto the shore near large wooden boatsheds. Camp fires were dotted across the beach. Beyond lay the wide mouth of the river Tyne, the natural highway that led far inland to the forts guarding the Wall. And on the far bank, above sloping rocks, a lighthouse, its beacon fire flickering in the evening gloom.

The imperial officials disembarked and were taken up to Arbeia fort in a carriage. After helping to unload equipment and cargo, the soldiers from Praesidium were ordered to follow on and find beds amongst the garrison there.

The Dux Britanniarum could not depend on his border garrisons to provide reliable intelligence regarding the Pictish pirates. Their homeland was far to the north, in hostile territory, and the landing points of their raids could neither be predicted, nor guarded. Other coastal frontiers around the empire faced a similar problem. Part of the solution was the maintenance of a fleet that could send out patrols, monitor shipping and perhaps provide some sort of deterrent against sea-borne raids. And if naval vessels could not intercept incoming raiders, then at least they stood a good chance of catching them in the act. If Praesidium was situated at Bridlington, then it is highly likely that it formed the nerve centre for the east coast defence and will have maintained naval squadrons within the Bay. If this was the case, then our view of Praesidium may need to be modified again, there may have been wooden boat sheds above the beach, accompanied by a shipyard for construction and repair. The legionaries may indeed have had some experience as shipboard marines, carried on the decks of oared galleys ready to board a Pictish boat or land at a beach or cove in time to cut-off the pirates' retreat.

A letter written by Sidonius Apollinaris in the 470s eloquently captures the frustration felt by the Roman commanders:

> [The sea-borne raider] attacks unforeseen and when foreseen he slips away; he dismisses those who bar his way, and he destroys those whom he catches unawares ... [the raiders] gladly endure dangers amid billows and jagged rocks, in the hope of achieving a surprise.[46]

Naturally, the deployment of lumbering Roman war-galleys would be of no use in such an engagement. It seems that much of the provincial Roman fleets were equipped with *liburnae*, a Roman term for the bireme, or fighting galley, with two rows of oars, an upper deck for marines and artillery. These vessels could carry out a wide range of naval activities, including the sinking of enemy ships. Ships of the British fleet would not all be *liburnae*, however. Vegetius, a contemporary of Gaius and Severus if they had existed, actually made a number of observations about the Roman fleet in Britain:

>...scouting skiffs (*scaphae exploratoriae*), having about twenty oarsmen on each side ... the Britons call *Pictae* (painted ships). They are used on occasion to perform descents or to intercept convoys of enemy shipping or by studious surveillance to detect their approach or intentions. Lest scouting vessels be betrayed by white, the sails and rigging are dyed Venetian blue, which resembles the ocean waves; the wax used to pay ships' sides is also dyed. The sailors and marines put on Venetian blue uniforms too, so as to lie hidden with greater ease when scouting by day as by night.[47]

The reference to blue camouflage is fascinating, it certainly emphasizes the British navy's primary role in the fourth century of observation and report, making land forces aware of the incoming threats. Vegetius also tells us that the Roman vessels also performed descents ('*superventus*', or sudden ambushes) on raiding ships.

The terror created by Pictish raids can easily be imagined when one reads Gildas' account of these concerted attacks:

>...like predatory wolves driven mad by the extremes of hunger that leap dry-mouthed into the sheepfold when the shepherd is away, the old enemy burst over the frontiers, borne along by their oars like wings, by the arms of their oarsmen, by their sails swelling in the wind. Everything they slaughtered – whatever lay in their path they cut down like ripe corn, trampled underfoot, and passed on.[48]

A number of partially preserved warships have been found on the Rhine foreshore near Mainz. They seem to typify the kind of lightweight patrol craft that Vegetius is referring to. The vessel described as Mainz Type A had both a sail and 15 pairs of oars, it was 21m long and 2.7m wide. The method of manufacture was distinctive of northern European shipbuilding traditions and it is obvious from Vegetius' remarks that similar vessels would have been built in Britain for use on the larger rivers and along the coast. The Romans in the fourth century called this type of river patrol craft a *lusoria* and the University of Regensburg has recently built a full-size replica of a Mainz Type A called the *Lusoria* (plate 20). The information gained during the *Lusoria*'s river trials along the River Danube has taught its crews much. What is life like on one of these fast patrol boats? The 'catwalk' that runs the length of the ship is broad enough only for one person to walk up and down (perhaps to keep the rowers in line!) but of no practical use as a place for troops to sit or stand during voyages. Indeed, the rowers are easily disturbed by any crewman walking the 'catwalk'.

A more practical proposition is to use this narrow central space for cargo (sacks, baskets, small casks), along with the small space around the base of the mast, and the bowcastle. If you were on board a *lusoria*, you were on a rowing bench! Researchers found that the vessel could be rowed for longer if a shift system was implemented, with three shifts taking it in turns – rowing for 20 minutes, taking a break for 10 minutes, then back to the oars. This method was found to be more efficient than allowing the full rowing crew to rest, and did not endanger the ship by letting it drift with the current.

Experiments with the reconstructed vessel also showed that a skilled cadre of rowers can quickly organise an inexperienced crew and have them operate the oars. Good manoeuvrability and a decent rowing speed can only be achieved by well-trained rowers, however. It is possible then, that infantrymen could be carried onboard these patrol ships (rowing when required), but more likely the sailors were also the soldiers, landing the ships and disembarking to ambush barbarian raiders.

On Patrol

Cloak wrapped tight around his shoulders, and shield thumping against his back, Gaius led the other soldiers down the main street, the via praetoria, of Arbeia fort. It was lined with columns in the exotic style of an Eastern city. Arbeia had been rebuilt sixty years ago following a catastrophic attack and fire. The first garrison to occupy the newly finished fort had come from Mesopotamia, at the eastern extremity of the Roman Empire. From baking deserts and the reed-choked banks of the immense Tigris river, bargemen and sailors were transferred to the north of Britain. Here the dark-skinned easterners must have felt very out of place amid snow, rain, fog and mud. They were expert sailors and provided a serious defence against sporadic Pictish sea-attacks. Many members of the garrison, the Numerus Barcariorum Tigrisiensium, still had the darker skin and black hair of their grandfathers.

Checking in at the headquarters to pick up their orders, the men then filed out of the north gate and down to the river. There they were rowed across the River Tinea as the sun rose up out of the sea and disappeared behind bands of cloud. Severus' teeth were chattering in the cold. They disembarked from the skiff and began their march. A squad leader from Arbeia had taken charge of them while they waited for their ship to complete its business and return to Praesidium. He had needed men to search local settlements north of the river and had decided that the visiting soldiers would do! There were no Roman roads, only wagon tracks, and the patrol soon left those to follow a narrow path climbing steeply through woods. That night, the men camped in the lee of a low cliff rising out of the forest, its rock face blackened by past camp-fires. Six men slept in two small tents, while Gaius and Bel-barak (the squad leader) sat up on sentry duty. The swarthy file leader explained that a disaffected chief's son had set himself up as warlord in the next valley and had begun raiding his father's settlements. Some of these raiders had also attacked Romans conducting business on this side of the river. This patrol had been sent to 'fly the flag' and make the warlord aware that Rome was watching him.

Next morning the group hiked down into the wooded valley. Each man wore a helmet and carried a full-size shield. Most had *spicula* and axes with them, Gaius, Severus and Bel-barak had brought *spicula* and *spathas*. The group had no tools, but had shared out a couple of tent canvases and various pots and pans amongst the men in the squad. They clanked and thumped their way past fields toward a local rath (farmstead). Smoke drifted lazily into the air and locals stood blank-faced, watching the patrol. The track ran through woods toward a second rath, and the squad marched on in that direction. Here the men-folk took an interest, watching with arms folded, grinning at the soldiers, joking and pointing. When something hit a Roman shield with a bang, Bel-barak barked orders and had the squad ready for action. Half of the patrol searched the yard of a roundhouse before moving inside, while Gaius and the others forced the onlookers to sprawl in the mud at spear-point. The farmers, men and women both, wore their hair long, and the men were sporting moustaches. A good deal of the colourful clothing was chequered. Dogs and children ran around making lots of noise. When men complained about the treatment some of the soldiers pushed their faces into the mud or kicked them. They were Roman soldiers.

Gaius heard the sounds of breaking cook pots and of furniture being upturned from inside the roundhouse. Shouting broke out and suddenly Severus came staggering out of the door. His face was bloody. The other legionaries also came spilling out, dragging men and women with them. They were furious at the sudden attack and one threw a firebrand onto the thatch, which caught light quickly. The men and women struggled and screamed to be free, but Bel-barak give the order and all were silenced with murderous chops. The remaining farmers, muddy and demoralised, watched the house burn and the children cry. The squad cleaned up Severus' face and bandaged his eye, then shouldered their arms to begin the return march. All the soldiers were pleased. The warlord would hear of Roman retribution, and the commander at Arbeia would be interested to hear of the native's surly and belligerent attitude. They could also not help but revel in the power and authority they wielded as men of the state, as Romans and legionaries, free to punish anyone they saw fit, out here in the wild-lands beyond the frontier.

Maurice, the sixth-century Emperor and writer on military matters, devotes a huge amount of attention in his book *Strategikon* to full-scale warfare.

But he does not ignore the theory and practice of light infantry patrols. These formed the day-to-day duties of most infantrymen most of the time. The deployment of small infantry patrols has been a standard information-gathering tactic from Pharaonic times up to the age of gunpowder. In the twenty-first century, little has changed. Daily patrols are sent out into the streets of Baghdad or Basra or into Afghanistan's Helmand province. The principal reason for organising frequent infantry patrols is the fact that they deny the area to the enemy. The regular presence of troops on the roads and paths, talking to locals and moving through villages prevents the enemy from doing the same.

The type of warfare waged by the *limitanei* forces is today referred to as 'counter-insurgency' (COIN). COIN forces patrol from established bases to dominate the countryside, gain the initiative, and keep in touch with the local population. Patrolling was a necessity for soldiers of the *limitanei* and it was in essence their central mission. They were the Roman border patrol, and as the frontier troops, they were tasked with defending that frontier and always being aware of enemy activity beyond it. A squad moves through occupied or disputed territories to gather information, scout out enemy activity, and attack its patrols. Meanwhile, aggressive patrols will set up ambushes, raid enemy camps, and seize prisoners for interrogation. Whether you are crossing the Rhine to patrol the German forests, marching along the caravan routes of Syria or hiking up into the English Pennines, you and your squad are carrying out the same basic mission: look for trouble and report back when you find it. Historically, very small groups of infantrymen are used for patrolling so as to retain the element of surprise. It is because of this that patrols must be totally self-sufficient.

Maurice had definite ideas about who should and should not go out on patrol, recommending that candidates be: 'intelligent and alert … reliable.' In case of capture:

they should look very manly and be a cut above the other soldiers in physical appearance, morale and equipment, so they may project a noble image … The officer in charge of the patrol should be well above average, selected for his alertness, intelligence, and experience. For this sort of assignment requires intelligence and alertness more than bravery.[49]

How often these rigorous demands on the quality of the soldier required for patrols wee followed is open to question! Maurice goes on to recommend that men who know and trust each other should be despatched on patrol, rather than a collection of soldiers chosen at random from several units. 'The men so detailed cannot be used to the best advantage since they miss the support of their friends and they do not know one another.'[50]

The *Strategikon* also gives a fascinating description of how Roman soldiers were arrayed for missions in the rugged wilderness well away from roads and battlefields. Maurice remarks how they:

...should be lightly equipped ... They should march without wagons ... nor should they have heavy armament such as helmets and mail coats. The heavy-armed troops should carry moderate-sized shields, short spears ... the light-armed men should have smaller shields, lighter bows and arrows, short spears, short Moorish javelins, and some metal darts (*plumbatae*).[51]

Although Maurice is more concerned with safeguarding the passage of a large army through wooded or hilly areas, he does provide a detailed description of how scouting patrols should move across rough country:

...not in close order as in the heavy infantry, but in irregular groups, that is, three or four armed with javelins and shields so they may protect themselves if necessary while hurling the javelin. They should also have one archer to provide covering fire for them. These little groups ... should not march along in one solid formation, nor should they be widely scattered, but they should be one after the other to protect each other's rear. If something should happen to the leading group, if for example, they encounter resistance from the enemy or get bogged down in rough terrain, the groups behind them may move up to higher ground without being observed and come down upon the enemy's rear.[52]

The modern infantryman is familiar with three types of patrol: the reconnaissance patrol, standing patrol and fighting patrol. All of these can be found within the *Strategikon*. The recon patrol gains information about the enemy by stealth and observation. It avoids combat, and is interested in locating enemy positions and assessing both their strength and extent, as well as the lie of the land and the activities of any enemy patrols. The Late Roman army was well practised in this type of operation:

While the enemy is still reported to be far off, only the scouts should be sent out when the general wants to gather information about an enemy's movements, the nature of the roads, or fortified places ... In hazardous circumstances more than one patrol should be sent out and in more than one direction. They should vary and be constantly changing according to the nature of the ground. They should be far enough apart so that if the enemy stays at a good distance from our men and manages to elude one of the patrols, they will run into others and be discovered.[53]

Maurice goes on to describe how an experienced patrol can estimate the strength of the enemy force from the ground that has been trampled and by the size of their camp. A good scout can also estimate how long ago they passed through the area by careful observation of tracks and the droppings of both horses and men.

A standing patrol is, essentially, static. It is an observation and listening post used to give advance warning of enemy movement and to prevent enemy infiltration. A Late Roman patrol of this type might be posted to guard the approaches to a fort or perhaps the approach road to an army on the march, resting at a marching camp. If the enemy is aware of an observation post, it is likely to circumvent it and fall on the main unit without warning. To avoid this, the standing patrol uses stealth, moving into position at night and remaining concealed throughout daylight hours. Maurice recommends that troops should man outposts around an unfortified camp that is within enemy territory.

> If the approaches are narrow, a few will suffice. In obstructed and open country, there should be more of them, in different places, in touch with one another, and further out. Vigilance is particularly necessary at night when the enemy can easily and freely move in to observe the outposts, and if weak can sneak up and surprise them. For this reason the outposts should be at a distance from one another and frequently change location.[54]

Modern standing patrols are often very small and explicitly ordered to avoid combat, but their Late Roman counterparts would certainly be able to defend themselves if attacked.

The fighting patrol is decidedly offensive. The soldiers assigned have been given a particular objective to achieve, which will involve striking at the enemy in some form. The infantrymen of a twenty-first-century fighting patrol conduct a variety of missions: from capturing prisoners or equipment to making surprise raids on enemy positions; from laying ambushes against men and tanks, to tracking down and eliminating enemy patrols. Maurice records the use of fighting patrols in the *Strategikon*:

> Before any fighting the first and the safest thing to do is to choose a few experienced and lightly armed soldiers and have them very secretly carry out attacks against some detachments of the enemy. If they succeed in killing or capturing some of them, then most of our soldiers will take this as evidence of our own superiority. They will get over their nervousness, their morale will pick up, and they will gradually become used to fighting against them.[55]

He goes further, describing the art of night attack, particularly using archers and javelin throwers, who are adept at attacking barbarian camps. The troops should only carry what is necessary and should regulate their march to arrive within a mile or so of the enemy camp two hours before dawn. 'There the army should stay in hiding and rest, and then attack the enemy just before dawn.'[56]

This remarkable fourth-century military handbook also describes the capture of prisoners in order to discover the strength and the plans of the enemy. How do you capture enemy soldiers? Maurice has advice for the officer in charge of the patrol:

> They should be trained for this just as for hunting, stalking them unseen and undetected. A few should show themselves and then draw back while others circle around as unseen and concealed as the ground allows. Individuals should show themselves in several places while the main body heads for another place where they can hide themselves through the night.[57]

Obviously similar tactics could have been used against barbarian patrols, cutting them off and wiping them out or capturing them.

In exploring the everyday experiences of the 'last legionary', details of life on the march cannot be ignored. All soldiers, in all periods, in all theatres, marched and pounded across country, mile after mile. Historically, the lot of a soldier has always been to walk and to walk and to walk – and then to fight. The image of legionaries spending a 25-year career in an unending series of battles with ferocious barbarians is wrong. Perhaps spending 25 years on guard duty and endless marches is a little closer to the truth.

The Roman roads that criss-crossed the empire were built to facilitate the movement of troops from one garrison to another, or to reach a trouble-spot in time to bolster the local defences. Soldiers were accustomed to marching long distances. Every soldier, then as now, was familiar with life on the march. His unit may be transferring to a new location lock, stock and barrel; or it may be moving quickly, without baggage and pack animals, to deal with a barbarian incursion or uprising. These marches would generally be made on the Roman roads constructed for that very purpose, but once in the area of enemy activity, or for those *limitanei* forces already up against the frontier, cross-country marches away from well-surfaced roads would be undertaken.

Vegetius tells us that recruits were trained to march 20 Roman miles (30km) in 5 hours at a 'military step', and 24 Roman miles (35km) in 5 hours at the 'full step'. This kind of speed was designed to get a legion, or part of, to its destination without becoming strung out or disordered on the march. On campaign, the soldiers would habitually travel at the much reduced speed of the baggage animals. Away from the Roman road network, marching across country, the speed of a unit would have been reduced even further. The experiences of modern soldiers bear out Vegetius' numbers, and it seems that both then and now, 20 miles (32km) was a good day's walk for a loaded infantryman.

The military step referred to by Vegetius certainly had no connection with the modern idea of marching 'in step' but was most probably a measured pace designed to ensure that the soldiers marched in a tidy and uniform manner. Taller men march faster than their shorter comrades. A US Army captain who trained recruits at Fort Benning described how: 'The shorter men are in the front of a long road march, while the taller men are at the rear, which enables the people with the shorter strides to set the pace.'[58] Certainly, the Roman legion could not swap men around like this, the accounts of the legion on the march described by Josephus in *The Jewish War*,[59] describe how every unit had its assigned place in the marching column. Learning a military step, or prescribed pace, then, taught all soldiers to pace themselves, to step a set distance and retain their place in the formation. It may be that the Roman height requirement for new recruits was designed to address this issue and help create a unit of soldiers with a uniform stride.[60]

Troops of the Legio Praesidiensis, like many other *limitanei* units, are unlikely to have marched out with wagons, mule trains and a full complement of baggage to relocate to another province very often. *Limitanei* troops, instead, would be much more familiar with fast armed marches to bolster defences at other points along the frontier, marching quickly, in armour, with weapons and a basic food ration. Of course the border troops were also familiar with the cross-country march, off-road, carrying a fighting load and supplies to last the duration of the patrol. The former might involve marching to Eboracum or Derventio, or to a point on the coast where Picts are known to have landed in force. The latter would involve cliff-top patrols, checking coves and beaches, moving through local villages, checking in at villa estates like Harpham and Rudston, and questioning travellers on the roads.

There was quite a homecoming for Gaius. Modesta and her father laid on a feast, and Severus was invited to join them, though his left eye still remained bandaged. The meal consisted of peeled apples served with honey, cooked chicken in fish sauce accompanied by cabbage and leeks fried with olive oil and caraway seeds. Oh how this compared to the barley soup and hardtack rations they had been eating on the *Diomedes*! When Modesta had served everyone wine with a little water she announced her news – Gaius was going to be a father! Severus clapped him on the back, while his father-in-law wept that Modesta's mother was not alive to see her first grandchild. There was a toast and many congratulations.

AD 394. There were tears this morning. Since one of the slaves had ran away after being beaten by Gaius, Modesta had found the leather import business increasingly hard to manage during the times her husband was away. And he was due to set off on a one-week patrol this very morning. Of course looking after their two-year-old son, Flavius, did not make things any easier.

'Pay Ursinus,' she insisted. 'We have a son and a business and I need you here, pay him the 600 *denarii*, just as Victorinus did last month. He will send another squad, and not yours. Please Gaius. Stay at home…'

He loved his wife, and he wanted to keep his business afloat, but he could not afford 600 *denarii*, and he was not the sort of man to let his commander down. He had developed a reputation for loyalty and hard work which had seen him rise to the position of *caput contubernii*, or squad leader. What had happened to Marcus Gavius, the walking skeleton? Last spring the legion had joined the Numerus Supervenientium Petuariensium from Derventio in a combined operation against Pictish raiders who had allied with deserters and rebels, in the moor lands. The Legio Praesidiensis had not suffered many deaths, but there were injuries. The Dux Britanniarum was visiting the moor land camp where the two units were based and had offered to take the most seriously injured back to Eboracum with him, for recuperation and then redeployment to what was left of the Sixth Legion there. Ursinus had pulled Gavius out of his tent. 'This man is suffering from fevers, he needs to be treated!' he lied. Gavius refused to go, saying he was fitter than any man in the legion, and that he could carry twice as much for twice as long. Ursinus again insisted, and despite Marcus Gavius' strident refusals, he was pushed onto a wagon and shipped off to Eboracum for treatment in the infirmary! That is how the legion got rid of Marcus Gavius and how Gaius became the file leader, eleven years after joining up.

The seven-day march was to head west past the Red Stone, then north into the Vale of Derventia, a wild land of marshes, where the men would then turn coastward and reach the sea at Two Bays. After staying overnight at the signal station, there, the patrol was to follow the cliff top path south back to Praesidium, stopping overnight at the Draco Point signal tower. Six, perhaps seven, days after setting off from Praesidium it would return. This was a reconnaissance and policing mission, but information gathered from the watchtower garrisons would be passed on to Sextus Aemilianus.

Marching Diaries

What were these marches like? The author has joined members of the research group Comitatus on a number of marches to investigate the properties of Late Roman equipment. These cross-country walks were intended to be highly authentic, but they recreated only elements of the Roman marching experience rather than duplicate a complete Roman patrol from start to finish. Each march has focussed on a different type of mission and a different load of equipment. Three marches in particular provided valuable information – the first, a climb to the summit of Scafell Pike, England's highest mountain, the second, a 12-km march along the highest and most rugged section of Hadrian's Wall, and third, a march along the line of a Roman road cutting across the North Yorkshire Moors. To gain useful results from the marches, each needed to represent some kind of Late Roman objective, and the planning of the expedition followed naturally from there.

The first march involved a walk from Hardknott Roman fort in Cumbria, up the Esk valley toward the base of Scafell Pike. From there the walkers would climb to the summit. Worries about what to take (and what not to take) plagued us even at the moment of departure. The weather was cold and we needed to be wary of rain, maybe even snow and sleet. It would certainly be extremely cold at the summit with wind chill factored in. The walk would warm us up, however, and of course, no-one wanted to be overburdened. We all wore Late Roman long-sleeved tunics of wool, woollen *bracae* and socks. We all wore a woollen *sagum* (rectangular army cloak) and each of us had a period hat to wear. Additionally, we carried ration bags, wool mittens and lots of water. To carry water we used leather waterbags. The extremely rugged terrain meant that this walk would be undertaken as a light troop unit, but we still had to be combat capable. The author took a long sword (spatha), recurve bow and quiver full of arrows. His companions took either short spears or *spicula*, as well as an axe or *spatha*. It was important that we have everything at hand for a fight. As a light infantry squad we were tasked with reconnaissance not combat, but every soldier was still required to pull his weight in a fight. No-one took helmets, although one walker did wear a scale armour corselet, and all the spearmen carried small round shields. We had settled on our choice of arms and armour without reference to Vegetius or Maurice, but once the walk was over we were delighted to find that the *Strategikon* recommended that light troops be sent into mountains in four-man squads, with the very equipment load that we had used. This vindicated both our approach and our choice of weapons.

We did attempt to rationalise our route, and came to two conclusions. At Hardknott Fort, a desolate posting if ever there was one, we could see the rugged nature of the terrain and imagine the plight of the soldiers stationed there. The thought occurred to one walker that a march up here in full kit might well have been a regular feature of life at the fort. A dip in the warm baths just outside the fort walls afterwards may just have made up for the exertion. Alternatively, we did compare Scafell Pike to other mountain ranges. Roman legions routinely crossed the Alps and campaigned in Armenia and the mountains of Turkey; Alexander's troops reached the Hindu Kush in comparison to which Scafell is but a molehill. So we thought we were justified in recreating a light infantry patrol in mountain country. Perhaps there were Scotti raiders snapping at our heels, or encamped at Wastwater, the other side of Mickledore Pass…

We marched. The sun shone out from a deep blue January sky. We sweated and sweated. Off came the hats, the cloaks, the mittens. Yes, we were fighting for breath as the inclines steepened. One man lost a knife whilst I snapped the sole of my boot and had to borrow a pair of spares. It goes without saying that the landscape was extraordinary. It was a stunning environment and to walk through this savage, untouched wilderness in Roman clothing, armed to the teeth, was an experience not easily forgotten. We passed waterfalls, crossed an old stone bridge and soon entered the Great Moss, a marshy bog in the cusp of the valley through which the Esk flowed. Here we stepped with care since no-one relished the idea of a soaking followed by sub-zero wind-chill at the peak. The party split up to find a way across the Esk and we met up later ready for the climb along a stream that came down from the high ridge. It was a punishing climb, with regular ten-minute stops. The shields really seemed to weigh the others down, and the soldier wearing scale armour was both overheating and suffocating. The group leader kept us going. The enclosed leather boots (*calcei*) did a decent job, but they did not grip the smooth rocks and did not stay particularly dry. Hobnails were lost, a seam or two was split, and (as already mentioned) the sole of my boots snapped.

At the top, after a frantic scramble on the scree slope, we crunched through snow to meet more traditional climbers who were surprised to see Romans clambering up to the peak. Of course the view from the top of Scafell Pike was stunning, the clouds below us, sunlight sparkling off of the Irish Sea and the fells receding away from us like the wave tops of a vast earthen ocean.

Our time was limited, and after a quick, authentic lunch, hunched down on a snow-covered, frost-shattered rock peak, we hastened down the mountain. We were chased by both nightfall and by a long tongue of thick mist which threatened to engulf the peak. At a breakneck pace we reached our cars as night fell. The march had taken eight hours in total and tested our legs and our backs to the limit. Our clothing worked superbly, the wool kept us warm and dry. The shields, well… we could have done without them. But my long sword did not prove a burden, and neither did my bow. The others found spears and *spiculum* to be quite helpful in climbing, and coming down the mountain I actually quite envied them. Two pieces of kit need particular mention: my scabbard chape did excellent service, without it the end of my scabbard would have been knocked to pieces banging on rocks, and my leg wraps (*fascia*) were excellent. My left leg-wrap came unwrapped right at the summit, but was easily re-tied.

On the way back my right leg went up to the knee in a bog and another walker had to pull me out, but when I later took my *bracae* off to wash I noticed that they were absolutely spotless. The leg-wraps themselves are absolutely black with dirt from rocks, ice, mud and bog, but they kept the *bracae* very clean.

The march along Hadrian's Wall was just as challenging, but threw up new problems. The plan was to camp authentically, at Winshields, just south of the highest part of the Wall. The following day, we would don a full load of armour and weaponry (a 'fighting load' in modern parlance) and march east, along the Wall past Housesteads fort to the temple of Mithras close to the unexcavated fort at Carrawburgh. This was a 10-mile march over rough terrain. At the end of the walk, we would return by modern transport to the camp site for a second night of authentic camping. The rationale behind the walk was that of a 'march to contact', a full day's march with the prospect of hard fighting at the end of it. I wore an Intercisa-style ridge helmet and a coat of ringmail, I carried a large oval shield, a spear and a *spatha*. Both of my comrades wore scale armour and carried *spathas*, one wore a Dar-al-Madinah-style *spangenhelm*, and carried a spear, the other wore a Burgh-castle-style ridge helmet and carried a *spiculum*.

There was an immediate problem with footwear, which has been discussed in Chapter 4, but once that had been resolved the march got underway. The mist clung heavily to the ridges and the Wall itself, the grass was damp and slippery. It quickly became apparent to me that marching in full armour was going to be difficult; the weight bore down heavily and turned every incline into torture. We passed mile castle 40, and then after Steel Rigg, mile castle 39. We passed the lake called Crag Lough, but it sat invisible on the other side of the Wall and the crags themselves were still wreathed in thick mist. The day began with fog, and although it brightened a little the weather was still misty and evocative. Over the Wall in places, where it sat on high crags, the rocks dropped away into the fog.

At Housesteads fort we picnicked, Roman-style, in the shrine of the standards of the HQ building. I ate little, preferring a few figs, some smoked cheese and bites of bread. I was exhausted and simply enjoyed the rest. I was almost out of *posca*, a legionary's drink which I recreated by adding a dash of red wine and red wine vinegar to water. I had brought a full litre, and it proved very refreshing – thirst quenching with a zesty tang. After lunch we jumped the wall amidst a growing crowd of onlookers and made our escape, passing Nag Burn Gate, a civilian gateway through the Wall. Up to Sewingshields Crags and the lovely woods there, we marched on. Over-heating. Shoulders getting more and more painful. The sheer weight pulling you down and down. And at times the constriction on your chest of straps and armour making it hard to lift an arm. I was getting thoroughly exhausted slowing down all the time. There were more turrets and mile castles, in a blur of lightening skies and staring at the grassy path ahead. At last we spotted the Mithraeum and the car park adjacent to it. Fantastic. Lifting off the helmet, armour, shield, *spatha*, belt and bags was like flying. I'd carried around 5 stone (30kg) of gear 10 miles – and I only weighed 10 and a half (70kg) to begin with!

There were lessons learned on this march. Although my comrades were not as fatigued as myself, they still found the going hard, but both certainly had better stamina and stronger legs. On level ground despite my heavy armour, I could maintain a fast and regular rhythm, but once the path began to climb that weight of armour almost brought me to a stand-still. Straps from the packs, waterskins, shields and other bags soon became very painful for everyone. Switching from one shoulder to another helped, but the best remedy was a piece of cloth padding (in most cases the soldier's hat!) to dull the pain. Wider straps that distributed the load more evenly would also have reduced the pressure. The shield was better out of the way slung on the back then held in the left hand, a free hand was usually needed to negotiate some climbs and to use the spear as a walking stick on tricky descents. Much of my food carried on the march remained uneaten. During the walk the body requires only a little food – bread, slices of smoked sausage, nuts, beef jerky and so on, but in small quantities. Only after the march had ended did we realise how hungry we were. Besides water, we took various other drinks with us; cider, wine and *posca*. The walker with wine was desperate for a drink of water by the march's end.

Next, a walk was planned that could explore some other aspect of Roman soldiering. From a light infantry patrol to a heavy infantry march, focus now turned to the possibility of carrying a full set of camping equipment on the march. This would include a canvas shelter, fresh food to cook in the evening and the following morning, as well as the pots and pans needed to prepare it. A proposal to carry the camping kit *in addition* to armour, helmet and large shield was quickly abandoned when the walkers experimented with the proposed loads. The march was planned to follow as closely as possible the route of a Roman road that crosses the North Yorkshire Moors. It would begin at the village of Goathland and head south-west, taking in an actual stretch of Roman road still visible on Wheeldale Moor, to end at the Roman practice camps at Cawthorn, where we had arranged to camp overnight in an adjacent field.

This walk was purely an exploration of how easy or hard it was to travel long distances along Roman roads and camp after the march. Perhaps we were skirmishers, scouts, messengers or a moor-land patrol. The weight of the canvas, bedrolls and cooking equipment precluded the wearing of armour and the carriage of heavy weapons. We all travelled light, with small skirmish shields, a spear, *spiculum*, some *veruta* (light javelins), a Saxon fighting knife or two.

The group set off from the Mallyan Spout Hotel in Goathland, North Yorkshire. We descended the gorge and moved swiftly along the rocks and boulders to the impressive 70-foot-high waterfall. Going was tricky, especially with all the camping gear we had strapped to ourselves. When it came time to meet the line of the Roman road, we scrambled and climbed straight up the side of the gorge following a stream bed. Now the heavy loads of blankets, cloaks, food, wine, pots and pans, tent canvas, javelins, shields, deerskins etc. began to drag. We met the Roman road and after a rest, began the long, comfortable tramp along it. It is now a modern minor road, but gave us a good impression of a Roman military route march; three men abreast, keeping up good conversation, trying to forget the pain of the straps digging deeper and deeper, getting almost to the bone. At some point, someone would call a halt and they would shift over the packs and shields to the other shoulder. The torture could begin again on the left side now…

We crossed a river via stepping stones and ascended the valley side, to eventually meet the Roman road on Wheeldale Moor. The original Roman flagstones remain in situ for a mile or two, and all the walkers felt a particular thrill marching at speed along an original Roman road in Roman military clothing carrying everything needed to survive out here for several days. Verisimilitude was heightened by the fact that we weren't strolling, we were chasing daylight to our intended campsite. Whilst on the remains of the road the sun went in, and hailstones came crashing down. The other walkers used their shields to ward off the hail, but my shield was strapped underneath other pieces of kit (shields need to be ready for action, against Picts – and hailstones!), my hat was doing duty as a padding for the knife-like straps of my baggage. I took the pain and carried on splashing through the marsh that surrounded the wreckage of the Late Roman road. How many soldiers had marched at speed across the road, in hail and rain like us? The hobnails crunched satisfyingly on the paved surface.

With the hail gone, we forded a fast flowing river and ducked into a forest to rest. We ate a wonderful lunch with wine, hardtack, smoked cheese and fish, fresh bread and other treats in the sunshine whilst sat on comfortable piles of dry pine needles. A brook bubbled past us. Certainly this was the best lunch of any march we had so far attempted. From now on, the weather turned; we heard tremendous thunderclaps to the west and watched the black clouds build up. Soon we were up and off, following more minor roads that tracked the Roman road leading us up to Cawthorn camps sitting on a grassy bluff. These Roman practice camps were used as training bases by local Roman legions – maybe thousands of young, inexperienced and half-baked legionaries camped up here for the weekend over the centuries.

We trudged up a very steep minor road to get to the top of the plateau. It was back-breaking and thoroughly exhausting work, with stops at every other tree. At the top the view back across the moor land was magnificent. It was time to establish our camp in the field we had arranged to use, and as we hunted for a suitable spot, snow began to fall. We had brought everything we needed for at least a three-day camp out on the hill (though only one was planned), from needle and thread to firestarting kit, food, wine, pans, bedrolls, tents, deerskins, axe, cups, and more… A great end to a fast-paced, hard-driven scenic march along Roman roads and foot paths, through forest, across moor land, down ravines and up a very steep hill.

As a marching exercise, this final experiment taught me the value of planning. Between the three members of the group we were carrying everything needed for a three-day patrol in the wilderness. For the Roman infantryman of AD 394, however, some of that kit could easily be left behind. Drinkable water was ubiquitous in Roman Yorkshire, the soldier would not need to carry two pints along with him, as we did. Wine was a luxury he could also have done without. One also wonders if a tent would have been carried, since it was common practice for Roman troops to find billets amongst civilians. Any roundhouse or barn might do, without any need of official sanction or paperwork. In extremis the cloak would become a makeshift shelter, and the soldiers would find a suitable wall or bank out of the wind, and wrap themselves up in that for the night. Assuming that the patrol was tasked with camping in the wilds, however, perhaps as part of a reconnaissance patrol, we felt justified in carrying the tent canvas.

The greatest problem encountered by the participants of these experimental marches was weight distribution. If you carry your own equipment and weaponry you must carry it over your shoulder. One appreciates the value of a capacious and well-padded rucksack when the shield strap, the waterskin strap, the bag strap, sword baldric, and strap for the bedroll all bite into the shoulder like knives. Having some straps across the left shoulder and others across the right alleviates some of the pain, but instead constricts the chest and makes taking any of the straps off (to get at a cloak or a shield, for example) a labour. It seems best, on reflection, to carry equipment in the following order: cloak first if it is a cold day (tie the cloak up in the blanket roll if it is too warm to wear, and remember that marching warms a person up), follow this with the bedroll and then the ration bag. The waterskin can go next, followed by the shield. To get at any of these items, each piece of kit on top of it has to first be removed, making the order very important. For the legionary, access to the shield is paramount. The waterskin will be needed on the walk and if strapped on too early the walker will be unable to lift it to his lips. We came to these conclusions through planning as well as trial and error. For the seasoned Roman legionary such matters were learned in training.

The legionaries following Gaius eastwards on the patrol first checked in at the Villa Claudius, picking up a jug of mead and fresh goat cheese from the kitchen. Everyone appreciated their presence, even though Claudius the Younger had hired men for his own bodyguard. These thugs had plenty of weapons and kept the tenants 'in order'. They were actually paid to protect the villa from bandits, rebels and barbarians. From the villa the patrol headed to the Red Stone, a six-metre-high holy stone standing like some finger of God out of the ground. They all touched the stone, reaching above the ritual blood-stains, and passed on to the evening camp. Each night they camped against a bank or in woods away from the path, making the best of the rations they had brought with them, mucking in and co-operating. The squad had a new recruit, but this man was reviled by the others and they barely spoke to him. The nineteen-year-old Veteranus had cut off his thumb to avoid the conscription, but despite that he had still been forcibly recruited into the Legio Praesidiensis. Useless in a fight, the man was given all of the jobs no-one else wanted. He was usually passed over for patrol duty, but stood guard at the fort night after night, or was detailed a week of latrine duties. When he did go into the field everyone cursed his name, but passed their gear to him. He was loaded down with blanket-rolls and equipment, twice as much as any of the other squad members. Veteranus never complained, though, he just got on with it. He spoke to no-one, but shuffled around wearing an unmoving mask of sadness and dejection.

In the Vale of Derventia, a marshy lowland between two long ranges of hills, the patrol slowed, picking its way along dry ground, avoiding the pools and stagnant reed-beds. Wooden poles, intricately carved with tribal holy symbols marked the safe path. They watched herons and geese on the water, and saw fishermen in dugouts, almost naked, smeared in mud. 'Savages,' declared Cassius.

That evening, the men tried to shelter under canvas from a rainstorm. They had found three large trees on firm ground, and erected the soaking tents beneath them. All seven men crammed into the two shelters and almost immediately the open-ended tents were filled with thousands of midges that were just as desperate to escape the rain. No-one ate or slept or got any form of rest the entire night, but simply fought to stay away from the rain and the insects. Gaius put Veteranus on guard duty that night, and he sat mournfully against one of the tree trunks with a hooded cloak pulled around him.

Unable to light a fire in the morning, the men of the *contubernium* ate hardtack and cheese. Gaius had the men pack up and set off marching east toward the coast. Everyone found the thick mud and the waterlogged fields treacherous to negotiate, and energy-sapping. Only Brocchus managed to stay immaculately clean during the passage of the flooded valley, to the frustration of his comrades. All of the pathways had become streams, but they led eventually to the signal station at Two Bays, and that is where the soldiers bedded down for the night, with wine and warmth and welcome company. Gaius, as squad leader, spoke at length to the *centenarius* Brigionus who commanded the station, and who recognised Gaius from his trip north on the *Diomedes* two years ago. He gave his thoughts on the Pictish raids.

'The Picts are getting bolder. Yearly they breach the Wall. Almost weekly they send ships along our coast, ships packed with warriors hungry for Roman gold and silver. With that booty they raise ever bigger war bands, and lead them south on even bigger expeditions.'

'We can stop them, though.' suggested Gaius.

'Perhaps. But it is unremitting, never-ending. Their favourite time to attack is sunset, when the east out to sea is dark and shadowed, and the land is still lit by the setting sun. The Picts can come out of the darkness and select exactly which part of the coastline they wish to pull up on. They might attack a place that very night, and be off in the morning; or wait up, steal horses and spend a day or two raiding one rath after another.'

'Do you receive warnings from local people of Pictish boats?' asked Gaius.

'We do. Although I prefer to take it easy, if I hear they are inland using stolen horses to raid the towns and settlements, I send out men to lie in wait close to their anchorage. Catch them on the way back, loaded down with silver and gold and all the nice things in life. It makes the slaughter all worthwhile. The locals don't get it back... but we've killed the Picts responsible. I get my cut of course. You are *caput contubernii* now,' he laughed, 'You know how to make a little money from this situation we are in!'

As dawn broke, the *contubernium* shouldered its arms and camping equipment, and set off south along the cliff-top path.

Carrying Food and Shelter

One wonders how much equipment a legionary carried with him. Luckily Vegetius gives us an actual figure with which to work. He says that: 'Recruits should very frequently be made to carry a burden of up to 60lb [60 Roman pounds – equal to 20kg] and route march at the military step, since on arduous campaigns they have necessarily to carry their rations together with their arms.'[61]

It almost goes without saying that the soldier, whatever he was doing, was heavily loaded with equipment – such is the sorry burden of the infantryman throughout history. Obviously, *what* he carried depended on where he was going and what he was intending to do. Marching into a full-scale battle demanded a different load to a cross-country patrol, carrying messages along the Roman roads, the crossing of a mountain to spy on the enemy, or redeploying with the rest of the cohort to a watchtower or another fort. We can identify three main equipment loads for the fourth-century legionary: the fighting load, the patrol load and the campaign load.

The fighting load consisted of the armour, helmet, large round or oval shield and all the weaponry that the infantryman needed to participate in a full-scale battle. Typically, as much armour as possible was worn, particularly by the file-leaders who took the front. This panoply was heavy; the author's shield weighs around 8kg, his suit of ringmail (short-sleeved and only hip-length) weighs 12kg. Add to this iron leg protection (greaves), a padded *subarmalis*, military belt, a *spatha*, a spear, helmet and five *plumbatae*, and his reconstructed fighting load weighs in at a total of 30kg.

Although he refers only to cavalrymen in Book VII of the *Strategikon*, Maurice advises his men to take with them cloaks and a ration bag with a little dried food or bread to the battlefield, along with a small flask of water. Although the aim is to fight unencumbered without the burden of packs and supplies, the veteran military leader recognised that a defeated enemy may flee to a fortified position and that it would be unfortunate to have to break off operations just because his troops did not have enough food and water with which to follow them.

Those soldiers sent out on patrol or campaign, away from the fort or the fortified camp for days, weeks or months at time, must reconfigure their kit. Survival on the march requires plenty of food and camping equipment and therefore a reduction in arms and armour. As we have already seen, the *Strategikon* clearly describes the types of weapons to carry across country, but little is said of rations or of tents. The expedition that Comitatus mounted across the North Yorkshire Moors in 2006 was in part an attempt to help define what a patrol would eat, what it would carry, how it would sleep – to fill in the blanks left by Maurice's (unusually) terse advice.

There are no surviving images of Roman soldiers drinking from water bottles, and the modern historical interpreter is forced to use his judgement in creating such an artefact. Some use circular iron flasks, similar in size and shape to American Civil War drinking canteens, but there is no evidence that they held water, in fact the mosaics at the Villa Armerina actually suggest they held oil for the bath-house. Ceramic flasks of a similar shape are common finds across the empire, and some believe that these too are drinking vessels, perhaps carried in net-bags or slung on leather straps across the shoulder (plate 28). After marching with military kit, the author feels that no Roman soldier would have need of a heavy and fragile ceramic water flask. If he carried anything at all, it is likely to have been a waterskin of leather. A peasant is depicted on a North African mosaic, drinking from a large goatskin waterskin. The Roman legionary would need something similar, only smaller. The skin might be hard, and lined with waterproof pitch, or it might be soft and flexible and contain a pig's bladder. Either way, the waterskin weighs nothing and is far more durable than pottery.

Marching rations need to be light in weight and preserved for later consumption, often by drying or smoking. These rations were designed to last for many days in the field. Ammianus relates how Julian rebuilt forts along the River Meuse during his campaigns against the German tribes, and provisioned them by taking part of the seventeen days' rations which the troops carried on their backs. It seems that seventeen-days-worth of rations may have been an accepted standard in the Late Roman army; the *Scriptores Historiae Augustae* tells us that some soldiers refused to '… carry rations for 17 days, as is normal practice, except in barbarian territory.'[62] The *Codex Theodosius* states that troops on the move should receive hardtack biscuits (*buccellatum*), bread, ordinary wine (*vinum*) and sour wine (*acetum*), salted pork and mutton.[63] It seems that hardtack and *acetum* would be consumed for two days, and on the third day the decent wine and bread would be eaten. We have other sources which tell us how bleak the marching diet was. Vegetius remarks that soldiers should have 'grain [i.e. wheat], wine, vinegar and salt at all times'. That wheat ration will have come as hardtack biscuits. The Emperor Hadrian lived the life of a regular soldier for a while and enjoyed '*larido, caseo et posca*', which was bacon fat, cheese and sour wine (also called *acetum*). Ammianus also mentions *buccellatum*. Avidius Cassius, a general who rebelled against Marcus Aurelius, ordered his troops to carry nothing except '*laridum ac buccellatum at que acetum*', i.e. bacon fat, hardtack and sour wine.

It would seem to be an exceptionally grim-sounding menu, but what would a typical meal-on-the-march actually taste like? *Buccellatum* (hardtack, or wheat crackers) would feature quite highly, as would bacon and lard. Using just those ingredients, Northern troops in the American Civil War concocted 'skilleegalee', hardtack crumbled into bacon and hot lard. The author has tried this for breakfast in camp, and it does the job just fine. *Buccellatum* can also be fried as it is, or soaked in water till mushy and then fried, or put in the pot with other ingredients. The American hardtack baked in factories for packing in boxes for Civil War armies was square or rectangular, flat and punched with holes that helped with the long slow process of desiccation. There is no contemporary depiction of Roman hardtack, but it is doubtful the crackers were baked in neat rectangular shapes for storage in boxes. More likely each piece of hardtack was ring-doughnut shaped. Paximados is a traditional Cretan bread that is still 'twice-baked' to a recipe that goes back to the Byzantine age. One style of Cretan paximados is ring-shaped and was until recently carried on a stick by some street vendors. Illustrations of ring-shaped paximados carried over the shoulder on a stick can be found in the Medieval period, showing a long tradition of doughnut-shaped hardbreads that most likely originated in the Byzantine period, inherited from a Late Roman practice.

Figure **25**. A traveller depicted in the *Liber ad Honorem Augusti*, an illustrated poem from late twelfth-century Italy. He carries traditional rural hard-breads over his shoulder on a long stick.

Perhaps the best illustration of this hardtack is of a traveller in the *Liber ad Honorem Augusti*, a panegyric poem from late twelfth-century Italy, written by Peter of Eboli. It shows a man on the road with a circular water-flask or bag over his left shoulder, and a metre-long stick that widens towards the end over his right shoulder with two ring-shaped loaves of paximados threaded onto it (figure 25, above). The author has had twice-baked hardtack in the Roman manner and found that a stick of that length can easily hold twenty individual loaves of hardtack. On the march, he discovered that the loaves fell onto the shoulder and quickly disintegrated, but that a loop of string tied to the top of the stick, threaded through each loaf and back up to the top, kept the paximados sitting high on the pole, and out of the way. To get at a loaf, the knot was untied and then retied a little higher. It is doubtful that Roman soldiers carried their ring-shaped hardbread threaded onto sticks (they had plenty of other equipment to carry on the shoulder), but the longevity of this shape and style of hardtack is impressive.

Remember that hardtack was a way to preserve the wheat ration. It was essential. Soldiers may even have ground it down in their mixing bowls (*mortaria*) to turn it back into flour with which they can bake fresh bread! Wheat or barley grains could also be carried, but they would need to be ground before use, using portable millstones carried by the *contubernium's* mule. Hardtack is a ready-to-eat wheat ration. Flour *can* be carried on its own. It is much more prone to damp and spoilage than wheat grains, however, but mixed with water and lard and slapped onto a flat stone warming next to the fire (or onto a frying pan) an unleavened bread can be cooked quickly. Alternatively, it can be used to cook up 'soldiers porridge', *pulmentum,* the staple meal of the legions for a thousand years, and surviving in Italian kitchens today as polenta. Wheat is always the major food source; flour or hardtack are essential for the legionary's survival.

We know that the Romans loved smoked cheese and so that might be on the soldier's marching menu. Smoked sausage would also travel well. There is no mention of beef jerky (known to the South Africans as biltong): strips of seasoned beef that have been cured and preserved ready for the trail, but beef was popular on Roman forts in Britain, and it would not be surprising if this subsistence food found its way onto the legionary's marching menu. Pearl barley and lentils are easily transportable and both foodstuffs can be soaked in water for several hours before cooking. Either can be added to a vegetable broth to create a very filling and tasty meal for soldiers relaxing after the day's march, or eaten on their own as a basic dish. Troops marching out of Praesidium on patrol may even have carried dried fish in their packs. The fish is dried by salting, a process which causes the fish to harden and shrink. In this state it may survive for months. To return it to an edible form, the fish must first be soaked in water repeatedly to flush out the salt. During the process the fish swells up to its original size at which point it is ready for cooking.

What about boiled eggs? A few apples? Some vegetables (leek, onion, radish, celery, cabbage, parsnip, carrot – take your pick). For a short patrol, how about a slice of beef or pork, perhaps a few lamb chops or chicken drumsticks? Of course the big factor here is: how far are you going? For a two-day hike your wife in the *vicus* can pack left-overs to fill your belly. For a week or two on the frontier or beyond, or a march to the Channel to cross for a campaign in Gaul, all your rations are going to be dried, salted or smoked. It must also be remembered that the local populace often feared the army more than the barbarians, since the army had government sanction to requisition supplies while on the march. Troops were even issued reaping hooks with which to harvest grain. They had a locust-like tendency to take whatever they liked from the farms and villages through which they passed. Maurice in the *Strategikon* exhorts his troops to avoid disturbing the crops of local people as they marched through friendly territory, but of course the fact that he remonstrates against the abuse meant that it was occurring!

To dwell on the contents of the legionaries' ration bag might perhaps be seen by some as irrelevant detail, obscuring more important matters. For these men, living hard lives, sharing night-time guard duties, digging out defensive ditches, marching hard across the British countryside in all weathers, food was the most important of matters. Battles in distant provinces fought by emperors and co-emperors against yet another barbarian tribe, or more likely against one another, were in fact the irrelevant details.

All of this food had to be carried in a bag, and every soldier must have had such a bag. But not a single one survives in the archaeological record from this period. Worse, there are no clear depictions of military bags in the third, fourth or fifth centuries upon which an accurate reconstruction could be based. Parts of a leather satchel have survived at Bar Hill, on the Antonine Wall, but this is of a much earlier date. It may represent the leather satchels depicted on Trajan's Column, in Rome. This monument dates from the first years of the second century and shows legionaries marching with slim rectangular packs slung from forked sticks carried on the shoulder. They are of a very modern envelope shape, with a triangular flap and a central ring closure. Such ration bags may have survived into the fourth century, but equally possibly, they may not. The forked pole carried on the shoulder with ration bags and equipment hanging from it is not mentioned in any Late Roman source or depicted anywhere but on Trajan's Column. It is extremely doubtful that the Roman forked pole survived much beyond the second century.

A soldier's pack *is* depicted on a fourth-century mosaic, but there is little detail and those details are indistinct. The 'Mosaic of the Grades' from the excavated Mithraic temple of Felicissimus at Ostia shows the ritual emblems of the grade of 'soldier' (a specific rank within the Mithraic religion). It includes a helmet, spear and a marching pack, that appears to be a teardrop-shaped leather or linen bag, with the top closed off, perhaps with a drawstring (figure 26). There does not appear to be any form of strap. This bag may have resembled a traditional sailor's duffle bag, with a circular bottom and cylindrical body, tied off at the top.

The bag on this mosaic might be thought of as a mosaic-maker's fancy, but the same pack turns up again in a Mithraeum – this time on a wall painting. Mithraic scholars Vermaseren and Van Essen described the appearance of a temple initiate depicted on poorly preserved wall paintings discovered at the church of Santa Prisca, in Rome. The only published photograph attests to a painting in a terrible condition, and the Italian authorities will not issue visitors' permits to view the temple. The two scholars, however, described the soldier-initiate in detail, wearing a long-sleeved bright brown tunic with two rows of purple piping at the wrists, plus a red-brown cloak. On his left shoulder is a military bag (*sarcina*) 'which he holds at its round buttoned-up end with his left hand.'[64] The

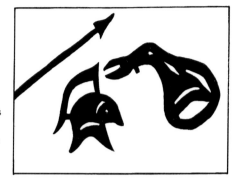

Figure **26**. The various grades of the Mithraic religion are displayed on the fourth-century Mosaic of Felicissimus, Ostia. This detail shows the emblems of the 'Soldier' grade, a spear, a crested helmet and a legionary's kit bag.

'round end' of this military pack fits the slight illustration we have from the Ostia mosaic. The observation about buttons is interesting, is the bag buttoned at the bottom? Without better-documented evidence, we shall never know.

There is better evidence, but it comes from the sixth century, from the Imperial Palace in Istanbul. Here in the East, the armies of Rome continued to wage war, to make peace and to intimidate the locals well after Rome fell in AD 476. A mosaic discovered there depicts the head and shoulders of a legionary, wearing a traveller's sun-hat, with a kit-bag thrown over his shoulder. The bag is a red-brown colour and its pleated texture suggests that it was made of thin leather. At the top, a drawstring closure can be seen, and it appears as if the soldier uses this drawstring to carry the bag over his shoulder (figure 28). Although the envelope-shaped satchel of the first and second centuries may have been used by the legions in the fourth and fifth, we can be much more certain that the duffel-bag appearing in the Istanbul mosaic *was*.

The marching pack of a legionary will have carried a lot more than food. From experience, there would be also a firestarting kit, a hand axe, a ball of string, a comb, a good knife, a whetstone, spare socks, wooden bowl and spoon, spare shoes or sandals, a candle stub, a pouch containing coins and other valuables, a few dice, and perhaps a spare tunic or a spare strap used to sling the shield over the shoulder (plate 22).

The Roman army was well equipped with tents, and writers in the fourth century mention them repeatedly in their accounts of the army on campaign. Unfortunately, no obvious depictions of military tents survive for this period, making any reconstruction difficult. We know from the archaeological record only of large, 3m square, leather tents used by soldiers of the Principate to accommodate a *contubernium* (eight-man squad).

Figure **27**. A simple shelter depicted in the sixth-century *Vienna Genesis* manuscript.

Fragments of tent leather from Newstead and Birdoswald were calf, others from Valkenburg were of goatskin. Each tent of this type was made up of panels of leather stitched together using a waterproof stitching technique. Junkelmann's recreated goatskin tent weighed 28.5 kg (leather alone), and once the rope, poles and pegs were added, it came close to 40kg. Just the leather alone is a substantial burden for a man on the march. The squad tent is certainly something that goes in the baggage train. Even if such large squad tents were still in use during the Late period, they are far too large to carry on foot and would only be erected once a fortified camp had been constructed while on campaign. The details and discomforts of life in a Roman marching column, on the road to war, within enemy territory are explored in Chapter 8. For all types of infantry patrols, the large squad tent will have remained behind at the fort or with the army's wagons (if on the march).

What of the 'field expedient shelter'? What did legionaries use for shelter when they weren't being followed by a baggage train? In many wars throughout history, the infantryman has had to find shelter where he could: in barns, ruined houses, foxholes, under fallen trees, dug-outs or simply crouched up against a wall. Many armies have issued their soldier with tarpaulins or blankets which have served as an improvised shelter. The *Strategikon* recommends that cavalry 'should take with them … small tents or a couple of heavy cloaks, the one for covering if needed and the other as a tent or shelter'.[65] Referring to a number of modern wilderness-survival books, the author discovered that a simple rectangle of cloth or canvas like this can be turned into a number of different shelter types. A single cloak, tied with string to a second, would make an acceptable shelter cloth in spring and summer (the campaigning season).

One of the shelter types in the book stood out: two short poles tied where they cross, with a larger beam using the cross as a support. This beam slopes to the ground at the rear of the shelter but provides the 'ridge' for a one-man shelter. It was recreated with a single blanket (rather than two cloaks tied together), an 8ft spear and two 3ft javelins. In the field-expedient manner I used string tied to the corners as tent loops, and along each side I pushed a pebble under the blanket as an anchor and tied string around it to create the loop. Scavenged wood served as tent pegs, the back of a hand axe as a hammer. Crawling in, I slept on my *sagum* and used my oval shield as a door to block off the entrance. It served well as a one-man shelter, but the cramped interior rendered it fit only for sleeping in; there was no room for other soldiers or for equipment. From experience, ironwork (helmets, spearheads, swords, armour, etc.) cannot be left in the open at night; dew forms at dawn and rust sets in only a few hours later. Iron equipment cannot be left on the ground or left uncovered, it must be brought into the shelter at night.

A second reconstruction focussed on a ridge-tent design, where a single pole is held up by two shorter uprights at either end. The canvas is thrown over the tent pole and the whole thing kept erect by the tension of the canvas once it is firmly pegged down. This design has had a long life and is still in wide use today. It is simple and effective, making it a good candidate for the type of tent used by the cash-strapped Late Roman army. This reconstruction was not based on idle speculation, but an attempt to recreate the only pictorial example of a Late Roman tent that we have. The illustration comes from the *Vienna Genesis*, a manuscript dated to the early sixth century. It shows a light-coloured canvas stretched over a central ridge which is held up by two shorter poles at each end (figure 27).

Figure **28**. This sixth-century mosaic from Imperial Palace in Istanbul shows a legionary with a drawstring bag over his shoulder.

I recreated this ridge tent using a spear as the pole and javelins as the uprights. The javelins were lashed to the ends of the spear using hemp string tied with a square lash. Two cloaks were tied together and thrown over the spear to be pegged out. This combined the literary evidence from Maurice with the pictorial evidence from the *Vienna Genesis*. To maintain some of the 'field expedient' feel of the experiment I again used the pebble and string method to create tent loops (no soldier is going to put loops in one of his beloved cloaks). Again, my tent pegs were made from scavenged wood. My recreation perfectly mirrored the *Vienna Genesis* shelter, though whether that particular tent was for civilian or military use we do not know. Probably it was a design used by everyone; the *limitanei* blurred the distinction between military and civilian in any case, but other items, such as footwear and tunics, were simply appropriated civilian designs. Federal troops in the American Civil War were using an identical design nicknamed the 'dog tent' or 'pup tent'. The lack of doors of any kind reflects its improvised nature, but it is roomy and comfortable. A blanket or a skin is required as a groundsheet, and at night for privacy or during rain or wind, a large oval shield can be placed at either end. In practical tests, I replaced the two woollen cloaks with a linen tent canvas of roughly similar proportions, this was mainly owing to the fact that my wool cloaks did not retain any of their natural lanolin, an oil in the sheep's wool that helped many Roman cloaks shrug off the rain (plate 21).

At Deurne, in the Netherlands, a single tarpaulin perhaps used for just such a purpose was discovered wrapped around several items of cavalryman's kit. This tarpaulin was probably carried by each individual cavalryman behind his saddle. The Deurne tarpaulin is very poorly preserved, but was probably made up of sixteen 72cm x 52cm goatskin panels (arranged in a 4 x 4 manner) sewn together, with a total size of 2.8m x 2.08m. Corner reinforcements were present and two of them bore signs of a now lost fastening (perhaps a loop and toggle with which several 'individual' sheets were joined together to create a bigger tent). Goat or calfskin may, in any event, have been cheaper than linen in ancient times, and perhaps easier to waterproof.

I tested this shelter in high winds and torrential downpours at the Festival of History held at Kelmarsh Hall, 2005. Both my equipment and I stayed dry and warm, but as the canvas got wet it stretched and several times the ridge pole slid over, until I secured it with a couple of guy lines. The tent pegs also needed repositioning to take the stretch into account. In all, the *Vienna Genesis* shelter-tent proved a successful experiment. It showed that the shelter is a viable design that can be erected in the field using materials and equipment commonly carried by Late Roman soldiers while out on patrol. With no real pictorial or archaeological evidence to show that Late Roman troops still used the elaborate eight-man tents of earlier periods, I suspect that a shelter like the one on the *Vienna Genesis* served the fourth-century legionary instead. It follows the tenet of the infantryman in all eras of history – 'adapt what you have to survive', and using your weaponry, shield and cloak to create your overnight bivouac fits well with the timeless military reality of the fighting man.

Gaius led his patrol along the rough path that wound along the cliff-tops, past fishing villages and the signal station on Draco Point. Looking down into coves washed by surging waves, his men expected to spot a Pictish currach at any moment, pulled up onto the beach. The *contubernium* was lively and excited, Brigionus had fired them up with his reports of Pictish raids. Gaius studied their faces while they ate lunch together on a shingle beach, sheltered by white chalk cliffs. He was still *caput contubernii*, or file leader, while Brocchus was his file-closer, his second. Severus and Cassius were now stalwart members of the squad. Veteranus, the unwilling conscript, was still shunned and abused by all the squad. Abruna the German had come to Britannia with his twin brother, Alatheus, along with thirty other captured prisoners. He was a willing and dedicated Roman soldier. Justinus was a recruit from AD 388, one of the unfortunate officers from the Sixth Legion that had been demoted and stripped of possessions, rank, wealth and honour for his support of Magnus Maximus. He now served as a common foot-soldier within the lowliest of infantry units. Justinus said little, but when he spoke he spoke with authority and experience. Over the past few years he had advised Gaius, but rarely contradicted or tried to countermand him.

Later in the day the patrol spotted a small ship, rolling with the waves, close in to the cliffs. It vanished from sight, and although there was a shingle cove in that area, it was isolated and did not lead to any local village or homestead. Gaius picked up the pace, and within an hour the squad reached the path that led down into the cove. A currach, skins stretched tight over the frame, sail still unfurled, sat on the beach. There were men down there guarding the ship, and others looking for driftwood. Picts!

Whispered orders were sent along the line, but before the legionaries could move into position a great roar took them by surprise. Armed men flung themselves from cover onto the shocked soldiers. They fumbled for axes and swords, tried to swing shields free of shoulder straps. The Picts screamed and shouted, creating confusion and scaring some of the newer recruits witless.

The German, Abruna, took the blow from a small square shield directly in his face and toppled backward. As he lost his footing a Pictish axe chopped at him and Abruna fell from view. The Picts were long-haired and bearded. All were clad in baggy tunics, all were bare-legged.

Gaius took several blows on his shield, then pushed forward, using the sword strokes taught to him by Ursinus many years ago. Shields slammed together. Gaius and his Pictish foe twisted and ducked. A hand axe cracked into his helmet, but the pressure on his shield fell away and Gaius looked up to see his opponent stumble away, clutching his neck. Gaius had got his sword tip past the Pict's defence and managed to catch his throat with the edge of the blade.

Seconds had passed, but it seemed longer. Around him Gaius could see that the Picts had been beaten off. Two or three were wounded but fleeing with their kinsmen, two more lay across the path unable to stand. Justinus used the butt-spike on the base of his *spiculum* to finish off the Picts, driving it home through the back of their skulls. The legionaries moved forward purposefully following Gaius' orders. Wary of another ambush they began to descend slowly to the beach, shields and javelins at the ready.

Gaius called a halt when the ship came into view. Some of the Picts were preparing to cast off, while others formed a defensive line across the beach. There might have been twenty of them in total. Obviously these raiders were themselves surprised to have discovered a Roman patrol within an hour of landing. They were reluctant to fight – perhaps they imagined more legionaries following behind, unseen. From the safety of the narrow path leading out of the cove, the Roman soldiers watched the raiders push the ship back into the waves. With sail billowing, the Pictish currach headed east out toward the horizon. Would it make landfall further south later in the day? Would it turn north and return to Pictland? Would it return to the same cove tomorrow?

There was no answer that Gaius could give his men.

The soldiers found Abruna's body at the foot of the white cliffs and whilst it was being brought up the path Brocchus looked at wounds sustained by Veteranus and Cassius. They were not serious. By nightfall the patrol had Praesidium in sight. The men were foot-sore, exhausted and hungry, eager to leave Abruna's body with Ursinus' deputy, and to wash and eat and sleep in their own barrack room once again. Before removing his muddy clothes, Gaius checked in at the *principia*, the headquarters building, giving a brief report to the officer on duty and accounting for each of his men in turn. Long patrols away from the fort seemed to provide the perfect opportunity for discontented soldiers to throw away their belts and desert. The squad leader was made accountable for the actions of his men, he had to bring them all back, or risk facing a punishment.

CHAPTER VII

Belief: 395–397 AD

The Emperor Constantius, Augustus, to Madalianus, deputy praetorian prefect: Let there be an end to superstition, let the madness
of sacrifices be done away with. For anyone who dares to perform
sacrifices in contravention of the law of the holy Emperor our father
and this decree of Our Clemency shall experience an appropriate
penalty and an immediate sentence of judgement. Received by the
consuls Marcellinus and Probinus.

Code of Theodosius 16.10.2

Outside the barrack block, men from the century of Ursinus mustered in
their civilian attire. They wore their best tunics and *bracae*, a good cloak and
the ubiquitous Pannonian hat. They were subdued. Ursinus led the unit out
of the fort where it gathered at the house of Statia, Abruna's widow. Gaius,
Severus, Brocchus and Justinus were detailed to carry the funeral litter. Four
others shouldered a second litter – this carried the body of Abruna's twin
brother, Alatheus. He had been on the sick-list for weeks with a lung illness,
an illness which had finally struck him down whilst his twin brother was on
patrol with the squad. They were to be buried together. It was a sad day, the
cohort had lost two of its most energetic and dutiful soldiers.

For the soldiers, the funeral would prove a novelty; the twins, although Goths, were both Christians. This faith had been the official religion of the emperors for almost a century, and although it had become extremely popular amongst the ruling elite and amongst those who dwelt in the cities, soldiers and the mass of rural Romans generally observed the old pagan rituals and spoke to the old pagan gods that had served their ancestors for generations.

A flautist led the funeral procession, whilst Statia, her two children and other members of her family followed immediately behind. It trailed through the *vicus* to the cemetery just out of town and by the side of the road. The men-folk wore their tunics unbelted and all either wore hats, or pulled their cloaks up enough to cover their heads. The women wore dark hooded cloaks.

Praesidium village was a small settlement with no Christian priest in residence. The unit's standard bearer, Silvanus, had instead agreed to officiate as he knew a number of Christian prayers, and had been a comrade of both the deceased. The graves had already been dug. Gaius and the other pallbearers carefully transferred the bodies to wooden coffins and then placed flowers and a new pair of hob-nailed boots in with them. The boots had been specially made for the men's journey to the Afterlife; and for that journey also, a single silver coin, bearing the face of Emperor Theodosius, was placed in the mouth of each corpse.

Although the inclusion of grave goods is commonly associated with pagan belief, such practices continued well into the fourth century, even amongst Christian communities. Hob-nailed boots, or simply just a handful of hob-nails were found in most of the first-century graves at Puckeridge, and the practice is still recorded at the Late Roman cemetery at Curbridge in Oxfordshire. A building containing a furnace together with 2,000 hobnails, was discovered inside the cemetery outside Cirencester, which could suggest that the hob-nails were created on site for ritual purpose, or even that 'funerary boots' were made especially for the burial.

Placing coins in the mouth, in the hand or on the eyes of the deceased was a practice that went back to pagan Roman and Greek belief. Charon the dread ferryman of the River Styx demanded payment from the shades of the dead who wished to cross in order to reach the Underworld. Hordes of ghosts who had been unburied, or buried without a coin, were believed to clamour at the deceased for passage across the Styx. This was certainly a pagan belief, but coins still accompanied many of the fourth-century burials within the generally Christian cemetery at Poundbury in Dorset.

There was a great deal of religious overlap and a mixture of beliefs, both pagan and Christian, that makes strict identification of a burial as one or the other extremely difficult. The graves of the twins, Abruna and

Alatheus, were aligned east-west, with their feet toward the rising sun, but some Christian burials were not orientated at all. On the other hand there were pagan cemeteries in Britain that showed a definite orientation. Likewise, some Christian burials included grave goods, some pagan burials did not. Archaeologists can speak of general trends, but of course these trends could also reflect cultural conformity as much as religious belief, especially within this transitory phase of Romano-British religion. Living within a community of pagans, a Christian may well follow the local burial traditions, particularly if buried *by* pagans. Is Statia pagan or Christian? Since the army organised and paid for his burial, and the pagan soldiers came to pay their respects with 'funerary boots' and freshly minted silver coins, the twins might appear to a modern archaeologist to be pagans. Perhaps the east-west orientation of the graves would provide a useful, though not incontrovertible clue.[66]

And of course, as Christian missionaries later discovered, the separation of pagan belief from Christian worship was a difficult task. Many of the old ways continued alongside a belief in Christ as Saviour.

With his calming voice, Silvanus the standard-bearer began the ceremony that would commit Abruna and Alatheus to the earth:

> 'Here twin brothers, side by side, give their bodies to the grave;
> The soil has brought together these whom merit united.
> Born of barbarian stock, but reborn from the baptismal font,
> They give their spirits to heaven, they give their bodies to the earth.
> Sorrow has come to Sagile their father and his wife,
> Who without doubt wished to predecease them.
> But with Christ's calming influence, great grief can be borne:
> They are not childless – they have given gifts to God.'
> ILCV 1516[67]

The family wept at their loss, while the soldiers looked on stoically. Each grieved at the loss of a mess-mate and a brother-in-arms. The legionaries were members of a close family, closer to each other than any friendship outside of the service, closer to each other than any relative or lover. No-one wanted to be the weak link, the man that let the unit down. Everyone wanted to suffer the same fate – good or ill. Being injured or wounded, or down on the sick list, brought on immense feelings of guilt at leaving the rest of the unit in the lurch.

As they looked down at the beech-wood coffin, the legionaries remembered the lives of the twins – how they had done their duty, helped men out, cheered up others. Silvanus finished the funeral service with a reading of the Lord's Prayer which the mourners repeated line by line. Dust was scattered and the party slowly broke up to return to the *vicus*.

Gaius remained behind with Silvanus to talk to Statia. After giving her his condolences he gave her a money pouch that paid for all her sons' weaponry and armour. In effect, the legion was buying these valuable items back from her. It was a token of course: with soaring inflation, the coins did not come close to representing the true value of the arms and armour. She accepted the purse with good grace, then thanked Silvanus for organising and paying for the funeral. The twins had contributed to a compulsory burial club throughout their military lives, and this reserve was used to pay for the joint funeral.

Almost nothing is known of the religious practices of soldiers in the fourth century. Traditionally, prior to AD 324, the soldiers participated in communal veneration of the legion's standards, held in sacred awe by the troops. The Christian writer Tertullian considered this veneration close to worship. These standards included the eagle, proud emblem of a legion, an image of the Emperor, the emblem or animal totem of the legion, the vexillum or flag bearing the name and titles of the legion and as well as others. These standards, carried on poles by junior officers, were locked in a sacred chamber, the shrine of the standards (*sacellum*), at the heart of the headquarters building, and were brought out for all official occasions. Roman soldiers were led in the communal worship of Jupiter, Minerva and Mars as well as any other gods favoured by the unit. There is no mention of priests living amongst the soldiers, but a wall painting from the Temple of Bel at Dura Europus (dated to the mid-third century) actually shows the garrison commander, tribune Julius Terentius, sacrificing before three statues. His men are lined up behind him, with right hands raised in prayer. Facing the tribune is the unit's standard bearer, holding the *vexillum* for all the troops to see. Does this mean that there was no need for a Roman military priesthood? Did the commanders carry out sacrifices on behalf of their men? Many altars are found on military sites dedicated by the commanding officer, and it is assumed that he is representing the entire unit, although his name is the only one appearing on the altar. The three statues in the Dura Europus painting may represent local Syrian deities, but are more likely to represent members of the imperial family. The worship of the Emperor and his family was state-organised. This imperial cult was always fervently followed by the Roman army, since it fostered an intense loyalty of the troops to the state.

Away from the parade ground or the grand cross hall of the *principia*, the soldiers could traditionally follow whatever gods they liked. Portable shrines, statuettes of gods, curse tablets and amulets are all common paraphernalia associated with this private worship. Gods, nymphs and spirits that were local to the area were always popular with troops.

Following Constantine I's adoption of Christianity as the official religion of the Roman Empire, the nature of religious worship within military

1. A front-rank infantryman of the Legio Praesidiensis. He wears ringmail armour and iron greaves, and his helmet is a common Intercisa type. The shield is a reconstruction of one found at Dura Europus in Syria, this example is decorated with the Christian '*chi-rho*'. He carries a *spiculum* and a *spatha*. Note the wide military belt. The legionary wears Gothic-style *hypodemata* boots.

2. The Deurne helmet, excavated in the Netherlands. Its precious metal gilding suggests ownership amongst the officer class. (Photo courtesy of Aitor Iriarte)

3. The *francisca*. A German throwing axe common to the Western legions of the fourth century.

4. Weapons of war. The sword (*spatha*), the thrusting spear (*lancea*), the heavy javelin (*spiculum*) and the light javelin (*verutum*).

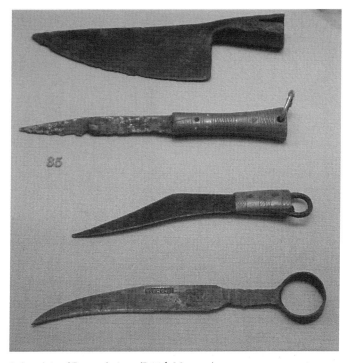

5. A variety of Roman knives. (British Museum)

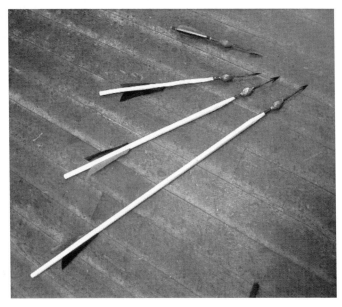

6. *Plumbatae*, lead-weighted throwing darts. Shafts have not survived, so these replicas have been fitted with shafts of various sizes.

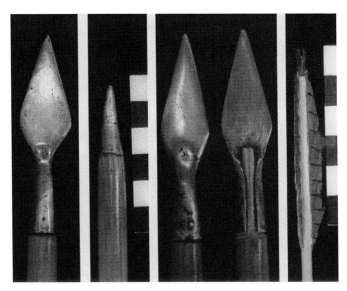

7. Reconstructions of Roman ranged weapons. Left to right: a leaf-bladed spearhead, a butt-spike, leaf-bladed javelin heads, arrow. (Courtesy I P Stephenson, from his excellent *Roman Infantry Equipment: The Later Empire*)

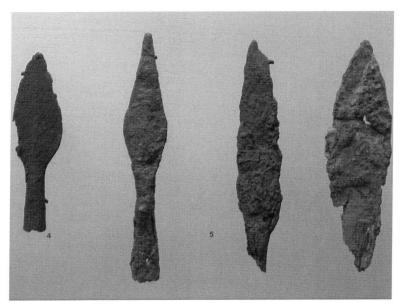

8. Spearheads. A variety of spearheads found at Vindolanda.

Above: **9**. Outside the barrack block. Through the door one enters a short corridor, with the squad leader's room to the left and the door to the squad room at the end.

Opposite above: **10**. The squad leader (*caput contubernium*) probably slept in the first room. Note the single bed, the storage jar (*dolia*) and hand-mill, used by the squad to grind its grain ration.

Opposite below: **11**. The back room of each 'pair' of rooms in the barrack block was probably the squad room. This reconstruction has seven beds.

12. The squad room may instead have been fitted out with space-saving bunk-beds, but so far, no evidence as yet been found to substantiate this theory.

13. The reconstructed gateway at the Arbeia Roman fort (in modern South Shields, England).

14. Many fourth-century soldiers had trades. Here, a cobbler replaces missing hobnails. He wears a Phrygian cap, and shoes based on a find from German bog-burials.

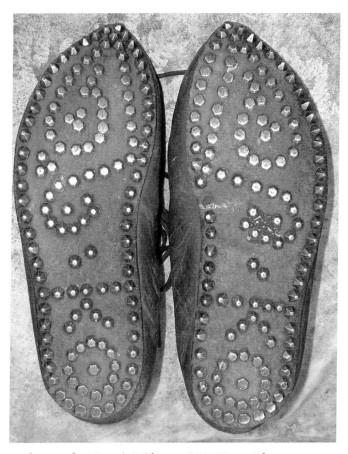

15. These marching boots (*calcei*) have walked 500km and the wear pattern on the hobnails is quite distinct. (Photo courtesy of Florian Himmler)

Above: **16**. The inner courtyard of the commander's house, reconstructed at Arbeia Roman fort.

Left: **17**. One of the fort's interval towers, viewed from the interior of the fort. These provided look-out posts and platforms for artillery, and allowed access to the wall-walk.

18. The commander makes the rounds with his adjutant. Within the safety of the fort, helmets and armour were often disdained by the troops on sentry duty.

19. Commander's dining room. Aristocratic luxury that contrasts sharply with the cramped conditions within the barrack blocks.

20. The *Lusoria,* a replica fourth-century patrol ship built under the direction of the University of Regensburg. (Photo courtesy of Florian Himmler)

21. A simple shelter based on an illustration in the sixth-century *Vienna Genesis* manuscript. This example has been erected using a spear and two javelins, and has space for two men as well as all of their equipment.

22. The *vexillum*, or flag, of the Legio Praesidiensis, reconstructed with the Late Roman symbol of Christianity, the *chi-rho*.

23. Simple *chi-rho* carving on a stone from Vindolanda.

24. Reconstructed legionary tools. From left to right: hand-axe, reaping hook, entrenching tool, pick-axe, turf-cutter and spade, next to a basket used for earth-moving and a hemp rope. The tools lie on a hessian sack.

25. Cutting turves in order to construct a rampart. The tool being used is found on military sites in Germany, but is not mentioned by contemporary writers.

26. The legionary's personal possessions. From top-left, moving anti-clockwise: horn comb, candle stub and holder, folding frying pan, wooden bowl and spoon, horn cup, spare shoes, hardtack (*buccelatum*) in a bread bag, as well as dried foods including lentils, barley and wheat. There is dried fish, a money pouch, a fire-kit, with flint and steel as well as charcloth, twine, a sewing kit and whetstone, camp knife, hand axe and reaping hook. At the back is a goatskin kitbag used to carry the possessions. Total weight: 6kg.

27. Folding frying pan and a small *patera*. (British Museum)

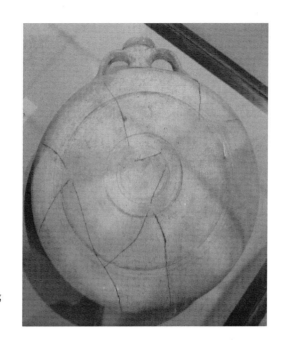

28. Ceramic flask, probably for carrying water or oil. (Dover Museum)

29. The battle-line. Two ranks of fourth-century infantry.

30. An example of a reconstructed Roman crossbow, or *arcuballista*.

31. Battle-line. Shields overlapped, spears lowered, the shield wall moves forward toward the enemy formation.

32. *Foulkon*. A sixth-century writer described this static defence against missile weapons as a *'foulkon'*. A more mobile version of this formation was called the *'testudo'*. (Photo courtesy of Stephen Kenwright)

33. Behind the shield wall. While the enemy cavalry approaches, the legionaries kneel down and brace themselves. Arrows and javelins will come splintering through the shield boards at any moment.

34. *Testudo*. This mobile defensive formation allowed legionaries to advance directly into an enemy missile barrage, while taking only minor casualties.

Opposite: **35**. Out of armour. The legionary is off duty, wearing a more colourful tunic, but retaining all of the symbols of his profession: the crossbow brooch, the wide military belt and the flat 'pillbox' hat. The cloak (*sagum*) is yellow-brown, the colour commonly associated with Roman military cloaks. In the fourth century, highly decorative roundels (*orbiculi*) like those here, were often woven into the fabric of the cloak. The soldier's footwear is based on a late third-century marching boot (*calcei*) found at Vindolanda.

36. Most fourth-century tunics were elaborately decorated with circular *orbiculli*, and bands (*clavii*) over the shoulders. Typically this decoration was woven into the garment whilst on the loom.

Opposite above: **37**. Off-duty soldiers and their families. Pannonian hats and leg wraps are visible, as are the heavy military belts of the period.

Opposite below: **38**. Reconstructed model of a Roman cargo ship. (Dover Museum)

39. Model of Dover lighthouse. (Dover Museum)

40. Remains of a granary at Housesteads fort, Northumberland.

41. Mithraeum at Carrawburgh, Northumberland.

Above: **43**. Multiangular tower, York. It is a surviving corner tower from the legionary fortress at Eboracum. The lower, smaller, stones are Roman, those above are medieval.

Right: **44**. Column from the north-eastern arcade of the fortress cross-hall at York.

Opposite: **42**. A town-house at Herculaneum.

45. The surviving walls of Saxon Shore fort at Richborough, Kent.

46. *Principia*, headquarters building at Housesteads Roman fort, Northumberland. (Photo courtesy of Dai Crawford)

units had to change – but how? The general assumption is that the soldiers of the empire became uniformly Christian almost overnight, but the truth is probably very different. In the first instance, the venerated military standards continued to be locked in the *sacellum* and continued to be paraded at the front of the legion on the march. A silver dish from Geneva, the Missorium of Valentinian I, clearly shows the Emperor clutching a *vexillum*, and a fourth-century glass beaker from Cologne, inscribed with the figures of four soldiers, depicts three military *vexilla*. The fourth-century writer Ammianus Marcellinus records the use of standards in battle,[68] and Vegetius records the continued use of the eagle standard that tradition-ally formed the focus of a legion's loyalty and devotion. 'Eagle-bearers [*aquiliferi*] carry the eagle. Image-bearers [*imaginari*] carry the images of the Emperor … Standard-bearers [*signiferi*] carry the standards; they are now called dragon-bearers [*draconari*].'[69] The fourth-century legionary continued to venerate the standards, and in many forts throughout Britain the shrine of the standards continued to be used to display these sacred objects. The *Strategikon* specifically tells us that even in the sixth century, the standards were blessed before hostilities began, they had not simply reverted to the status of flags and mundane signalling devices.[70] Vegetius does not mention the mounting of a cross or *chi-rho* symbol on a pole, as a military standard, but the latter symbol certainly appeared on some depic-tions of *vexilla* (plate 22).

There is no record of fourth-century commanding officers leading their men in Christian worship. Although the emperors continued to be vener-ated by the army as near-divine, this may have had little if any Christian association. No emperor of the fourth century could ever have been regarded as the 'head of the Church', and in fact the Emperor Theodosius, ruling during the period so far covered by this book, was at times domi-nated by Ambrose, his bishop in Milan.

In the sixth century the armies of the Eastern Empire called on God when they were about to enter battle: '…the command is given: "Ready!" Right after this another officer shouts: "Help us."[*Adiuata*] In unison eve-ryone responds loudly and clearly: "O God."[*Deus*]'[71]

Embodying this group identity of a military unit was the use of Latin in the forts as a *lingua franca*, and also the annual swearing of an oath to the emperors. The symbolism and language of Christian belief may also have helped to form a corporate identity for the fourth-century armies of Theodosius, but much more important to the troops was the personal reli-gion that they practised in the barracks or with the family in the *vicus*. This had always been the case. Local gods, spirits of the household, ancestor spirits, the tutelary god of the soldier's part-time trade, and so on, were the accessible religious forces that soldiers felt most comfortable in turning to. No doubt the officer class was Christian or had Christian sympathies, but it was difficult to impose the new religion on every soldier and rural peasant on the Roman frontier. There are an extraordinarily small number of finds from military sites that have some Christian association, which suggests that the forts were certainly *not* hot-beds of Christian belief (plate 23).

Throughout the military zone in Britain the temples and shrines used by the army show the patterns of use or disuse as those in the more settled, civilian areas. The army does not seem to be a special case. In this military region, for example, some pagan shrines are abandoned in the early or mid-fourth century, but others were in use throughout that time. A number continue in use well into the fifth century, after the legions depart, and some shrines were established or re-established during the second half of the fourth century. There is evidence of a late resurgence in pagan worship throughout the British countryside. Many Romano-British shrines were refurbished or built anew, and both the quality and quantity of finds there indicate that the shrines were well supported and popular. Some, like those at Maiden Castle and Jordan's Hill were established on the site of former hill-forts. The most impressive of the new pagan shrines is undoubtedly that of Mars Nodens at Lydney in Gloucestershire. Here a temple to the healing god, sited away from towns and cities, was accompanied by a bath house and a guesthouse for pilgrims who came to seek the favours of the gods.

Christianity was practised in Britain, but it was most popular in those areas well away from the military frontier, on the secluded villa estates of wealthy noblemen, particularly, and in the larger cities with more cosmopolitan populations. Even in these locations, however, the new faith was not all-conquering. Many of the beautiful fourth-century villa mosaics continued to display pagan motifs, sometimes (such as at Frampton villa in Dorset) side-by-side with Christian iconography. The search for churches (buildings specifically dedicated to Christian worship) still continues with few firm identifications. A number of possible candidates have been located, notably at Silchester, Caerwent and Canterbury. More commonly there seem to be rooms set aside for worship within large houses, such as Lullingstone villa in Kent. In urban centres these may in fact be the homes of church leaders where the local congregation met.

January AD 395. With a roaring fire in the hearth to warm up the room, Modesta laid out her new pottery on the table. She had recently returned from a three-day visit to Eboracum, and had brought back with her a fresh load of tanned hides for the business, a new Saxon slave girl and a basket of new pottery. The pots were from the Derventio kilns and were cream coloured, decorated with fashionable red dots and stripes.

Gaius entered the house, trailing snow into the room. He was pleased to see his beloved wife and son again, but perhaps not so pleased about all of the new pottery. Modesta soothed his money worries with a generous serving of lamb stew, washed down with Celtic beer.

Figure **29**. Mithras. This marble bust was found at the Walbrook Mithraeum, London.

'No olive oil' he remarked, but he already knew there would be none in the food; the supplies had been intermittent for the past five years. Modesta had also sold the only oil lamp they owned (the one they used at the table when entertaining guests) and instead they used clay pots filled with animal fat to light the room. They spat and produced smoke, but it was winter and they needed the light to eat by.

The couple shared their experiences over the last three days. Gaius had very little butchery work to do at this time of the year; meat had already been cut, salted and stored for the winter. Instead he had been part of a construction detail blocking up the northern gateway. It was little used these days and with increasing Pictish activity in the area it only served as a weak point in the fort's defences. It had been hard, cold work, but was now complete. Tonight Gaius looked forward to a gathering of friends and a small religious feast, a feast in celebration of the god Mithras (figure 29, above). Immediately the couple began to argue. Modesta had become a recent convert to Christianity after meeting several women in Eboracum who invited her to meet the local bishop. She had brought this new faith with her to Praesidium and this had not gone down too well with Gaius.

'I thought you had decided to forget about the birthday of Mithras. That was on 25 December, and now it's January.'

'No, we had to postpone the ritual, Aufidus and Cattullinus were both at Danum fort. We agreed to wait a couple of weeks, rather than hold the ceremony without them.'

'I won't help,' Modesta insisted, 'we were told that Mithras is a false god, that his followers are ridiculing Christians.'

That evening Gaius warmly welcomed the seven followers of Mithras into his home, only Demetrius was strangely absent. They shook the snow from boots and cloaks. Against the back wall they hung a linen cloth, painted with the image of Mithras slaying the Bull of Life. First a pot of incense was lit, and then a bowl of wine mixed with water was passed around for each man to drink from. To the soft chime of cymbals and the shiver of a bronze rattle, Meraclus began the chants: 'Hail to the Fathers, from East and West, under the protection of Saturn! Hail to the Lions for new and many years! Hail Nymphus; hail young light!'

These strange titles were ranks within the religion. Gaius led the ceremony, though he was only a *Heliodromos* ('Messenger of the Sun') a senior initiate into the cult, but not the Father who should actually have led each worship. The Father of the Mithraic cult at Praesidium was Marcus Victorinus, a veteran *centenarius*. With the increasing strictures against paganism, Marcus Victorinus had found it more and more difficult to get away from the fort to lead the Mithraic worship. Like all of the officers, in public and in military affairs he was a Christian. This was, after all, the religion of the state and of the upper classes, should Victorinus shun the worship of Christ, it would do his career no good at all. Meraclus continued: 'We must get through dark times in piety. To the very end I have borne on my shoulders the accomplishments of divine orders.'

The cult was an old one, and a cult that in AD 395 was almost dead. It had once been extremely popular, with *mithraea* (small subterranean temples) in every large city of the empire, and in large cities and at ports there were often many mithraea to cater to the huge numbers of initiates. Several forts in Britain had a *mithraeum* in the civil settlement outside the fort walls, including Housesteads and Carrawburgh (both forts on Hadrian's Wall) (plate 41). The cult was popular amongst soldiers; it was tough, masculine and fostered a brotherly comradeship, and a supportive male-only community that assisted fellow initiates, and helped them to face dark times with bravery and stoicism. There was no place for women in this religion, and indeed the worshippers had to be initiated with a rather unpleasant series of rituals before being allowed to join the first rank of members (the Ravens). Further initiations were possible that could see an experienced cult member rise through the grades, as Bridegroom, Soldier, Lion, Persian, Heliodromos and finally Father. This was a sun cult with aspects of magic and astrology that had its origins in the Persian east. Mithras was a sun hero, a champion of the world who slew the Sacred Bull and fought against demons to bring life to the universe.

The *mithraea* were always small, typically holding a congregation of around twenty people, yet there must have been many more followers of Mithras in the typical garrison. The cult was extremely popular amongst the army and actually carried from one province to another when units received new postings. Perhaps the worship of Mithras at the stone-built temples outside Roman forts was quite exclusive, limited only to the officers of the fort. With officers gathered together, sharing ideals and drink, breaking bread and swearing secret oaths of brotherly loyalty, the *mithraea* might have resembled elite officers' clubs. The cult was not elitist, however: poor men, freedmen, senators and hard-working Roman tradesmen could all become initiated, although one suspects that membership was by invitation only. Did lesser ranks worship in barracks? Did they perhaps use the temple on a rota system?

This very military religion quickly vanished from sight after AD 324, however. It was seen as a parody of Christianity, a dark, bloody and secretive version of the Saviour that Christian writers utterly condemned. *Mithraea* were attacked, some were refurbished but ultimately all were abandoned by the end of the fourth century. It seems very unlikely that a Christian mob broke into the *mithraea* on Hadrian's Wall, smashed the statues and toppled altars. The historian Peter Salway believes that the destruction of the subterranean temples may well have been the result of an order from the military authorities.[72] Was this the Christianised officer class attempting to display its loyalty to God and Emperor? Pagan sacrifice and the old imperial cult had never been mutually exclusive, but when Christianity became wedded to the cult of the emperor and his family, the wealthy nobles and military men of the empire were forced to abandon the old gods. The fourth century was rife with treason trials and the dispatch of imperial agents into the provinces to pursue allegations of disloyalty, whether true or not. Without an officer membership, the *mithraea* that had served the fort garrisons for a century or more were abandoned, and all outward signs of the cult in Britain vanished.

This chapter speculates on the survival of the cult amongst the rank and file of the legions, albeit in a much-reduced and very low-key form. Soldiers have always been lovers of tradition and known for their stubborn refusal to give way to new ideas. Mithras the Bull-slayer may not have been given up so quickly or so easily by the men in the barrack rooms.

With a flurry of snow that made the lamps gutter, Demetrius suddenly burst open the door. He looked breathless.

'The Emperor is dead!'

The little group were incredulous that Theodosius, such a well-established and unassailable emperor, could have died so suddenly. Demetrius told them how he had been detained with other subordinates at the *principia* to hear the news directly from the mouth of Sextus Aemilianus himself. There was no mistake. On his deathbed the dying Emperor had named his commander-in-chief (*Magister Utriusque Militae*), Stilicho, the guardian of his two sons, Honorius and Arcadius. These boys were to reign over the two halves of Theodosius' great empire – Honorius the West and Arcadius the East. It seemed that Stilicho was now the most powerful man in the empire.

For the friendly gathering of Mithraists inside Gaius' house, the reign of Theodosius became the only talking point of the evening. Much of the talk revolved around the endless rounds of laws and decrees that made it increasingly difficult for pagans to worship the old gods in the traditional manner.

Past emperors, since Constantine I (AD 306–337) had strengthened Christianity and secured its place as the religion of the imperial family, the imperial bureaucracy, the army and of the state. However, little was done in the first half of the fourth century to actively discourage interest in the traditional gods. When Theodosius became Emperor in AD 379, this situation soon began to change. Animal sacrifice was banned, this was the one pagan rite that the Christian clergy abhorred, and linked with fears of divination. Offerings, incense and libations were all still perfectly legal.

In AD 391 Theodosius had begun to pressurize the pagan cults with a new law that forbade all access to shrines and temples. Worship continued but was forced to move into private houses, or was carried out in the guise of festivals or community gatherings. Out in the countryside, of course, these laws had little effect. It was a fear of rioting and of Christian mob violence that forced pagans living within the cities to adhere to Theodosius' new laws. Outside of the cities, where there were no rampaging mobs, no militant temple-smashing monks or disapproving Church authorities, the mainly pagan population carried on as before – almost oblivious to imperial religious edicts.

Violence against temples continued unabated, however, in Egypt, Gaza, Petra and also in Gaul, where Martinus of Tours was leading a vociferous anti-pagan crusade. The Emperor Theodosius had not sanctioned these violent acts, but his silence was taken by the extremist bishops and monks as approval.

In late AD 392 another law, even more restrictive, was decreed. This law was designed to purposefully eradicate all traces of pagan worship, pagan belief and pagan culture. Sacrifice was now punishable by death, and every symbol, offering and libation, every garland, sacred lamp and social custom associated with the pagan tradition was now banned. Civic officials could be heavily fined for not enforcing this ban.

For the inhabitants of Praesidium, and for those living nearby on the villa estates or farmsteads in northern Britain, such restrictions may not have made a great impact on their lives. It may well have been a different story within the cities of the province. In places like London, Cirencester and York the presence of imperial officials together with bishops and established Christian communities (albeit small) may have led to some enforcement of the vigorous new anti-pagan edicts.

Theodosius' last great act was the defeat of a rival emperor in the West in September AD 394. Arbogast, Theodosius' military commander in the west, had been a powerful political figure, but rather than taking the throne for himself, this Frankish general had been instrumental in the elevation of Eugenius to the purple. Arbogast was a pagan and Eugenius immediately made concessions to the pagan aristocracy of Rome's senate house. Theodosius, ruling from Constantinople in the east, could not tolerate this turn of events and war had been inevitable. What was more, for some contemporaries (and no doubt Theodosius himself) it was seen as a war between pagan tradition and Christian belief. The battle was fought on the banks of the River Frigidus beyond the eastern Alps. Eugenius' army had marched beneath the standard of Jupiter, Theodosius' army had marched beneath the *chi-rho*, the symbol of Christ. The Christian forces contained many barbarian allies fighting under their own commanders, Alans, Huns, Goths and the Visigoths under their leader Alaric.

The fighting had been bitter. The situation suddenly and miraculously changed when a wind picked up and blew steadily and forcefully across the battlefield into the eyes of Eugenius' forces. His troops could not see the enemy, they could not hold their shields in place and worst of all, their missiles were blown back toward them or fell short. Stilicho, Theodosius' general, exploited this 'divine wind' and hurled his men into the rebel line. The Battle of Frigidus was trumpeted as a victory of Christianity over paganism.

Gaius and his mess-mates would not have been troubled by this momentous battle, by what it signified or by its outcome. The foot-soldier often has greater worries, bigger problems; boots, food, work details – hunger. When the news of Theodosius' death had circulated around the fort on the day following the Mithraic meal, the only word on the men's lips was 'donative'. The child Honorius was now Emperor of the West under the guardianship of the general Stilicho, and this would mean a donative would be paid to every serving soldier; much-needed gold and silver. In the weeks and months that followed the accession of the boy-emperor, no donative was forthcoming. On 1 May, when the *stipendium* was due, there was still no donative, only poor excuses put forward by Sextus Aemilianus. The *annonae* was pitiful, a handful of clothes and boots for each century, the worst that Gaius had ever seen. Again there were excuses: 'the supplies are late because of the cold winter', 'Saxon raids on the south coast have meant fewer supply boats are getting through', and 'the war with Eugenius has temporarily affected supply'. In reality, the empire was struggling to clothe and feed its vast army. Constant cross-border attacks by large barbarian groups had significantly affected the economy of the empire. Displaced farmers meant fewer taxes, and fewer taxes meant less money with which to pay the troops their *annonae* as well as the much-anticipated donative.

The troops at Praesidium and their families were hopeful that the situation would improve later in the year. Unfortunately the processes that would bring down Roman rule, Roman government and Roman life within the British provinces, had already been set in motion. The Visigoths who had fought in the vanguard of Theodosius' army as allies and who had spilt much blood at the Frigidus River in his service, were now sent back to their eastern Danubian territories. Alaric, their king, was not happy with the situation. He had led the Visigoths into battle for Theodosius twice now, his allotted lands were being raided by the barbarian Huns (from whom the Visigoths had fled into the safety of the empire a generation ago) and, most important of all, he wanted a top job like so many other barbarian leaders. Stilicho himself was a Vandal, one of the Germanic tribes pushing up against the frontiers of the empire, his predecessor Arbogast had been a Frank and Gainas, another highly placed Roman general, was a Goth. To force the issue, Alaric led his troops on a violent rampage through the Balkan provinces, sacking several Greek cities without opposition.

Throughout AD 396 and 397 the men of Legio Praesidiensis felt the pinch. Promises of pay kept them going, but life was harder than it had been only five years ago. Few shipments of replacement arms and armour came in from Gaul, and clothing was in very short supply. Food had become such an issue that the tribune had ordered forcible requisitions from surrounding farms. At the Villa Claudius, close to the ancient Red Stone, the owners had been 'bought off' with a bag of gold and threats on the lives of Claudius' family. The aristocrat fled to Eboracum with his family whilst his bailiff at the villa continued to manage the estate. Nearly all of the agricultural produce went to Praesidium now, with only a little retained for the subsistence survival of the farm-workers themselves.

That summer Gaius and his men spent time at the villa, cowing the workers, helping to organise the harvest, helping themselves to fruit, honey, fresh meat. The hot, lazy summer of AD 396 proved a good one for the *contubernium*, and one which they would look back on with fond memories.

AD 397 was still a year of making do. Supplies were still almost non-existent and Sextus Aemilianus sent out parties into the local farmsteads to collect much-needed equipment. Shovels, pick-axes, ropes, new pottery, wicker-baskets and oxen were all in short supply. The soldiers took them from the farmers, countering their refusal either with legal argument or with outright threats to burn down their round-houses.

CHAPTER VIII

On Campaign: 398–399 AD

Even in friendly territory a fortified camp should be set up; a general
should never have to say: 'I did not expect it.'

Maurice, *Strategikon* 8.1

AD 398. Belts continued to be tightened, although the legionaries were
still extracting the maximum amount of supplies from surrounding farmsteads. The tribune Sextus Aemilianus had brought forward the retire-
ment date of twenty of his long-serving veterans, and they were settled on
abandoned farmland further inland. In this way he had cut the number of
mouths to be fed, and created a few more farmers from which to extract
food. The veterans, the squad's own lazy Cassius amongst them, were not
happy about their settlement.

Gaius was on a foraging expedition with his squad. They had come
to a stretch of the white chalk cliffs that towered 600ft above the ocean,
cliffs that were home to thousands of seabirds flown in from the open
sea to nest. Locals had often come here to collect eggs, but the sport was
a dangerous one. A man was lowered on rope to the ledges where he
collected eggs quickly, avoiding the suicidal attacks of angry kittiwakes,
guillemots and gannets. This expedition told of the desperate plight of the
legion: too many mouths to feed, too dependant on the long chain of supply that connected forts with cities with farms. Yet the legion was luckier
than others. The *limitanei* forts had at least made measures over the last

century to become at least partially self-sufficient. The mobile field armies that were billeted inside cities and that moved from one military crisis to another, were totally dependant on receiving rations and pay from central supplies.

From the high cliffs, Gaius looked north to the signal towers at Draco Point and, close to the horizon, Two Bays. Both were now abandoned, the troops could not be properly supplied and their garrisons were too small to effect any sort of local requisition. They would be regarrisoned once the supply crisis in the south had abated. It was simply a matter of crushing the Saxon pirates, Gaius had been told. Ursinus the *centenarius* had even told the men that they could expect back-pay, once the Channel was made safe enough to send across legionary pay chests.

The squad marched home. It had a couple of baskets of eggs and twenty seabirds, shot out of the sky as they wheeled over the crashing surf, using an improvised method of arrows tied to coils of string. The birds, mainly guillemots and razorbills, with a couple of puffins also, had been reeled in and tied to a spear. They would be well received by the men of the cohort. Six-year-old Flavius ran out to meet his father. He had Modesta's looks, but Gaius knew he would make a good soldier, because although he was covered in cuts and bruises, he felt no pain. He was fearless.

In the evening, he and Modesta sat outside the barracks under the veranda and ate dinner with Flavius and Severus. They ate a bowl of creamed wheat, guillemot fried with onions and garlic and boiled eggs drizzled with a spicy fish sauce. Severus played with Flavius; he was like an uncle to the boy, and Gaius' closest friend. The man had matured and mellowed and finally settled into army life, despite losing his right eye from a recurring infection of his face wound. 'Uncle Severus' now wore a leather eye patch, and consequently Flavius thought him the greatest and most fiercest soldier in the legion!

Outside the barracks opposite sat the swarthy sailors of the Numerus Barcariorum Tigrisiensium, the Tigris bargemen from Arbeia. The entire unit was on the move to the south coast of Britain. There it would assist in the transfer of Britain's field army back to Gaul where it was needed by Stilicho. The bargemen were resting at Praesidium for a week before continuing to the southern port of Dubris. Bel-barak strolled across to join the diners. Like the rest of his men, he was looking forward to returning to Arbeia. The field army was led by a Count and had been sent across from Gaul following the defeat of Magnus Maximus back in AD 388. Theodosius had feared more rebellion amongst the British garrisons – this field army had been a show of strength. But now, Bel-barak told Gaius, it was desperately needed. Alaric, the Visigothic king, had spent the past three years laying waste to northern Greece, battling with Stilicho's small army and playing power politics with both Honorious and Arcadius, boy emperors of the West and the East.

'There might yet be civil war,' he warned. 'and whomever Alaric sides with has the best chance of victory'.

Bel-barak later returned to his men. He had been pleased to see Gaius once again, and was saddened that Severus' had lost the eye that had been injured whilst on patrol across the River Tinea. As a parting gift he presented Modesta with a small pouch of fragrant incense.[73]

By the end of the week, the Tigris bargemen had put to sea, destined for southern shores. The men of the Legio Praesidiensis were also on the move. A new order had come through from the Duke's headquarters in Eboracum, shocking everybody. The entire legion was to be mobilised and put into the field immediately, it was to rendezvous with other *limitanei* units at Cataracticorum, ready for a strengthening of northern defences. Rumour was rife that a massive barbarian attack had gotten underway.

Marching to War

There were times when an entire unit was mobilised and sent out onto the road. Often this was the result of a redeployment, the legion (or part of) had been issued orders to move to a new fort, a fort that could be as close as 5 miles away, or as distant as 300 or 1,000 miles away. If this was the case the unit assembled in a marching column (*agmen quadratum*) carrying all of its arms and armour, ration bags, cloaks, and personal items. A baggage train would also be assembled, and local ponies and mules, bought for the purpose would be laden with supplies, equipment and tools. Wagons pulled by oxen would be similarly loaded, the unit would have amassed a huge amount of baggage and belongings that needed to be transported, everything from hobnails to rope, paint to axes, mattresses to clothing. On a march like this the legionaries would leave their helmets and armour in the wagons and carry only their shields and weapons. Ration bags would be stuffed with food, both dried and fresh. Travelling within the empire to the new posting, the troops could remain off-guard to some degree, although by the late fourth century barbarian invasions and raids could suddenly transform entire frontier zones into 'enemy territory'.

When the legion marched out of the empire, across the frontier and into the *barbaricum*, the nature of the marching column changed entirely. Expeditions into Persia or into regions recently invaded by Goths or other Germanic tribes always comprised many legions, together with cavalry, guard units, headquarters elements, and local allies (*foederati*). In all, tens of thousands of men might be on the march to war. Within enemy territory the possibility or reality existed of attacks from hostile cavalry or skirmishers. On the battlefield, men were mentally prepared to fight, but strung out for a mile or more, out of armour with weapons thrown into wagons, concentrating on their own place in the column and unable to see where it is headed, men were unready for war and prone to panic should they come under attack. To minimize the danger to his column, a general was advised to know the route well, to keep his plans secret and to send out scouting patrols along the line of the march in order to foil ambushes.

Vegetius described the ideal formation for a column marching to war. At the head is placed the bulk of the cavalry and behind it the infantry. In the centre of the column is placed all of the baggage, the wagons, pack animals and the servants. Finally, the rear-guard should be composed of light cavalry and skirmish troops. Additional light or heavy troops could be deployed to screen the baggage portion of the column, and protect the vulnerable flanks. When a commander suspected (perhaps via information provided by scouting patrols) that an enemy force might try to ambush the column, he might reinforce one part of the column or another with additional troops. These troops, Vegetius tells us, are best employed as a reaction force, able to quickly move to intercept an enemy ambush or pursue fleeing attackers. Consequently, picked cavalry, light infantry and archers were preferred for this type of duty.

Both Vegetius and Maurice warn of the panic and potentially deadly confusion that arises when a column on the march comes under attack, and both provide a measure of advice to mitigate that confusion. Marching with hundreds of other soldiers, overburdened with equipment and supplies, trying to keep in formation, trying to keep one's footing and not slip or trip, it is not surprising that legionaries would neither expect nor be easily able to react to a sudden attack. The author has discovered from past experience that unless one carries a shield in the hand and does not sling it on one's back, it is difficult to bring it around ready for instant use. Indeed one of the strongest pieces of advice given by the ancient writers was that troops should carry their shields and spears in their hands (rather than packing them in the wagons, one suspects). The chaos that ensued when the baggage train became panicked could be lessened by putting experienced servants in charge of the animals under military-style standards. To these standards the servants, wagons and mule-handlers could rally.

Within hostile territory, the great fear was that gaps might open up along the column, either from units marching too slowly or too quickly. The officers were tasked with regulating the speed of individual units in order to retain the cohesiveness of the column. When an attack occurred on a disorganised column, the gaps could be penetrated and parts of the column isolated and surrounded. Vegetius again stresses the critical effect on morale that a surprise ambush could have: 'Those who have gone far ahead wish to get away rather than go back. Meanwhile those who are in the rear, deserted by their comrades, are overwhelmed by the violence of the enemy and their own despair.'[74]

The baggage train was an essential part of any army on the move and was never left unprotected. The soldiers' servants, children and other members of their family would travel with the baggage train. If the safety of the baggage was not assured, then the troops would become distracted and dispirited. Of course the wagons and pack animals of the train carried all of the troop's supplies (mainly grain, flour or *buccellatum*) as well as vital equipment, armour, weaponry and ammunition. According to Maurice, each *contubernium* should have had its own wagon, which carried a millstone, tools, *plumbatae* and caltrops (spikes thrown onto the ground as a defence against sudden attack). Other wagons carried *ballistae* (bolt-shooting artillery) as well as the tools required by carpenters and metalworkers. It seems that the oxen which pulled these wagons were branded in order to identify the unit to which they belonged. Pack-horses also accompanied the army in Maurice's day, and these could carry a *contubernium's* tent.

Mention has been made of servants, and there are almost no contemporary descriptions of what these servants did at the fort, where they slept or who was responsible for feeding them. Servants, who seem to have been slaves, were certainly owned by those soldiers who could afford them and their duties within the marching column are described in detail by Maurice. Some men could claim wages for the upkeep of their servants if that man had a specific title or job while on campaign.[75] Poor soldiers could club together to maintain a servant that served them all. If there weren't enough servants to handle the pack animals and wagons, then the commander was forced to assign a few of his most inexperienced troops to the task. The servants were given weapons (mainly javelins, *plumbatae*, bows and slings) with which to defend themselves and the baggage train, if it came under attack.

In the field of logistics, the Roman army is justifiably praised. No other army in the ancient world came close to matching the administrative efficiency with which Rome supplied and resupplied its legionaries in the field. Planning, record-keeping and a sophisticated road network all combined to keep troops fed while on the march. The type and amount of rations allocated to troops was discussed in Chapter 4. However, since the soldiers of a Late Roman unit were actually paid in food, were higher ranks given a larger portion of the marching rations? Officers actually received the same rations as the lower ranks whilst on the most arduous campaigns. It would be impractical and unnecessary to award larger portions to some men and less to others, particularly if food was scarce. When the Roman roads ended and the legions stepped beyond the frontier, resupply was a much more precarious affair. We know that rations were apportioned equally to every man, rather than according to rank and status, 'on the understanding that after the emergency there was restitution to these men from the State.'[76]

The expedition of the Emperor Julian into Persia in AD 363 proved to be such an emergency. Despite success in battle, his men were starving; their ration bags were empty and crops in the region had been burnt to deny them to the Roman invaders. Nevertheless:

> …food carried by the baggage-animals of the tribunes and counts was distributed to relieve the pressing needs of the rank and file. Instead of delicacies fit for a royal table, the Emperor, who was to take his frugal meal under the poles of a tent, had prepared for him a scanty ration of porridge which even a common soldier would have spurned.[77]

Autumn AD 398. The great northern road that connected Eboracum with the garrisons on the Wall split just north of Cataractonium. Gaius and the rest of Legio Praesidiensis were following the western branch that would take them across the high moors to eventually reach the west coast of Britain. He had never marched in such a large formation. The entire garrison was on the move, wagons laden with tools, provisions and tents, servants, slaves, women and children. At the head of the column marched skirmishers, next came the main body of troops with the baggage train following on behind. At the rear marched more troops equipped as skirmishers. Sextus Aemilianus rode with his officers at the head of the heavy infantry, and it was here that the legionary standards were being proudly held aloft by the *signiferi*. The legion was marching in the company of a cavalry regiment, the Equites Taifali, which had been part of the British field army but had not accompanied it on its march south to Dubris. They were the sons of German barbarians that had been defeated in battle and then organised into a Roman unit to fight in Britain.

The seven-day march had been hard, although it had not left the Roman roads. The pace was slow and everyone carried so much equipment that the hard surface drove hobnails up into the base of the foot. Mile after mile there was much cursing and complaining. When a bag or shield strap broke there was a desperate scramble to pick up the equipment and quickly improvise a repair; no-one wanted to have to push and shove their way through the column to find their place in it once again. At night Gaius helped pitch the squad tent, as well as a number of smaller shelters for the families and servants. The women baked bread, the servants and children collected firewood, and each *contubernia* ate wheat porridge or bacon with hardtack biscuits. The oxen and the mules had to be fed and watered too. These night-time camps were not fortified, but set up on flat ground close to a stream. Water for drinking and cooking was collected in large leather waterskins and in jars – but often it was fouled because the cavalry had watered their horses upstream and stirred up all the mud on the river-bank. The troops of the Praesidiensis were furious with the Taifali.

Food was carefully rationed; the troops had been ordered to leave a substantial supply of grain at the fort for a small detachment of cavalry that was to garrison Praesidium in their absence. These 110 Dalmatian cavalry had originally been billeted in Eboracum with the Duke's head-quarters, but their own unit was stationed at a shore fort on the south coast. The Duke wanted Praesidium manned by an effective force whilst the Praesidiensis were on campaign.

Lavatris, a fort on the high moor land road, was the column's destina-tion. Here, troops and civilians alike were rested and refreshed before tak-ing to the road once again. The local garrison of the fort was meagre: 240 infantrymen of the Numerus Exploratorum ('the Scouts'). The Scouts were an unconventional bunch, made up mostly of archers and javelin-throw-ers, and this rough-looking unit was ordered to lead the column west.

The road skirted the northern side of a wide moor-land vale and here the land was featureless and barren. Cold rain began to fall from a dark sky. At the sudden sound of bugles, the column was suddenly and chaoti-cally broken up; men of the Praesidiensis were called to arms with much fumbling of shields and straps. Amidst the commotion no-one knew the cause of the alarm, everyone feared that the enemy was blocking the road further ahead. The Praesidiensis formed up in a battle-line, four men deep. Shields were readied, the red star emblazoned proudly on a blue background. Sudden fear almost overwhelmed Gaius, but he looked through the rain, along the line, and the steady determined faces of his comrades settled his nerves. From his place in the front rank he could see a small Roman tower on the nearby hill and smoke was billowing down the slope. For an hour, the legionaries maintained their formation until some of the Scouts returned from their reconnaissance. The tower garrison had been butchered; there was certainly, from the evidence, a force of Picts in the pass and its size was unknown. Immediately, the tribune gave the order to construct a fortified camp.

The Fortified Camp

Troops on the march may be vulnerable to enemy attack, but when resting for the night in camp they are in much greater danger. For centuries, the Roman army had taught its soldiers how to lay out a temporary marching camp and organise its construction and see to its defence. So valuable were these skills that the building of marching camps was incorporated into the legionaries' training regime. Substantial practice camps from the early imperial period have been discovered in northern Britain. One of the best preserved is found on the road from Malton Roman fort to Goldsborough signal station, at Cawthorn.

When battle seemed imminent a fortified camp provided the Roman army with a place of retreat, should the fighting go against them. This 'last-ditch defence' could prove critical, and even turn the tide of a battle. In AD 355 the Roman commander Arbitio suffered a disastrous rout against the warlike Alemanni following an ambush. The fleeing legionaries managed to link up with their units and returned to the marching camp where they took stock of the losses that had been inflicted upon them. 'On the following day the Alemanni, encouraged by this success, advanced more boldly upon the Roman entrenchments;' the Roman troops dared not leave the safety of their camp until three tribunes charged out of the gateways with their soldiers behind them and 'fell on the enemy like a torrent and put them to a disgraceful rout; it was not a pitched battle but a succession of quick skirmishes.'[78]

Vegetius explains in some detail how these camps were constructed, and should best be used, but he also laments that the Late Roman army no longer bothers to build them. However, a fourth-century camp has been discovered at Ermelo in the Netherlands and Ammianus Marcellinus, giving his accounts of campaigns in the period, makes reference to the use of fortified camps. It may be that individual commanders made the decision to erect a marching camp based on the situation and the capabilities of the men under them. Barbarian recruits were sometimes extremely reluctant to engage in camp construction, as Ammianus relates:

> We had with us … two of Magnentius' legions which had recently arrived from Gaul. These were strong and active men, admirably suited to fighting in open country, but quite useless, indeed a positive nuisance, in the kind of warfare to which we were restricted. They were no help in working the artillery or constructing defensive works.[79]

In essence, the temporary marching camp consisted of a level area surrounded by a ditch cut into the ground, with the soil or turves thrown up to create a rampart on the inside of the ditch. The space within this simple fortification needed to accommodate all of the infantry within the column as well as the wagons, beasts and servants of the baggage. Cavalry needed space and was frequently camped outside of the rampart. Passageways across the ditch and through the rampart were required, there were traditionally four of these gateways, with the main gate (*praetoria*) and rear gate (*decumana*) the most heavily trafficked. Following the layout of the unit's home fort, the headquarters tent was pitched in the centre of the camp, and the *contubernia* pitched theirs in measured rows, alongside their fellows in the same cohort. Although camps in the early imperial period were of a standard regular layout, those constructed in the Late Empire could be triangular, square or semi-circular, to suit the demands of the site.

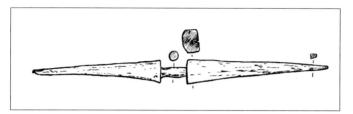

Figure **30**. Palisade stake from Welzheim (after J. Beeser).

There were three possible levels of defence: a single rampart of turves only 3ft high suitable for an over-night stop; a ditch cut 7ft deep and 9ft wide with a backing rampart made up of the excavated soil; and finally a ditch 9ft deep and 12ft wide that would have an inner rampart 4ft high made up of the excavated soil. This last fortification was intended to prevent a determined attack. The added height of the rampart gave the ditch an effective depth of 13ft.

Any of these defences could be enhanced by the use of wooden stakes, carried by a legion on the march (figure 30). When the Emperor Julian wished to cross the River Rhine unopposed by Alemanni forces, he armed 300 of his soldiers with stakes and had them row across under cover of darkness. There, with the wooden stakes, they established a bridgehead camp under the noses of the barbarians.[80] Examples of these stakes or *sudis*, have been unearthed at Welzheim and Oberaden in Germany, they were thick, of square-section, and sharpened at both ends. Those at Oberaden were inscribed with the mark of the unit that owned them. In modern experiments, a single line of these stakes have proven extremely flimsy, since, being double-ended, they cannot be hammered into the ground. Three can be lashed together, however, using the narrow hand-grip at the stakes' centre, to form a stable and very formidable obstacle somewhat resembling a modern 'tank-trap'. Mounted atop the earthen rampart, this fence could provide an effective barrier from behind which the soldiers could defend the camp. Caltrops (*tribuli*) were routinely scattered in the grass in front of the ditch as an additional protection. These were small iron traps, with four spikes, twisted so that as they lay on the ground, one spike always pointed upwards ready to catch an enemy foot or hoof unawares.

The *Strategikon* provides details of sixth-century camp-construction methods, and it seems that much had been preserved from earlier Roman practice. Its author recommended that four gateways be left in the ramparts, and that two roads be marked out that intersected the centre of the camp. Although he acknowledges that Late Roman camps can be constructed in a variety of shapes, he recommends the classic rectangular camp of earlier periods.

Wagons of the baggage train were parked around the inside edge of the campsite, up against the earthen rampart. Did the servants and families sleep with the wagons? Or did they bed down in the soldiers' tents? Contemporary writers are silent on this subject, as they are with most aspects of the soldier-servant relationship. However, one would expect the servants to remain with the wagon or pack animal to which they were assigned. Here were the personal items: any loot from raids or battle, perhaps group rations, spare clothes and the *contubernium's* weaponry and armour. All needed guarding. Soldiers often scratched or hammered their names onto objects that they owned; often enough to tell us that theft must have occurred within the legions!

In later centuries, and perhaps in the fourth century, too, the small tents of the light skirmish soldiers were pitched just inside the line of wagons. A broad area was then left for the missiles of an enemy attacker to fall harmlessly into, and then the tents of the *contubernia* were pitched in ordered lines within the central area of the camp. Senior officers that camped close to the gateways were responsible for guarding them, and for preventing troops from leaving camp without permission (perhaps to desert to the enemy, or to engage in unauthorised pillaging). Activities within the fortified camp, such as preparing to move off, beginning work or knocking off for the evening meal, were signalled by trumpet calls – just as they were back at the fort.

Just how thoroughly prepared the Roman army was to fortify camps whilst on the march is illustrated by the sophisticated range of tools available to them (plate 24). These tools are listed in contemporary writings on the Roman army, and their physical remains are found in abundance on military sites. Every legionary was intimately familiar with these implements, used on a daily basis to fell trees, cut and dress timber, dig out ditches and erect ramparts. More than likely, the typical soldier of the frontier *limitanei* was far more familiar with his pick-axe and mattock than he was with his *spatha* and *spiculum*! In the fort of course, the whole range of Roman tools was available to the legionary, from blacksmith's tongs to carpenter's planes, leatherworker's awls to the stonemason's mallet. On campaign, however, a smaller set of tools was needed, and these tools had won battles in the Roman past. Caesar's victory at Alesia in Gaul (52 BC) was in great measure due to a concerted campaign that involved digging miles of defensive ditches, piling up earthen ramparts and erecting impregnable timber palisades. Alesia was won by the pick-axe, not the gladius.

In the first century, the legionary carried with him his arms and armour, as well as other essential equipment that included 'saw and basket, axe and pick, as well as a strap, reap hook, chain and three days' rations, so that there is not much difference between a foot-soldier and a pack-mule!'[81]

Both hand-saw and axe were useful in cutting timbers ready for fort or palisade construction, while the pick and basket were used to shift earth and dig out the defensive ditches. The strap of leather or rope may have been used to carry turves on the shoulder, as legionaries are shown doing on Trajan's Column (from around AD 100).

We know from military handbooks that the legions of the fourth century relied on exactly the same pieces of equipment as their first-century predecessors, in addition to a number of others. A squad wagon of the Late Roman army contained pick-axes (*dolabra*), hand-axes, an adze, a saw, a mattock (*ligo*) or two, a hammer, a couple of shovels, a basket, sickles (*falces*) and some coarse cloth (perhaps for making sacks). These tools were shared amongst the squad, just as the work was to be shared. When it came time to construct the marching camp, some members of the *contubernium* could help fell trees, while others might be lifting turves, digging the perimeter ditch or sawing timber to create new palisade stakes. All could work simultaneously with the tools they had at their disposal. One tool that has been recovered by archaeologists from several military fort sites is a semi-circular blade with a socketed mounting. There is no mention of this strange tool in the Late Roman army handbooks or in literature from earlier periods and it does not appear on carvings from any period. Yet the tool seems to have been quite common in the north-west provinces. In form it closely resembles a modern gardener's lawn-edger and by common consensus it appears to be a 'turf-cutter', used to cut out and then lift turves ready for stacking to create a rampart.[82] Each turf (1ft wide, 1½ft long and ½ft deep) becomes a 'brick' of soil held together with grass, and can be stacked like a brick, with the grassy sides facing one-another. Turf ramparts are of course much more stable and faster to construct than ones from loose soil. The author has constructed a replica turf cutter and it was used expertly by several members of the Comitatus research group to lift up turves across a 25 sq m area (plate 25).

The squad was allocated its place along the perimeter, it was to construct 8m of the rampart. Gaius handed out the tools, but the men retained their spatha and axes; of course shields and spears were close by. Some of the Numeri Exploratorum began a patrol of the area, while others stood guard. The Taifali sat in the saddle ready to gallop into action should the alarm sound a second time. Many of the servants and other civilians were terrified. They cowered beneath the wagons to hide from the rain, as well as the imminent threat of battle. Meanwhile the soldiers of the Praesidiensis put their backs into it. Brown heather had to be cut back before turves could be lifted. These were stacked up waist high against a line that had been marked out by the *ducenarius*, commander of the first cohort. No attempt was made to dig out a defensive ditch since there was little enough depth to the soil, and rock seemed to outcrop all over the place. While Gaius kept his men going, he now saw the *ducenarius* marking out lines within the ramparts – these were for the tents. Servants began pulling wagons into position, erecting tents and trying to light fires in the rain.

Three hours later, the men were finished. Gaius was shattered, shivering, soaked and muddy, and collapsed into the tent with his fellows before Ursinus could nominate some of his squad for guard duty. The patter of rain on the tent, the constant shouting of officers and the threat of enemy attack ensured that no-one but Brocchus got any sleep. He slept soundly, and, as always he was immaculately turned out, not a spot of mud on his clothing or boots, his hair combed and tidy. They let him sleep. Before dawn a number of the Scouts returned from the west. Their report quickly circulated. There were over 500 Pictish warriors in the pass, as well as 100 Scotti mercenaries and an equal number of legionary deserters, all apparently working together.

At dawn the soldiers were astonished to see a bedraggled column of Roman troops mixed with civilians marching into the fortified camp. This was the tiny garrison of the next fort along the pass, Verteris. Out of food, their foragers and scouts attacked, the demoralised soldiers of the Numerus Defensorium ('the Protectors'), had been forced to flee the barbarian raids and trek toward Lavatris. They were grateful to be admitted into the fortified camp, but there was not enough space for all, and the rations carried in the wagons would struggle to feed everyone.

In the morning the Taifali, the Scouts and the First Cohort of the Praesidiensis were ordered to march along the pass. The rest of the unit followed orders and waited at the camp in the rain fruitlessly for two days. No word came from the expedition, and not a single courier or supply wagon reached them from further east. At night Gaius had his men cut heather to make mattresses, but they still felt like they were laying all night in a stream. Everything was wet, every spare item of clothing; the rawhide on shields was falling off; boots and shoes were coming apart, hardtack was soft and flour had spoiled. Each morning blankets were wrung out, and everyone awoke shivering. Two days in these conditions seemed unbearable. Gaius was woken on the second night by the sobs of those around him, especially the young soldiers like Veteranus, and the women and children, crying in the anonymity of the dark.

Out of the bleak mist came a rider. The enemy force had been harassed, and it had fallen back to a point not far from the camp. The Praesidiensis was to march immediately down the valley to block any escape.

Facing the Enemy

The Picts only appear in Roman accounts from AD 297 onwards; before that time nothing is written of them. The name (*picti*) was given to them by Roman writers and means 'Painted Ones', referring to the tattoos worn by their warriors in battle. It is likely that the great Pictish confederation that existed in the north-east of Scotland was a development of the earlier tribal system of the iron age Celts (whom the Romans knew as Caledonii). However, the Pictish language certainly had little in common with the language of other British tribes. The Picts may have emerged from obscurity as a very ancient tribe established in north-east Scotland and the Orkneys, who moved to fill the vacuum left following the Roman annihilation of the Caledonian people around AD 200.

Like many other northern barbarians, they were a heroic, warrior people, with a tradition of inter-tribal warfare and of loyalty to powerful chiefs. Unlike other barbarian folk, the Picts seem to have been far more politically organised. There were seven Pictish kingdoms, and their kings could have deputies and also sub-kings, they also owed fealty to a High King of Pictland. Rule was hereditary. Some historians believe that it was this High King who orchestrated the raids and attacks into Roman Britain.[83]

Pictish raids are recorded as beginning in AD 297 and they culminated with the *barbarica conspiratio* (barbarian conspiracy) that Ammianus Marcellinus reported as occurring in AD 367. It was this catastrophe that embroiled Gaius' father and mother in Chapter 1. According to Gildas, a clergyman from Britain in the early sixth century, there were three 'Pictish Wars' before the middle of the fifth century. The first began (according to Gildas) after Magnus Maximus had left for Gaul, the second has been connected with the military eulogy of Claudian quoted above, that credits Stilicho with a successful campaign against the Picts in AD 398. Rather than a war in the accepted sense, these 'Pictish Wars' were more probably periods of Pictish raiding that were just more intense and more wide-ranging than normal.

Pictish armies were interested neither in conquest nor in fighting large-scale battles. They were only interested in short-term raiding ventures, the chief prizes of which were slaves, cattle and booty. These raids would benefit the leader of the expedition, who would generously award gifts from the booty to his warriors in return for continued loyal service. This 'gift-giving' held heroic societies together through a system of obligation and reward. As is often the case, the method of war employed by the Picts shaped the army and its equipment. A force was typically small; even the largest numbers that have come down to us rarely exceed 300 warriors. This was a fast and mobile force, often unencumbered with baggage, that could cross rough terrain and disappear into forests or across marshland. In this style of warfare, a force pillaged and looted as it moved, and had little need of elaborate supply lines. Armour was not worn; helmets, if worn at all, were simply taken from Roman casualties. The Pictish style of warfare favoured mobility, speed and man-to-man combat. Consequently, the shields depicted on Pictish inscribed stones are small, either round or square, and were used in combination with spears, javelins and axes. A few fragments of swords have been found, and by no great accident these resemble Roman *spatha*. They will have been prestige weapons, carried by the chiefs and warriors of rank.

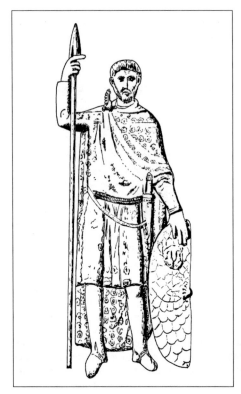

Figure **31**. The *magister militum* Stilicho. Born a Vandal, he commanded Rome's armies and dictated policy after Theodosius' death.

Individual prowess in battle was everything to the Pictish warrior who would be conscious of the presence of bards on the field. The job of the bard was to remember the exploits on the battlefield and retell them in the mead-hall back home, praising the brave and shaming the cowardly. It is unsurprising then that the heroic warriors stepped forward out of the battle-line to challenge men of the opposing army. Common Pictish dress was a knee-length tunic of colourful plaid and a cloak, but legs were bare and feet often unshod. Gildas makes a number of references to Picts fighting naked which certainly followed a Celtic tradition in the Highlands of Scotland. The aim of fighting naked was three-fold: it demonstrated a disregard for death or injury, it may have shocked and alarmed soldiers of other cultures, and it allowed the famous Pictish body tattoos to be seen. It is likely that these tattoos had magical significance in battle, a significance that would be lost if hidden beneath clothing.

Gaius' preparations for imminent battle against the Picts in AD 398 are of course conjectural. Claudian, a staunch and vocal supporter of the *magister militum* Stilicho (figure 31), wrote eloquently in AD 400 of his great exploits and achievements:

> Next spake Britain clothed in the skin of some Caledonian beast, her cheeks tattooed, and an azure cloak, rivalling the swell of ocean, sweeping to her feet: 'Stilicho gave aid to me also when at the mercy of neighbouring tribes, that time the Scots roused all Hibernia against me and the sea foamed to the beat of hostile oars. Thanks to his care I had no need to fear the Scottish arms or tremble at the Pict, or keep watch along all my coasts for the Saxon who would come whatever wind might blow.'[84]

Claudian speaks here of a campaign in the British provinces against the old barbarian enemies. Some historians take this passage to mean that Stilicho came across to Britain himself to wage a war against the Pict, Scot and Saxon. However, the situation with Alaric and his Visigoths balanced on a knife-edge in the Balkans, it seems doubtful that the commander-in-chief would risk such a remote enterprise. More likely Stilicho was simply taking credit for the hard work of the *Dux Britanniarum*! It is this campaign against the barbarians dated to the years AD 398 and 399 (or both) in which Gaius, Severus and his comrades in the Legio Praesidiensis find themselves.

From Claudian's account of Stilicho's military activities against the barbarians in Britain during this time, we know that the *frontier* was breached. Was the Legio Praesidiensis involved? Of course, we have no way of knowing. All we have is a mention within the *Notitia Dignitatum* that lists the Praesidiensis as part of the Gallic field army in the 420s. In Chapter 2 we discussed how this unit was probably transferred to the field army in Gaul before the *Notitia Dignitatum* was updated, which makes a transfer from the fort at Praesidium likely in the late 390s. Helping us to pin down a specific event to explain the redeployment, Claudian describes how Stilicho had 'a legion' transferred from Britain to the Continent at this time: 'There also came a legion, protector of the furthest Britons, which curbs the ferocious Scot and has watched the tattooed life draining from the dying Picts.'[85] The Praesidiensis seems a likely candidate for transfer to the field army, and there are several other units, too, which probably originate from Britain but nevertheless find themselves fighting Visigoths alongside *comitatenses* units in the Gallic field army. Claudian, a poet who flouted military terminology in every verse, may have meant a legion of 1200 men, or 500 or 5,000. We have no way of knowing. More likely is the transfer of *several* units to Gaul, which Claudian described poetically as 'a legion'.

We assume that only the most combat-capable units, active in the recent Pictish war, were taken abroad by Stilicho. This is a logical assumption that has no evidence to back it up, it is a suggested turn of events that uses the facts as known. In this way the Praesidiensis and other transferred units find themselves fighting Picts in AD 398. What follows, then, is conjecture – events and occurrences that fit all of the available facts, but, like all aspects of Gaius' life, are a work of fiction. The events below provide an illustration of the method by which the British units may have been transferred to Gaul. Bear in mind that the campaign, the battle and all of the units involved are conjectural.

Cresting a heather-clad rise, the Legio Praesidienses looked down toward the Pictish host which stood astride a rocky stream-bed. Hundreds of barbarians screaming and shouting formed up in four loose lines, with knots of naked heroes forward of the main host. The Numerus Exploratorum had split into four cohorts and all were attacking the Pictish front, while the Equites Taifali were spread out along one flank. Pictish cavalry seemed scattered around as if they were trying to reform. Sextus Aemilianus with his guardsmen watched the First Cohort of Praesidiensis as it edged closer toward the enemy line. The Praesidiensis' *tubator* signalled clearly across the low valley lifting the spirits of the engaged Roman forces. Gaius was on the frontline in full armour. Behind him marched Carosus, brought across from another *contubernium*, then Severus, Justinus was next, half-way down the file and acting as the half-file leader. Veteranus was behind him with a clutch of javelins and a quiver of *plumbatae*. Brocchus brought up the rear of the file of men, looking clean and dry despite the awful conditions of the past three days. Gaius marched through the heather at the front of the legion in line with the other heavily armoured squad leaders, each one followed by the men of his *contubernium*.

Facing the enemy, the legion's second-in-command gave the order to stand ready, *'Parati!'*. Shields were locked, spears thrust forward with a growl. Now he began the battle cry *'Adiuta!'*, and the men as one screamed in unison, *'Deus!'* (Protect us O God). The Picts pelted the legion with javelins, many thundered into shields with some force, some spun over the shields to bounce off helmets, a number of the points caught men in the faces. The legion advanced still further and the order was given to throw their own javelins. Spears were planted firmly in the soft ground. Severus passed *veruta* to Carosus and Gaius and these three men, along with the first three men in each file along the front of the legion, cast their missiles as one.

Now the fighting began. The Pictish heroes, covered in mud and tattoos, were gathered into wedge formations that charged into the frontline. Other warriors hung back waiting to rush in and exploit any weakness. Close up, the men looked savage and awful, with staring emotionless eyes, teeth flashing beneath large moustaches. Gaius braced with the other front-rankers. Severus and Carosus pushed him forwards and he took the charge of the Picts on his shield. He and Carosus had gotten their spears past the Pictish shields and into bodies, there was pushing and shoving on both sides. The savage screaming men were chopping over the shields with axes and lunging with spears. He felt he was being pushed backwards and almost tripped on a body under him. He kept stabbing past the shields of the enemy with his spear, his shield was pressed up against him. A Pict with brown beard and yellow teeth was pushing up against it, trying to get a long knife around the edge and into a Roman. Justinus stabbed his spear past Severus and Carosus into the man's upper arm.

Shouts and screams filled the air, everything was pushing and slipping, ducking away from blows and staying upright. At times the lines came apart and both armies shouted at one other, to later clash together, another bout in the bloody game. And then the Picts fled. Too many heroes had fallen it seemed, too many warriors at the back were fleeing the battle, and the resolute fighting of the Praesidiensis had a demoralising effect on the Pictish frontline.

As they began to run, huddled together in gangs and small groups, all order gone, the legionaries tried to run after them, elated at the fight's finish. The ground was all stream bed, rocks and heather and the armoured soldiers had no chance to keep up. Instead, Gaius gasped for breath as he leant on his blood-smeared spear, to watch the Equites Taifali ride them down. The Scouts, too, joined in the merry chase, peppering the isolated groups with arrows and javelins.

The Roman troops were flushed with victory. In the afternoon they retired to the fortified camp and they spent a happier evening, nursing wounds and discussing the battle. Gaius had lost two fingertips on his right hand and his left shoulder was in agony. Veteranus had been killed by a javelin in the chest, Gaius realised that it had been Veteranus' body that had almost tripped him up. Severus was a nervous wreck. He had kept his place in the formation, but once the fighting had ended he had broken down and lay in his wet blanket shaking. Justinus was having an arrow removed, it had slid along the inside of his shield before entering his left forearm, but had not gone in too deep. In the next squad tent Gaius could hear sobbing and the groans of wounded. A legionary in the tent had been hit in the face with a hand-axe and survived, but Death would surely claim him by dawn. Another was sobbing and spluttering, during one of the clashes he had bitten off his own tongue.

With the Picts defeated or chased away, supplies soon came up and the Roman army was able to return to Lavatris, with its baggage and families in tow, for rest and recuperation. There were more manoeuvres that year. During the winter Gaius and the men, along with their families and servants, were garrisoned at Uxellodunum, a large fortress further west, built originally to accommodate a thousand troops. Praesidiensis shared the fort with detachments from several other units mobilised throughout AD 398 to push the Picts out of northern Britain.

The legion continued to campaign in the west throughout AD 399, until being ordered to spend the winter at the grand legionary fortress of Eboracum. This fortress was huge, and had been built to accommodate in excess of 5,000 soldiers. Its present garrison numbered only around 150, men of the Sixth Legion left behind as a caretaker unit, but their families were being turfed out of the barrack blocks to make way for the Praesidiensis as well as a number of other units fresh from the Pictish campaign. The units assembled at Eboracum were composed of the Legio Praesidiensis, the Equites Taifali, the Numerus Defensores Seniores (the 'Defenders'), the Numerus Exploratores (the 'Scouts') and the Tungrians (from Vercovicium, a strongpoint on the Wall).

CHAPTER IX

To War! 400–402 AD

Explore carefully how soldiers are feeling on the actual day they are going to fight. For confidence or fear may be discerned from their facial expression, language, gait and gestures. Do not be fully confident if it is the recruits who want battle, for war is sweet to the inexperienced.

Vegetius 3.12

AD 400. The Legio Praesidiensis was in Eboracum [York], but the legionary fortress was straining to hold so many infantry and cavalry units at one time. The Duke of the Britains, who had his headquarters within the fortress, decided to billet the men of the Praesidiensis out amongst the population of the town, a common practice amongst the elite *comitatenses* field armies. Talk was rife that the build-up at Eboracum heralded the formation of a new and improved British field army to replace the one shipped across to Gaul in AD 398. That meant greater prestige, better pay, more chance of promotion and, most importantly of all, more reliable supplies.

Eboracum in AD 400

York, with its crucial river-crossing in the heart of enemy territory, had been founded by the Roman military eager to subdue the local tribes. The legionary fortress was established in AD 71 on the northern bank of

155

the River Ouse. It was soon accompanied by a civilian settlement to the south-west, immediately between the fortress and the river. The town also spread across the River Ouse and this southern section was linked to the fort by the all-important bridge. By the early third century, the settlement had been granted the status of *colonia* by the Emperor. This was an important legal distinction that enabled the city to govern itself through a senate (*curia*) of local aristocrats (*decurions*) elected to office. A century later York was a thriving and cosmopolitan city of perhaps 3,000 inhabitants (contrast that to Roman London's 10,000) with its own city walls (probably built in stone), its own forum, temples, wharves and warehouses, smart town-houses with mosaic floors and under-floor heating, shops, public baths, and street fountains – all laid out to a neat, rectangular plan. York had become the impressive second city of the British provinces, and one of the four provincial capitals (plate 42).

In AD 400 the fortress was still occupied and maintained, although there was now some industrial activity occurring within the walls. The local garrison, the Sixth Legion, was significantly reduced in numbers but the fort continued to operate in a military capacity (plate 43). The civilian settlements north of the river around the fortress seem to have been abandoned by the late fourth century, yet the *colonia* south of the River Ouse continued in existence through to the end of Roman rule in the early fifth century. Perhaps the locals immediately outside the fortress sought shelter within the walls during the barbarian crises of the 360s and then remained there. The *colonia* had its own stone wall defences.

Other changes had occurred. The main road leading from the south, across the bridge and into the fortress had been narrowed during the fourth century. Timber booths or stalls had been erected on either side, perhaps to catch passing trade with food or other saleable items. Large and impressive houses had been built in various locations throughout the city during the early part of the century, and these houses, with mosaic floors, hypocausts and courtyards were probably the smart residences of administrators, wealthy merchants and retired military officers.

Archaeologists have identified several building remains that have been overlain with deposits that have become known as 'dark earth'. A stone building on Wellington Row as well as a house excavated at Bishophill Senior and at 5 Rougier Street were overlain with this dark, silty deposit made up of decayed plant material mixed with domestic refuse, often finely broken up. Layers of this 'dark earth' have been discovered at other Roman town sites in Britain, and they seem to have become more common after the departure of the Romans in AD 410. There is no consensus of opinion as to what 'dark earth' actually represents. To some, the deposits are evidence of decay and abandonment, of roofless buildings overgrowing with vegetation and used as refuse pits by locals who can no longer rely on the struggling urban authorities to remove their waste. To others, the dark earth represents a new phase of timber dwellings with thatched roofs that spring up within the cities – signs not of decay but of a post-Roman survival.[86] For others still, the earth is brought in from the fields to either support urban agriculture or to beautify the fortified area of the city with prestigious gardens.[87]

The trend in Romano-British towns is for falling population levels and declining local economies.[88] Some of the urban buildings uncovered by archaeologists in towns like Verulamium (modern St Albans) were obviously neglected and ruinous, some public areas were clogged with rubble or refuse. Buildings destroyed by fire during the late fourth century seem never to have been rebuilt, wooden lean-tos and huts were constructed either within or against empty town houses, and mosaics that formed the centre-piece of a Roman dining room have been covered over with gravel floors or scorched by the cooking fires of later tenants. Domestic rubbish has been found piled up in adjacent rooms.

The city was an invention imposed upon the British people by the Roman state shortly after the invasion of AD 43. More used to living in scattered farmsteads and upon fortified hill-forts, the British were induced to live within the newly established urban areas. For Rome the cities acted as administrative centres for the gathering of taxes and as economic power-houses for the maintenance and feeding of the legions. In the time-honoured tradition, local aristocrats were encouraged to sponsor the construction and maintenance of public buildings. Rome did not fund the growth of cities directly; this was a local provincial concern. There was certainly no free-market economy fuelling construction by demand. In the third and fourth centuries the financial pressures on the landed gentry became intolerable ,and many fled the cities for their villas in the country. Here they could lavish their fortunes on extensions and wall paintings, hypocausts and mosaic floors. The cities began their inevitable decline once the aristocracy had turned their energies, and their wealth, toward the country estates.

Eboracum had changed since Gaius had been there last. He had been forced to close his cowhide import business in AD 394 which had necessitated a trip to the city in that year. Many buildings had been boarded up, although many thought it a temporary measure. Some of the houses that had been neglected a long while had been torn down. Gaius remembered seeing a gang of workmen pulling down a wall with chains and iron hooks. A bystander told him the gang were artisans that had once toured the province installing mosaics in all the great villas. That was 394, when the sewers had still worked and the streets had still been clean. Now no-one paid for the necessities. In AD 400, less than six years later, Gaius was shocked at the difference. The streets had taken over from the choked sewers, filth ran freely down toward the river. There were large piles of animal dung at every crossroads. Many of the wooden boards had come off the abandoned town houses. Where the roof had collapsed the rooms had become rubble-strewn and weed-infested refuse piles. Plenty of high-class buildings were now home to the less well-off inhabitants of Eboracum: petty traders, criminals, labourers, prostitutes, refugees from the countryside, and out-of-work artisans. All were eager to live rent-free and close to the main thoroughfares.

Threading his way down a street choked with wooden houses and lean-tos, Gaius gazed on poor craftsmen and petty artisans desperate for work and unable to afford the customary rents. He suddenly spotted Claudius, the owner of the grand villa at Red Stone that he and his men had turfed out and bought off. The rich man and his family were now lowly refugees, buying food at high prices, without land, wealth or skills to sustain them. The timbers used to build this street of shanty-houses came from the roofs of the buildings on either side. The Sixth Legion had been through here last year and stripped off all the roof tiles as soon as regular deliveries of fresh tiles stopped arriving. Now flooded and useless for habitation, the town houses at least afforded good timber for the shanty huts.

To ease the cramped conditions within the fortress, the Dux Britanniarum had ordered that the troops from Praesidium be billeted with local families. Gaius and Modesta followed the legionary clerk to their new billet; it was the river-side house of a wagon-driver and his family. Looking over the cramped conditions, Gaius turned back to the street. Within the hour, he and Modesta, Flavius and their two slaves were making the best of things in a townhouse. Recently abandoned and boarded up, Gaius had kicked in some of the hoardings and lit a cooking fire on the floor. The family members now had four rooms between them!

From summer AD 400 through to autumn AD 401, Gaius and his family lived reasonably comfortably within the town house. Flavius was now nine years old and helped his father re-establish his butchery business in Eboracum. The family still received army pay (although a great deal was still owed to them) and some of this helped to pay rent on a shop front along the main street. The business helped them survive their year in Eboracum, a strange year where Gaius spent more time at the butcher's chopping block than the fortress fencing post. Customers always asked Gaius' how he had lost his two missing fingers, but he never told the same story twice!

When his presence at the fortress headquarters was suddenly ordered, Gaius feared that he had unwittingly broken some military law. In his smartest tunic and cloak he stood waiting in the echoing hall, over 20m across and almost 70m long. Eight huge columns stood on either side of the hall, and light filtered in from glass windows high above (plate 44). This was the largest building Gaius would ever stand in. While he leaned easily on a fat column base, legionary officials and soldiers on business hurried about looking anxious and over-worked. To his horror, Gaius was then led into the private chamber of the *Dux Britanniarum*, Caelius, Old Coel Hen, the Duke of the Britains who commanded the military forces of northern Britain. The duke was a bald-headed man, dressed in sumptuous white linen, embroidered with gold and silver. He wore a purple Pannonian hat and sat with his advisors at a desk covered with scrolls and wax tablets. The wall behind the duke was beautifully painted; one colourful panel depicted a columned shrine topped by a grimacing actor's mask.

The meeting was short and direct. It had come to the duke's notice that a *centenarius* once attached to his staff was now serving as a common foot-soldier in Gaius' *contubernium*. This Justinus, a loyal man, no matter what the previous emperor had to say, was to be re-instated as a *centenarius* and given command of a cohort within the Legio Praesidiensis. Gaius was given credit by the duke for treating the disgraced officer fairly and without bitterness.

Despite the number of advisors in the room, and the maps and plans that littered the desks, there was no hint of the immense changes about to take place. A re-deployment was about to change the lives of every soldier in Eboracum, yet the *Dux Britanniarum* himself had no knowledge of it. Momentous events were taking place over in the Alps…

Rome and the Goths

After the death of the Emperor Theodosius in AD 395, his eldest son, Honorius, ruled the West from the imperial capital at Mediolanum (modern Milan). Just a child, his rule was only nominal and it was Theodosius' senior general, Stilicho, who effectively governed the western half of the empire. History looks favourably upon Stilicho; he seems to have had a sincere desire to protect all of the work that Theodosius had done stabilising the empire after disastrous encounters with the Gothic tribes. He did not approve of the growing rift that had developed between the western and eastern halves of the Roman empire. This was not the result of sibling rivalry, but of separate and equally powerful courts filled with generals and advisors pulling in two different directions. Stilicho's aim to reunite the east and the west could easily have appeared to the courtiers of Constantinople as a desire for conquest.

Caught between these two powerful and competing imperial households were the Goths, led by their ambitious chieftain, Alaric (figure 32). These barbarians had been allowed to cross into the empire a generation before, but had been mercilessly exploited by the Roman officials they had encountered. Pushed too far, prohibited from farming or from travelling, forced to sell their own children in return for dog meat, they fought back with weapons smuggled across the border. Retaliatory pogroms against other Goths, already peaceably settled in the Balkan provinces, were carried out. This was war and it and lasted until AD 382. During the Gothic War, the Emperor Valens was killed along with the bulk of his army in a catastrophic defeat at the Battle of Hadrianople in AD 378. Valens' successor was Theodosius, who, though inexperienced and with his legions in tatters, was able to restore the Roman defences and finally achieve a settlement with the barbarians in AD 382. The Goths were settled within the Thracian provinces as allied troops that Rome could later call upon in time of war.

When Theodosius faced the usurper Eugenius at the Frigidus River in AD 394, he called upon his barbarian allies, especially Huns and Alans, and a huge contingent of Goths who were treaty-bound to fight for him. As we saw in Chapter 7, the battle was won by Theodosius, but at a great cost in Gothic blood. Those tribesmen who survived, left the battlefield with bitterness and regret, and it was Alaric, their chief, who became a focus for the frustrations. Theodosius died only months later, and it is likely that Alaric and his warriors considered their treaty obligations now void. They had made their peace with Theodosius, not his son Honorius. In AD 395 Alaric led his Goths back to Thrace, and during this journey they sustained themselves by looting, despite being inside Roman territory. They went on to plunder Macedonia and Thessaly, and even marched on Constantinople, the eastern capital, but were incapable of taking a city so well defended. The Roman general Stilicho marched out his meagre western armies to challenge and subdue Alaric, but the Goths were too strong.

In AD 396, Alaric led his warriors south into Greece, where they plundered and extorted the ancient city-states. Stilicho mobilised his legions once again, this time attempting to relieve the Greek cities by landing a force at Corinth. However, his troops had been hastily recruited and half-trained, or pulled piece-meal from garrisons on the Rhine frontier. The dispirited general was again forced to return to Italy and to the imperial capital of Milan. The Goths retired to Illyricum (the lands of the former Yugoslavia) over which the Eastern Emperor Arcadius, had actually given Alaric full military authority. Arcadius' advisors had spotted the potential of the Goths as allies in the struggle against the Western Empire. East and west were being split apart!

Unfortunately, in AD 401 Stilicho was forced to turn his attentions to the upper reaches of the river Rhine where the barbarian Vandals and Alans were threatening the provinces of Raetia and Noricum. With the commander-in-chief fighting fires elsewhere, Alaric led his Gothic army almost unopposed straight into northern Italy – the very heart of Rome! The Goths were able to plunder several towns successfully and even besiege the city of Aquileia for a time. At the end of AD 401 Alaric settled his troops into winter quarters. Milan, the current seat of Rome's western government and the home of the boy emperor Honorius, was within his grasp. Even an unsuccessful siege of Milan might force the boy and his frightened advisors to award Alaric with high office, perhaps even that of *Magister Militum*; a Gothic Alaric in place of a Vandal Stilicho! Why not? Gainas, another Gothic chief who had also led warriors into battle at Frigidus, had been promoted by Honorius' brother, Arcadius, to the rank of Count and had been given command of the Eastern Empire's field armies.

Figure **32**. Gemstone of Alaric, the
Visigothic king who was both an ally and
an enemy of Rome.

With Alaric and his Gothic army wintering in northern Italy and prepared to strike against the capital in the spring, Stilicho had to move
quickly. He made a rapid tour of the Rhine frontier and stripped the forts
of troops. These *limitanei* units were forced to join the field armies ready
for the defence of Italy. They would never return to the border forts that
they had manned for decades.

Stilicho also sent an urgent request across the Channel for troops from
Britain. The *Dux Britanniarum* was obliged to co-operate. It is likely that
Stilicho dispatched a senior officer to Britain in order to organise the redeployment and take charge of the units as they marched south. However,
the poet Claudian, our main source for this historical episode makes no
mention of such an intermediary.

The Legions Leave Britain

Do we know which units were transferred to Gaul at this time? Claudian
refers to a 'legion', which is an extremely imprecise term, particularly
in this period, and when one considers Claudian's loose and poetic language. All it tells us is that 'troops were moved from Britain to Gaul by
Stilicho.' The *Notitia Dignitatum*, the register of officials which gives us a
good idea of which military units where were in the Roman empire after
400, would seem an excellent place to search for answers. But the western
sections were first written in the 390s and updated a number of times until
perhaps 420. There are several inconsistencies, double entries, and unex-
plained omissions. Some of these inconsistencies can help us keep track
of units. Those military units in *The Last Legionary* that accompany the
Praesidiensis southwards to Gaul all appear in the army lists for the Gallic

field army, as well as in the British army lists. Since we know troops were only ever withdrawn from Britain after AD 383, historians can confidently assert that these units were transferred away from Britain to the Gallic field army (and not the other way around!). These units are detailed in Table of Unit Transfers. The heading 'First Entry (on Continent)' gives the entry for the unit as it appears either in the Gallic field army (*magister equitum Galliarum*) or the field army of Illyricum (*comes illyricum*) in around AD 420. Both armies had seen extremely heavy fighting in the previous two decades, and it is quite likely that some of the units in Illyricum had been redeployed from the Gallic army.

Table of Unit Transfers
(Possible *Notitia Dignitatum* Unit Transfers from Britain)

First Entry (on Continent)	Second Entry (Britain)	Third Entry (Britain)
Defensores Seniores (*magister equitum Galliarum*)	Numerus Defensores (*dux britanniarum*)	-
Exploratores (*magister equitum Galliarum*)	Numerus Exploratores (*dux britanniarum*)	Numerus Exploratores (*comes litoris Saxonici*)
Secunda Britannica (*magister equitum Galliarum*)	Secundani Iuniores ? (*comes britanniarum*)	Legionis Secundae Augustae (*comes litoris Saxonici*)
Abulci (*magister equitum Galliarum*)	Numerus Abulcorum (*comes litoris Saxonici*)	-
Equites Honoriani Taifali Iuniores (*magister equitum Galliarum*)	Equites Taifali (*comes britanniarum*)	-
Seguntienses (*comes Illyricum*)	Segontio - a British fort (*Antonine Itinerary Iter XI*)	-
Tungri (*comes Illyricum*)	Cohors Prima Tungrorum (*dux britanniarum*)	-
Pacatianenses (*comes Illyricum*)	Numerus Pacensium (*dux britanniarum*)	-
Praesidienses (*magister equitum Galliarum*)	Praesidium - a British fort (*dux britanniarum*)	-

Most of the units in the table share remarkably similar names which allow historians to make a tentative match. Sometimes the order in which the unit is listed also helps, particularly when troop units from Britain are all listed together. The odd couple of Praesidiensis and Seguntienses are equated not with a similarly named unit found in the British army lists, but instead with distinctively named forts that are found in the province. According to the *Notitia Dignitatum* a unit of Dalmatian cavalry (*equites Dalmatarum*) occupies Praesidium whilst the Praesidiensis are in Gaul with the field army. Segontium, the eponymous Welsh fort of the Seguntienses, is not given any garrison in the *Notitia Dignitatum* or listed under any military command, yet archaeology has shown that Roman troops were certainly stationed there well into the mid-390s. While possible, it is unliekly that it was Stilicho who removed the garrison, summoning the men of Segontium to the defence of Italy? Although troops still garrisoned Segontium up until AD 394, this was a skeleton force only, and the bulk of the garrison was transferred away in AD 383. It is likely that the Seguntienses shipped out to Gaul to fight for Magnus Maximus – not Stilicho.

The reader might reasonably wonder why a unit would be listed in two places at once, defending Hadrian's Wall in one account, yet fighting in the Gallic army against Goths and Vandals in another. This highlights the great difficulty that historians have with the *Notitia Dignitatum*. It is a wonderfully rich document, but it is clear that several amendments were made, perhaps to record a unit's deployment into a new province, or to record the fact that the unit was occupying two forts simultaneously. Other explanations are also possible. These amendments were carried out from around AD 395 until AD 420 (at least for the sections which document the Western Empire, which are the parts that concerns us). And it seems that some parts were altered without any cross-checking or deletion. This explains (for example) why the Numerus Exploratores are listed as the garrison of two separate British forts (both Portus Adurni, on the south coast, and Lavatris, in the Pennine Mountains) while also turning up in the Gallic field army!

When were these units transferred to the Continent? Although Magnus Maximus did march to the Channel in AD 383 with a substantial portion of the British garrison behind him, the *Notitia Dignitatum* was compiled after that event. It is doubtful that troops transferred so long ago would still be listed as occupying their home forts. Claudian then records the possibility of troop withdrawals from Britain by Stilicho to meet the crisis of AD 402 and is the date favoured here. However, a second date is possible. In AD 407, Constantine III, a British general elevated to the purple by the remaining troops of the province, took his soldiers into Gaul and fought with Romans and barbarians alike to seize power there. The first five units listed in the Table of Unit Transfers could have been transferred to Gaul either by Constantine III or by Stilicho… there is no way of knowing.

Illyricum was a war-torn province in the region of former Yugoslavia and the current bolt-hole of Alaric's Visigoths. Beyond the Alps and the Adriatic, it was a province far removed from Gaul. Those British units listed under the Count of Illyricum (Seguntienses, Tungri and Pacatianenses) were probably dispatched to the Continent much earlier than units transferred to Gaul. The Seguntiensis are likely to have left Britain in AD 383 with Magnus Maximus, while the other legions are more likely to have been transferred in AD 401. But this is just conjecture. For the Praesidiensis the argument is a little more clear cut. If Constantine III withdrew the last vestiges of troops from Britain, utterly emptying the forts, then from Praesidium he would have taken the Dalmatian cavalry stationed there (and listed in the *Notitia*). Troops of the Praesidiensis were already in Gaul and they had most likely come across at the behest of Stilicho. This is a fact.

No-one is sure whether or not Constantine III took a substantial military force with him. What was left to take? The *Notitia Dignitatum* records units within the British forts, but modern archaeology suggests that few forts were occupied beyond AD 400. Crucially, the last Roman coins found in Britain in any number are those struck by Arcadius and Honorius up to AD 402. Since the bulk of coins only entered the province in military pay-chests, the implication is obvious: there were no organized Roman legions left in Britain to pay. The theory that the ambitious general instead took barbarian allies as well as mercenaries across to Gaul with him certainly has some merit.[89]

November AD 401. On the road again. Travelling light. Travelling fast. A huge column of men moving south on the Roman road, heading for one of the southern ports. Orders from the *magister militum* Stilicho himself. His representative, a dashing Count with large German moustache and a crimson cloak, arrived a fortnight ago in the company of forty Huns. These mounted bodyguards from the distant realms of the east far beyond the frontiers of empire, were bizarre in appearance, with twisted faces and stooped bodies. Their clothing was baggy and loose and their hair was long and straight.

The *dux* was commanded to empty his entire fortress and send the troops to Italy, a fortress he had spent a year stocking with *limitanei* soldiers ready for a grand campaign into Pictland. But Alaric the Goth, like a hungry wolf, had slipped into Italy for the winter, and come the spring he would have Honorius by the throat, the empire would be his and he would feast on its flesh. Stilicho's envoy addressed the assembled troops on the parade ground: 'Friends of Rome, the time has now come for you to exact vengeance for outraged Italy... Reflect that all the fierce peoples of Britain and the tribes who dwell on Danube's and Rhine's banks are watching and stand ready. Win a victory now and so be conquerors in many an unfought war. Restore Rome to her former glory; the frame of empire is tottering; let your shoulders support it. A single battle and all will be well; but one victory and the world's peace will be assured… the scene of war is the very centre and heart of Italy. Protect Father Tiber with your shields.'[90]

No-one travelled in November. There was no pasture for animals, no surplus of food to carry on the road and a lack of good travelling weather! Away from the well-made Roman roads, local tracks only ever proved useful in dry weather.

Freezing rain lashed the *contubernium* as it marched south. Gaius led the small unit; he tried to stay in time with the men of the next squad ahead of him. Severus cursed their luck over and over, swearing to Nemesis and Dis. Whilst their armour and helmets sat in a wagon that rumbled along the paved road, the legionaries were ordered to tramp through the mud-filled and partially flooded land on either side. Pannonian hats were pulled down low. Hooded cloaks were pulled tight. Legs wrapped up in cloth bindings. Yet the hard rain penetrated everything and everyone. The families were in the rear, stumbling along behind the wagons. There was no future for them at Eboracum – for good or ill, their future lay with the men marching to war.

In the evenings the column arrived at a roadside settlement or a villa and turfed out the occupants, whatever their station. Soldiers crammed into the dining rooms, bed chambers, the corridors and outbuildings to get out of the rain. Those bringing up the rear had to pitch tents in courtyards or up under the eaves. No-one cared about the owners. After four days of almost-continual rain, the troops were desperate for a slice of comfort, just to be dry for one night. Anything that could burn was thrown onto the fire: tables, chairs, cabinets and beds were all chopped up for firewood and burnt against the walls of houses and villas. Sleeping by a roaring fire one night, Brocchus began to cough. It would worsen each day they marched.

On the twelfth day, the bedraggled Praesidiensis camped outside the walls of Rutupiae, a port on the Channel coast (plate 45). The Taifali were with them, as were the Prima Tungri, and the Defensores. The rest of the column, mainly the Pacatianenses and the Exploratores, had been sent to Portus Adurni where they would embark on ships separately.

It took a week to get the Praesidiensis across the Channel. The men of Ursinus' cohort had sat under wooden verandas out of the cold wind waiting their turn to board a ship. The square and squat fort with its massively thick walls certainly impressed Gaius. While they waited their turn, bored and hungry, Ursinus brought across a number of men. There had been too many losses. Gaius' squad now had only three men, and one of those was sick. He ordered Gaius to fall in behind Gabinius, who commanded a squad of five healthy men. Now Gaius found himself demoted to the rank of a *milites*, or common legionary. Gabinius was tough, but looked like he enjoyed watching Gaius being stripped of his rank. Severus bemoaned their position. He had heard terrible things about Gabinius and did not trust him.

The Second Augustan Legion who garrisoned the fort, were grim and uncommunicative. When Ursinus' cohort discovered that the unit preceding them had all drowned when their ship had capsized in bad weather before reaching Gaul, it refused to board the next vessel. The flamboyant Count simply ordered the Second Augusta to drive the last of the Praesidiensis onto the waiting ship at spear-point. And so, on a stormy grey sea, Gaius, with his friend Severus, his wife Modesta and his son Flavius, made the crossing to Gaul. Britannia had seen better days, but once the Goths had been dealt with the pay would return, and the legions would be there to spend it! Life would return to normal and Gaius would once again sleep in his room at the fort of Praesidium. Unfortunately, Severus reminded him that he would first have to shovel out a mountain of Dalmatian horse manure! As their ship, the white-sailed *Quadriga*, passed Dubris heading south toward Gaul, Modesta and Gaius looked back at the British coastline. The lighthouse at Dubris shone fiercely in the dark evening sky, reminding them both of the watchtower on the headland above Praesidium. Likewise, the white cliffs here were a perfect match for the cliffs of the Ocellus Headland. The couple was sadly reminded of a home far away. And the snow-dusted shoreline of Gaul began to loom ominously into view…

After landing at Bononia the cohorts were called up one by one to receive seventeen days' rations. No-one had been told whether there would be a resupply along the way, but Ursinus had told then it was at least thirty days' march into northern Italy. There was a day of reorganisation before the column left the port and the sea behind it. Hills were white with snow but the road was clear and the going good. Recent hard frosts had frozen the muddy tracks on either side of the paved road.

Evening camps were not fortified and there was little formal organisation, with individual units making their own *ad hoc* arrangements. Sextus Aemilianus ensured that the Praesidiensis maintained a well-run camp each night. Brocchus, Severus, Gaius and his family camped together, sharing out food, sharing tents.

The column passed many empty buildings and even an entire roadside village – abandoned and weed-grown. Cities were always grim and dour places, poorly garrisoned, with the few inhabitants watching silently as the troops filed through. Ambiani, Noviodunum, Remi. At Durocatalaunium five days later, the locals barred the gates of the city and refused the army entry, for fear it was a force of Germans. By the time the column had reached Andematunnum in the Roman province of Germania Superior, the food was being rationed out. The terrain was becoming more rugged and the civilians were flagging. Snow flurries warned of the dangers ahead. The land southwards was carpeted with thick snow.

There were some supplies to be had in Andematunnum, assigned to legion and cohort by hardened fighters of the *Cornuti*, one of Emperor Honorius' crack fighting forces. These men were here to speed the column on its way and lead it through the Alps to the imperial capital at Mediolanum. Now it became a forced march. The pace was unrelenting, the weather worsening and the rations lean. Through a blinding white landscape the column moved, fresh snow replenished from day to day with further falls. The families suffered, although many of the children were able to sit in the wagons. Everyone felt the cold. Gaius wore three tunics beneath his soldier's cloak, as well as a hooded cloak over the top. With leg-wraps over his trousers, a Pannonian hat, woollen wrappings around his frozen hands and long scarves wound around his neck and face, he should have braved the cold. But when the chill November wind blew it cut him to the bone. His missing fingertips burned furiously, bringing tears to his eyes. They tramped on through the snow, gritting teeth against the cold and the continual abuse hurled at them by the cock-sure *Cornuti*.

'Stinking British peasants!'

'Cowards, hanging back for fear of a good fight!'

'Keep up, this is how the real army marches!'

'Faster! Faster! We need you to die in Italy, not here!'

Within a week Gaius passed bodies lying in the snow; exhausted and frozen, these men had dropped out of the column. They looked poorly dressed, but this simply reflected the need of the men immediately behind them for good boots and extra cloaks. These bodies would be almost naked by the time the end of the column had snaked past.

Severus choked on tears. He bore the misery, the cold, the hunger and the fatigue badly. In the evenings, during the brief time allowed for rest, he called for death and said it held no horror for him. Gaius was more concerned about Brocchus. His illness was obvious now, wracking coughs and a fever, yet the man still shouldered his burdens and marched with the rest of his fellows. He never talked or ate, but drank all the water he could get.

Not that there was food to eat. Rations brought along from Andematunnum ran out quickly, men could be seen breaking *buccellatum* up into halves, then quarters, then sharing the pieces out. Rumour flashed through the Praesidiensis that rations had been seized up ahead by the Equites Taifali and the Cornuti, but nothing reached Gaius or his bitter, angry comrades. As the column approached Besontio (modern Besançon) the pace increased, there were great storehouses there – food! But when they arrived there was almost nothing. Units of the Gallic field army had been through the week before and stripped out the wheat and smoked meat, the *buccellatum* and the salted pork. What was left amounted to a handful per man, many gave this up to feed their families.

Cornuti drillmasters kept up the pace, beating anyone who slackened. As soldiers dropped into the snow to await death, the *Cornuti* ridiculed them: 'The weak can die here, we need only the strong! Every man who drops dead makes us stronger!'

So hungry was Gaius that he volunteered to join a flank patrol, a couple of squads sent away from the column watching for enemy activity, perhaps German raiders, bandits, deserters ... Gaius knew it was the only chance he had of finding food, and his luck was in. The patrol had struggled through snow drifts, sapping their strength, but they had found a farmhouse, empty and partly collapsed. Inside they found rotten eggs and a large loaf of bread, green and mouldy – and frozen hard. The legionaries ate the eggs whole, shell and all. Gaius divided up the bread between the patrol members and each man hid it in his cloak.

To misery and exhaustion was added ill-feeling. 'The Goths cannot be worse than the Cornuti,' wailed Severus. Gaius was suffering terribly with his boots and his feet had been numb for days. The road climbed inexorably into the Alps, shields, packs and bags grew heavier as the ground grew steeper and the drifts thicker. One night, Brocchus took off his boots to examine his feet. Like Gaius, he'd had no feeling there for days, and in the moonlight Gaius could see that his toes were black. Brocchus wrapped his feet in a dry blanket, but come the morning could not put his boots back on – his feet had swollen in the night. With the determination and fatalism of Mithras, he was forced to walk barefoot in the snow. At midday Gaius looked around for Brocchus, but he had gone. One more casualty on the roadside; his neat and fashionable clothes probably already stripped from his back. That hit Gaius hard. He remembered the days in garrison, the jokes about Brocchus' spotless tunics, the long patrols, the battle against the Picts, the gruelling march across Gaul. To end here in the snow, halfway up a mountain, with not an enemy warrior in sight. Tragic and wasteful.

Below the top of the pass, between two snow-capped peaks, the column halted for the night. Many of the wagons had been abandoned long before, those with forethought like Gaius put on their heavy armour rather than leave it by the roadside. Thefts were now rife; any food was hidden and eaten in secret, lest others seize it for themselves. The Cornuti, however, did not seem to want for food and the suspicion was that they were hoarding rations meant for everyone. This suspicion was confirmed a few days later when the column descended the mountains into Italy. A heavy hailstorm had Gaius, Severus, Modesta and Flavius cowering beneath shields. The hailstones were as big as hazelnuts, big enough to hurt the mules of the Cornuti. While they were running up and down, one of the mules ran into the fourth cohort of the Praesidiensis and the troops pulled off the packs to find bacon and *buccellatum* – enough to feed a cohort! By the time the Cornuti had arrived to reclaim their goods the rations were safely hidden. Only the mule remained, and they were lucky to get that back uncooked!

With the slopes now behind them the march became more bearable, and rations arrived in plenty from the local Italian towns. Spirits were raised, and soon enough the impressive imperial capital of Mediolanum came into view. Walled, fortified, garrisoned, supplied – this impregnable base was to become the Praesidiensis' home for the next three months.

It is probably at this time that the Praesidienses, along with the Defensores, the Secunda Britannica, the Pacatianenses and perhaps the Tungri were all promoted into the field army, now becoming *pseudocomitatenses*, rather than *limitanei* forces. From now on they were part of the mobile army, garrisoned in cities, receiving regular supplies and some of the best equipment. They may also have received higher donative payments. To earn these privileges, the new *pseudocomitatenses* would have to fight more often and more fiercely than they had as *limitanei*, and would be out on the road when not inside the cities.

Mediolanum (modern Milan) had become the de facto capital of the Western Roman Empire during the early fourth century. Rome had become too distant from the critical frontiers; meanwhile Mediolanum was perfectly sited to transfer troops to battlefronts in the west, the north and east toward the Danube provinces. Around Milan, across the broad Italian plain, were scattered the workshops and arms factories that kept the legions supplied. The Emperor Theodosius had spent his final years at the western capital, and his son, Honorius, continued to govern the empire from Milan. It was from this north Italian capital that Stilicho, his *magister militum*, commanded the military might of Rome.

In the spring of AD 402 Alaric roused the Goths from their winter camps and headed west, directly toward Milan. His army threatened the heart of empire. The darkest hour, dreaded by Romans for centuries, had at last arrived. A vast barbarian army was only miles from the capital, intent on destruction and death. Both Gothic and Roman armies manoeuvred around Milan, until both came to battle south of the capital at the small Roman town of Pollentia.

The Experience of Battle

Troops were deployed from a marching column into a battle line, front facing the enemy. With units formed up alongside one another, the battle line could stretch for some considerable distance. This ancient formation had stood the test of time and proved extremely effective in battle.

Of course the line needed to be more than one man deep! Any breaks in the line would be exploited by enemy soldiers who would push through the gap and begin attacking the flanks and the rear of the other soldiers. Consequently the Late Roman commander typically arrayed his forces eight men deep; this was a single 'file' (*acia*) – a squad of men stood one behind the other. There was a great advantage to be had in putting so many men into the line. The eight men added weight and impetus to any charge, pushing the front rank onto the enemy's formation. They could step up to replace fallen front-rankers, which in theory, kept the front line straight and prevented gaps from opening up. Rear ranks could provide fighting support, with the second and third ranks thrusting with long spears past the front-rank as well as casting javelins. Meanwhile the rear ranks hurled *plumbatae*, or shot stones and arrows.

To this basic formation, generals added innumerable twists to suit conditions on the battlefield. The *Strategikon* advises commanders to use battle lines only four men deep when they are supported with a cavalry force, but recommends that the line should regularly be sixteen men deep! This would seem to represent two squads or files doubled up. The idea is simple. With large files sixteen men deep, the commander always has the option to divide the depth (or the files) by two, halving the depth and consequently doubling the width of the front line. He can do this again to create a force four-men deep; and again to create an impressive-looking battle-line only two men deep, but exceptionally long.

The *Strategikon* also tells us that soldiers had a set place in the formation, and did not just turn up on the day and stand wherever they pleased! Each eight man *contubernium* made up a 'file' of soldiers stood one behind the other, with the file leader (the squad leader, *caput contubernii*) at the front. This man was experienced and well paid, he had the fighting skill and the armour to face the enemy first. His second, the file-closer, stood at the rear. This man was equally experienced and equally well armoured. If the battle-line needed to turn around (to the order '*Transforma!*') then the new front-ranker would still be a seasoned veteran. But it didn't stop there.

'Of the sixteen, the eight most competent are stationed in the front and in the rear of the file, that is, positions one, two, three, four, and sixteen, fifteen, fourteen, thirteen... The remaining men, the weaker ones, should be stationed in the centre of the file.' [91]

The commander often wanted to make his front line broader, perhaps when faced with a broad enemy line across the battlefield, or to try and prevent the enemy line from easily slipping around the side of his formation to flank the troops. The clever distribution of troops by experience throughout each file enabled the Roman battle-line to always remain strong, both front and rear, no matter how many times the general halved the files. To the command of '*Exi!*' the file divided in half, every other man stepped to the left and created a new file of eight men which marched to the front. If the command was given again, the eight-man file divided in half, every other man again stepping to the left to create a new file of four men, which once again marched to the front. The ingenuity of this system is obvious. The width of the battle line could be extended up to three times, whilst still keeping tough, armoured men in both the front and rear lines, and the weaker men, perhaps inexperienced and unarmoured, in the centre of the file. The command for a file to march back into its original place was '*Intra!*'

Roman organisation and training had sustained the empire for centuries and allowed it to defeat many foes on many fronts. In particular, the sophisticated military training of the legions allowed their commanders to alter an army's formation in order to counter almost any threat. For example, when the battle-line was facing an enemy, yet a hostile force appeared directly behind, the commander could order it to create a 'double phalanx' with the command '*Medii partitis ad difallangiam!*' The first half of the file halted in its tracks; the rear half faced about and marched forward forming the double battle-line, back to back and ready to take on the enemy from both front and rear.

If the enemy suddenly made its presence known behind the battle-line instead of at its front, the commander may have wished his strongest legionaries, his file leaders, to close with the foe first. To do this he shouted: '*Muta locum!*' and the file leader turned right and then marched to the rear of the line, every man after him following in his footsteps.

When attacked by heavy cavalry, the Roman legion could form a *foulkon*,[92] which was essentially a static, anti-cavalry formation (plate 32). To the command of '*Junge!*' the troops closed up to create a denser mass of men. At the command '*Ad foulkon!*' the front-ranker knelt down with his shield stood on the ground in front of him. The man behind him locked his shield on top of that to form a wooden wall, whilst the third man held his shield above his head like a roof. The first two ranks held their spears forward at an angle and planted in the ground to resist the charge, whilst the men of the third and fourth rank held them over-arm ready to thrust forward at any foe that approached the shield wall.

A tried and tested formation that enabled the legion to advance upon a foe despite a withering barrage of lethal missiles was the *testudo* (tortoise). To the command '*Ad testudo!*':

> The men in the front ranks close in until their shields are touching, completely covering their midsections almost to their ankles [plate 34]. The men standing behind them hold their shields above their heads, interlocking them with those of the men in front of them, covering their breasts and faces, and in this way move to attack.[93]

This formation was usually used when the front-rankers lacked adequate armour protection, particularly when attempting to approach a well-defended fortification. It was a defence against missile fire, but it was not invulnerable. At the second battle of Cremona during the civil war of AD 69, legionaries formed a *testudo* to attack a Roman military camp. As it approached the rampart, the formation was split open when large stones were rolled down upon it; poles and long spears were then used to push the remaining shields apart. Other tactics were used: there are reports of millstones and stone column drums being heaved over the sides of city walls to smash apart a *testudo* and maim or kill the soldiers inside it.

A manoeuvre termed the 'boar's head' (*caput porcinum*) or 'wedge' (*cuneus*) could be employed where a weak point in the enemy line was observed. The formation was triangular: wide at the base, with a heavily armoured veteran at the apex. The *cuneus* dashed forward of the main line and charged into the enemy's front rank with as much force as the soldiers within it could muster. Tactically, the *cuneus* broke the front line almost immediately, as long as hard fighting could hold open the breach. An opponent who had some prior warning of the wedge attack could close ranks and brace for the impact, which meant the manoeuvre was not useful in all battlefield situations.

A final tactical arrangement was not a formation at all: the mobile group (*globus*) was a detached body of men sent for some battlefield mission, perhaps to kill an artillery crew, defend a breach in a city wall, or drive away skirmishers. The men ran out to perform their mission and then returned to the battle-line and to their assigned places in the formation. Often a *globus* was countered by another *globus*!

Each of these manoeuvres had their place, but when it came to defeating an enemy unit in battle, the standard attacking formation was a battle-line with shields and spears at the ready (plate 31). The cry from the commander was '*Dirige frontem!*' ('Straighten that line!'). As already discussed, no man could lag behind for fear of allowing the enemy a way through the line to attack Roman soldiers in the flanks. No man could step forward for fear of exposing himself to enemy attack. Ammianus Marcellinus described the conduct of troops fighting against the Persians in AD 359: 'while we were still in doubt about our tactics, some of our men were rash enough to run out in front of our line and were killed.'[94]

'Move!' came the command. The line advanced onwards toward the enemy formation. Tensions were high. The older and more experienced soldiers in the front ranks were able to pace their advance and keep a grip on their fears and emotions. Those in the rear were also veterans who would not flee. It was those soldiers in the centre of each file, new recruits and the unarmoured who might well falter or hesitate. The file-closer in the rear urged the men on, pushed them on, and was under orders to beat anyone who so much as whispered during the advance.

The unit was within one bowshot of the enemy force. '*Parati!*' roared the commander. Shields came up to face the enemy, and spears were levelled with a roar. Individual members of the opposing force could now be seen. This was disconcerting: it meant that the time was rapidly approaching. Here the psychological aspects began to take hold of the proceedings. Show no weakness, look the part, sound mean and angry. Who is the hardest? Who will keep on fighting until the enemy is dead? Within a bowshot, this kind of warfare now prevailed. It was machismo and bluff; bravado and chest-beating. Who is the fiercest? Who are the killers? Who is going to win?

This sizing-up of the opponent was important. There had been occasions in ancient warfare when a unit had actually fled the battlefield simply because it was terrified by the appearance of its foe.[95] One classic Roman tactic was to remain utterly silent upon the battlefield, disheartening almost every foe who encountered it. Such discipline! This went against every natural human urge, which needed to express the abject fear and tension and adrenaline rush which wracked every soldier on the field. The Goths and the Celts screamed and yelled, pouring forth curses and insults, and proclaiming their noble lineages in front of the legions. The Romans remained silent. Only in the final moments did the Roman legions give voice to their ferocious emotions. This was called the '*barritus*'.

'*Adiuta!*' cried the commander; '*Deus!*' cried the troops. (Help us – O god!). Repeated over and over as the lines began to meet, this refrain gave strength to the troops. Shout loud, show your conviction, show your willingness to win!

The historical research group Comitatus has successfully recreated Late Roman drill using Maurice's *Strategikon* as a guide, and the author has participated in many of these exercises. The commands are simple and easy to understand, and the manoeuvres themselves are just as simple to execute. There is no evidence that the legions ever marched 'in-step' despite the reference that the Roman writer Vegetius makes to the 'military step'.[96] As one individual in a large formation, the soldier has to regulate his stride to maintain his position. The soldier on the right-hand side of each line is the marker to whom all others match their pace. One glances often to the right while marching in formation.

Forming the static *foulkon* or the mobile *testudo* can be a cramped and exhausting experience (plate 33). In experiments it was easier to put taller men in the second line who could stretch over the first rank with their shields. For some of these second and third rankers a few minutes holding the large oval shields overhead became quite tiring; Roman formations may have come under missile barrages that lasted much longer than that. Pushing forward with the *testudo*, a soldier can only see the back of his own shield, and he must take small, measured steps in time with the other men. With shields locked together, a sensible rhythm was found to be essential and it was helpful for the soldiers in the *testudo* to chant quietly in order to build up that rhythm. Stumbling along blindly meant that obstacles on the field were unseen until trodden on, and being so closely bunched up it was very easy to accidentally stamp on a neighbour's foot with heavy hobnailed boots.

Training exercises were also recreated by Comitatus, using both blunt weapons and cavalry. One experiment brought together two lines of Roman legionaries; two battle lines in opposition. The field was muddy. At spear distance the points were lifted high to prevent serious injury and the shields of each line collided. Here a pushing match began, and the slippery conditions brought one man down quickly. Soon after, one line broke when a pair of heavily built soldiers pushed their way through. The line began to break up at that point. With shields overlapped, the author was disconcerted to find that at one point the line bent and all the shields turned, too, forcing the author around. As the opposing line pushed through, the shield was twisted right around and the author with it, so that he had his back to the enemy. You are attached to your shield, where it goes – you go!

Trials were also conducted that pitted cavalry against a battle-line. Again, for reasons of safety, the infantry did not engage the cavalry with spears, but formed a large defensive formation, shields forward, men standing ready. Surging past the line the horses seemed huge and powerful and each soldier was aware of the danger should one fall against the shield wall. As spears and swords came crashing down onto the shields, one had to strain upwards to absorb the blows. Repeated attacks tired the shield arm, to be of any use the shield had to be raised high to protect the head and shoulders. Javelins thrown from horseback slammed the shields back with a sudden impact, and for the unwary they were cracked into the face. One man acted as spotter, peeping over his shield to let the rest of the troops (hunkered down behind their shields) know what was coming next. The cavalry retired to pepper the battle line with arrows, and although blunt-headed, they were shot from powerful recurve bows and impacted the shields with significant force. One soldier was hit by an arrow on the upper calf, bringing him down with the pain, and the author, despite feeling safe with iron greaves protecting his shins, was hit on the toes. Both men dropped out of the formation, the shield wall quickly closing the gaps they had left. Had the arrows been sharp then the injuries would both have been debilitating.

For the fourth-century legionary, arrows would cause the first casualties. Archers in the rear would begin shooting over the formation into the enemy when within bowshot. Slingers, who were also behind the battle line, would likewise begin shooting at this point. The line advances closer to the opposing army. Spears were planted in the ground (with the ferrule or spear-butt) and the front rank threw *plumbatae* that arced down onto the enemy. Tests in armour and helmets with heavy shields have shown that a range of 70m is perfectly feasible with these hand-thrown missiles. The advance continues until the range drops to 20 or 30 metres. The lines are very close now, and the Roman soldiers can see the faces of individual opponents. Spears are planted once again and javelins are thrown, either *veruta*, the light javelins that could be thrown in a withering barrage, or *spicula,* the expensive iron-shanked javelins, perhaps carried by the first rank of the formation. Once the *spiculum* had been thrown, the front-rank-ers would need to draw their *spatha* and prepare to fight hand to hand. Meanwhile the ranks behind will support the front-rank fighters with their spears, able to reach over the shoulders of those at the front (plate 29). The *Strategikon* seems to support this idea: 'The heavy infantry … in the front line … hurl their lances like javelins [*spicula*?], take out their swords and fight … The men to the rear keep their heads covered with their shields and with their lances support those in front.'[97]

This implies that the front rank (and possible the rear rank, too) carried the heavy javelin known as the *spiculum,* while soldiers in the rest of the formation carried spears (*lancea*). This all-important phase of hand-to-hand combat was termed by Vegetius '*ad spathas et ad pila*' ('to broadswords and to javelins'). The first two lines of troops were expected to carry out most of the killing. They were to stand their ground and have the self-control not to pursue a fleeing enemy.

There is today no way for us to truly understand what it was like to stand in an ordered battle-line of several thousand soldiers, waiting for the order to march towards a rival army. The experience of actually engaging in ancient warfare is equally incomprehensible. This was killing up close. Marching slowly toward the threat, facing an army numbering thousands; men trained to kill, armed and armoured. A slow stumbling towards a terrifying physical ordeal that could well end in one's body being dis-membered, disembowelled or trampled. No easy way to escape, trapped, hemmed in by a thousand comrades on all sides. And no release for that mounting anxiety, that growing fear bubbling up – no way to scream or cry or make a tearful appeal. This is the legion. A steady advance into the enemy line. Every step bringing that inevitable moment closer. Silence to be maintained. Keep marching. No lagging behind or the file-closer belts you with his spear, and if you cry or wail, your comrades despise you because you've just told them exactly how they feel themselves… Was it like this?

The accounts of Greek writers and poets, historians and playwrights have preserved some telling clues that can shed light on the experiences of the Late Roman legionary. The abject fear of the soldier in the line is certainly attested. The playwright Aristophanes made several allusions to Greek hoplites loosing control of their bowels before the clash of armies.[98] Other sources describe how soldiers chattered their teeth involuntarily, or strained to retain control of the shaking bodies that desperately wanted to be elsewhere.[99]

What was it like to stand facing another army on a battlefield? At what point did bravado turn to solemn realisation and when did that turn to fear? Was it at the sight of the enemy? Was it during that moment when both battle-lines began to close the distance between them? Or was it at the sight of faces and men's glaring eyes, the sight of dipping spears and naked blades? Silence was enforced amongst the legionaries, but for the Germanic tribes, the Persians, Alans, and Huns there was no such restrain and their armies gave vent to a continuous and collective warcry designed to intimidate their opponents. At the moment of impact, spears were levelled and the formation crashed into the enemy battle-line. Spears were aimed at any visible gaps between the shields, which meant they would slide up into thin air, or thrust directly into a face or throat, a thigh, a shin or a groin. Doubtless many spears missed their mark and snapped against the enemy shields, since the natural human urge would be to duck one's face down below the shield as it came within range of the opposing spear-tips.[100] 'There was not any yelling, but there was not silence either; instead that particular sound was present which both anger and battle tend to produce.'[101]

This roar of rage, panic, distress and fear was accompanied by the tremendous thunderclap of shields taking a beating from spears, javelins, spatha and other shields – a continuous smashing and thumping of men hacking and stabbing at the enemy in desperation. Livy, describing the battle of Lake Trasimene fought in 217 BC records: 'the groans of wounded men, the thud or ring of blows on body or shield, the shout of onslaught, the cry of fear.'[102] In his play *The Acharnians*, Aristophanes uses this well-known sound as a synonym for war. The war-cry would go up in moments of crisis:

> The Cornuti and Bracchiati, veterans long experienced in war, intimidated the enemy by their bearing and put all their strength into their famous war-cry. This is a shout which they raise when a fight is actually at boiling-point; it begins with a low murmur and gradually increases in volume till it resounds like the sea dashing against a cliff.[103]

In the front rank the legionaries would be shield to shield with the enemy, that is: almost face to face. Both were desperate to knock the other out of the fight or be killed. It was that simple: fight or die. The slightest hesitation or mistake, a wrong move or missed blow would result in one's own death. High stakes indeed. The pressure of the entire formation squashed the front-rankers up against their foes, forcing the conflict, trying to push the opposing frontline back and over. The men in second and third rank were able to stab overhead with their spears. Of course spears could also be lowered; the second and third rank were quite capable of bending down to stab their spears between the legs of their own front-rank to impale and shatter the shins of the enemy warriors. Front-rankers wore greaves, and they needed them!

There was always a significant danger of wounding one's own men. These spears were double-tipped with sharp butt-spikes, and inevitably men behind the first few ranks will have been wounded (perhaps badly) by these weapons. The first few ranks were not checking behind them as they thrust fiercely and continuously into the enemy line. Cramped formations and battlefield conditions increased this risk. At the Battle of Hadrianople in AD 378, the Roman legionaries were trapped and desperate: 'The ground was so drenched with blood that they slipped and fell, but they strained every nerve to sell their lives dearly, and faced their opponents with such resolution that some perished at the hands of their own comrades.'[104] If blood and guts would make men slip and slide, then corpses could trip them up. Ammianus also describes how 'gleaming helmets and shields rolled underfoot' at the battle of Strasbourg.

The line may have moved forward, pushed onwards by men in the rear shoving with their large oval shields, or it may have been itself pushed backwards. The killing would have continued on the frontline, with men falling, and being replaced by second and third rankers. After an hour of this, every soldier involved in the fighting would have been mentally and physically exhausted. The pushing match (which the Greeks called the '*othismos aspidon*') would always prove crucial. At the Battle of Strasbourg in AD 357, 'one moment our men stood firm, at the next they gave way, and some of the most experienced fighters among the barbarians tried to force their foes backward by the pressure of their knees.'[105]

Ancient battles were never about killing all of the enemy and counting the dead, neither were they the massed one-on-one fights of Hollywood movies; they were more akin to linear rugby scrums, walls of men pushing for advantage while trying to kill those men leading the push. At times, the crush was horrendous:

We were so tightly packed that the bodies of the dead remained upright in the press because there was no room for them to fall, and a soldier in front of me, whose head had been split in two equal halves by a powerful sword-stroke, was so hemmed in on all sides that his corpse stood there like a stump.[106]

When the formation lost ground, the men in the rear grew worried. Was the battle lost? Were the men up front retreating, pushing back in their haste to flee? And the panic would spread with the rear ranks trying to run, to save themselves before the enemy hacked their way through each rank until it got through to theirs. This was how the majority of battles were ended. The resolve of one formation crumbled and it broke and ran. Sometimes the front rank realised how perilous its position was and did try to turn and run, but often it was those in the rear, fearful and ignorant with a ready escape route, that broke ranks. Men from both Roman and Gothic armies fled from the Battle of Ad Salices in AD 377: 'The fugitives on either side were pursued by cavalry, who hacked at their heads and backs with all their strength, while at the same time men on foot hamstrung those who had got away…'[107]

Pursuit, either by the enemy infantry or by supporting units such as cavalry or skirmishers, often made short work of men on their own or fleeing in small groups. The formation that broke and ran was often butchered. Losses to the defeated were always far in excess of the losses suffered by the victors. Ammianus, who is recognised as one of antiquity's most impartial and unbigoted writers, records that during the battle of Strasbourg, there were only 247 Roman deaths, while the Germans lost over 6,000 men. Likewise, during Julian's successful encounter with the Persians at Ctesiphon in AD 363, 2500 Persians were killed for the death of only 70 Roman soldiers.

Head wounds are frequently recorded by contemporary writers, and Ammianus twice mentions survivors clutching severed right hands. Obviously this is one of the most vulnerable parts of the soldier when fighting in the battle-line. But there was no end to the gruesome ways in which men could be wounded or killed on the ancient battlefield:

Others, half-dead and hardly able to breathe, sought to catch a last glimpse of the light with their dying eyes. Some had their heads severed … so that they hung merely by the throat; others who had slipped in the blood … were suffocated under the heaps of bodies which tumbled on them, and died without receiving any wound.[108]

The spectacle of the field following the bloody conflict shocked men of the age. No-one could become inured to the sight of thousands of human bodies rent and split, chopped and twisted into strange unnatural shapes. Blood pooled under the corpses. Unlike the modest entry and exit holes created by modern firearms, ancient weaponry routinely severed major arteries. Wounds were large and bleeding unrestrained. Few battle commentators ignore the stunning amount of blood running from the corpses.

Livy, a Roman historian in the reign of Augustus, paints a bleak picture of the field of Cannae following the victory of Hannibal in 216 BC:

> All over the field Roman soldiers lay dead in their thousands, horse and foot mingled, as the shifting phases of the battle, or the attempt to escape, had brought them together. Here and there wounded men, covered with blood, who had been roused to consciousness by the morning cold, were dispatched by a quick blow as they struggled to rise from amongst the corpses; others were found still alive with the sinews in their thighs and behind the knees sliced through, baring their throats and necks and begging who would, spill what little blood they had left.[109]

While dispatching the wounded, the victorious troops would comb the battleground searching for booty, and almost anything and everything was fair game. Generals rarely interfered with this customary reward for the hard fighting of their men.

Day-break. April 6, AD 402. Gaius woke to the trumpets. Soldiers across the fortified camp were rousing. Modesta made a fire, while Flavius ran to fetch water. Severus was pale, and he packed his gear in silence. After they had eaten, everything had to go onto the wagons. The two men had left their ringmail out on a blanket in the morning sun. Two helmets, a pair of greaves, a *spatha* and an axe, sat nearby. Javelins and spears were laid out on a nearby tree-trunk. Ham fried with apples and black pepper, served with lots of *buccellatum* made a satisfying meal. While they ate, Severus and Gaius watched the turmoil of the camp. Everything was in motion. There was no panic before the battle, but a constant movement; none of the thousands of soldiers could stand to be idle for a minute. No-one wanted to be hurrying at the final bugle-call, leaving equipment behind, or forgetting to repair straps and buckles.

'Do we need food?'

'Yes,' replied Gaius. 'Let's take a small bag of *buccellatum* and the rest of the apples.'

The men prepared for war, speaking little, pulling on the ringmail shirt, strapping on belt, scabbard, knife, greaves, waterskin, ration bag. Modesta and Flavius and taken down the simple shelter. One of the slaves had died in the Alps, the other had run away in Mediolanum. The family wealth was in a small wooden casket that Modesta carried with her. It was not much. Man and wife said their goodbyes. This was a battle like none they had seen before. The forces on both sides were vast, tens of thousands on each side. And Alaric and his Goths had a reputation that preceded them. Modesta did not cry. She trusted in God, placing around Gaius' neck her silver *chi-rho* symbol. He let it be, knowing that it did her good to know he was wearing it. Flavius, now nine years old, threw his arms around Gaius and then around Severus. He touched the leather eye-patch tenderly, as he always did before they parted. 'Ulysses!' said Severus, as he batted Flavius on the head playfully. That was him getting his own back: the boy had called him 'cyclops' too many times.

Mid-morning. The men of the Praesidienses stood brigaded with a second unit, the Geminiacenses. This pairing up of units was a tradition of the field army. Both regiments had been marched up to the left wing of the enormous battle line. To their left, on the very end of the line were the Cornuti and the Brachiati, tough *auxilia palatina* units that they had met before.

'Pigs!' grunted Severus.

'At least the pigs are on our side,' retorted Gaius.

The waiting seemed to last for hours. Riders thundered up and down the line, carrying messages between tribunes. Stilicho himself, a white-haired man with closely trimmed beard, spoke to the tribune commanding the Cornuti. They seemed in good spirits. The men were sat on their shields, trying to keep dry on the wet grass. At last the trumpets blared the signal and with screams and shouts from commanders and *centenarii,* the battle-line rose and began the steady march toward the enemy. Several times the march stopped for no reason. Groups of horsemen, perhaps scouts or dispatch riders, galloped across the lines once again. Again the officers screamed their orders and the line stepped out once again. Gaius was in the second rank; Severus was behind him in the third. Gabinius their squad leader marched ahead of them both, clad in bronze scale armour and wearing a helmet with a nasal bar to protect his nose. He had fitted a horsehair crest of scarlet to his helmet that nodded as he walked. Gabinius was an Illyrian, son of a fisherman, who had large, brown eyes and an olive skin. He looked soft and pampered, yet had a heart of iron and a fierce temper.

There were fewer horsemen riding past now, and the standard-bearers and officers that had been seen out front, were nowhere to be seen. Had they formed up into the battle-line? Gaius' view was good. Better than most. Past that infuriating horsehair crest he was able to look upon a grassy field, which seemed to turn into ploughed soil in the distance before rising gently to a very low hill. There were trees dotted along the base of the rise. A hint of smoke blurred in the cold, blue air above the rise. That must be the cooking fires of Pollentia, thought Gaius, if only they could imagine what was about to happen here.

Trumpets and tubas began to bray their orders. 'Ready for action', they blared again, picking up the tempo, 'March to contact'. Severus began to swear quietly to himself. A murmur ran through the Praesidiensis, and Gaius could hear file-closers hissing at their men. Suddenly they could hear the voice of the standard-bearer: 'Silence! Observe your orders! Do not worry. Keep your position. Follow the standard. Do not leave the standard to pursue the enemy.'[110] Other standard-bearers were shouting the same refrain, across a mile of battle-line.

Now he could see the Goths and from the murmurs that ran through the line, so had the rest of the battle-front. A sea of oval shields in plain colours swathed about the lower slops of the hill and along the fields. In number they were uncountable. From the hedge of spears and lances there were many ranks.

An awed silence descended upon the Roman force, broken only by laboured breathing and the jingle and rattle of equipment as they marched forward toward the ploughed field. Now came a low rumble, slowly growing to a shout, the mighty roar of thirty thousand men, rolling across the field toward them. Gaius heard someone to his right weeping, and behind him a Christian pleading to his God. Trumpet calls halted the Praesidiensis yet again. Who else was moving? Was anything happening? He could see only straight ahead, his view all around blocked by the men of his unit.

'Maybe they are talking. Alaric and Stilicho. Maybe its not going to happen. We can go home. Maybe he's buying him off.'

Gaius did not answer Severus.

'*Silentium!*'

Now they could see the Goths more clearly, between a hundred and two hundred paces distant. Gaius' mouth was dry. It didn't look like a barbarian rabble. There were gleaming helmets, battle-standards, scale and ringmail. He could hear the distant shouts of German voices, and the host gave a thunderous roar that raised every hair on his neck. Now the chiefs began to shout incessantly, over and over, at the Romans or their own men Gaius knew not.

The Goths took to chanting together, a hideous and terrifying sound which seemed to shake the earth. The Roman trumpeters replied and the battle-line began to march again, with the Praesidiensis stepping onto ploughed earth. A man began screaming and shouting in the rear. Heads twisted around; soldiers hesitated. Were they being attacked from behind? Were they trapped? The screaming stopped abruptly; 'Keep your position! Follow the standard!'

'Arrows! Slings!' A storm of hissing arrows and sling bullets passed overhead and a sudden activity in the enemy line was proof that they had landed amongst them. A second hail of arrows and lead shot was released from the Roman missile troops behind the formation.

There was more shouting from the Gothic chiefs and the enemy battle-line seemed to quiver and shake. They were running toward the Roman front!

'Halt!' Far away to the right, the Praesidiensis could hear hundreds of men shouting. Goths? Romans? The fierce enemy continued to close, despite several more deadly barrages. What use are arrows?

'*Plumbatae!*' That was the order to grab a handful of lead-weighted throwing darts and ready them. Gabinius had five strapped inside his shield, Gaius had seven sticking out of his ration bag, handed to him as he took his allotted place in the line.

Seventy paces. Sixty paces. 'Ready... Ready... Throw!' Gabinius and the rest of the front-rank stepped forward and threw the darts underarm, Gaius threw his a second later, stepping slightly to the right of Gabinius. A thousand white fletchings falling upon the Goths resembled a snowfall. Gaius heard shouts from behind and the order '*Testudo!*' Rogue *plumbatae*, easy to mis-time that release even in practice. 'Throw! ... Throw!' Fifty paces, forty paces. They could see men falling, others tripping, the Goths should be closer by now, they must have slowed. Some raised shields over their heads. They had stopped!

Suddenly, a score or more of Gothic cavalry raced past, horses panting, kicking sods of earth high into the air.

'March out!' This was serious business, Gaius was dreading this order. Every other man in the file stepped up to create a new, shorter file. Gaius was now on the frontline, Severus beside him. From this vantage point he could see left and right down each way. By God. The numbers of men, receded into the distance. Far to the right both lines seemed to merge, and dust hovered them in a cloud. Far away trumpets bleated in futility. He could see more horsemen charging down between the opposing lines, but could not tell whether they were friend or foe. The spectacle entranced him.

'March!' The legionary behind him hit him in the back to make him move.

'Javelins!' He planted his spear in the plough-soil and took three of the light javelins, the *veruta*, being passed to him from behind. 'Throw! Throw!' Gaius dropped the weapons in his haste, and they clattered about his muddy boots. 'March!' Damn, he hadn't time... he took his spear and looked up just as Gothic javelins thundered into the battle-line. The crash of shields and the startled shouts shocked him, he hadn't seem them throw the weapons. His shield smacked him in the face and he staggered back onto the soldier behind him, his face on fire. He was disorientated. There were more orders; the Goths were booming out their chants and it sounded too close. He was pushed back to his feet, his face was numb and hot, he tripped over a javelin, a Gothic *angon* with an iron shank, its tip stuck into the rim of his shield.

God. They were at ten paces. The fury-filled faces of bearded Goths, spitting insults, screaming, brandishing shield and spear defiantly. Waiting for the moment or the order.

'Ready!' came the Roman order. Every legionary swung around his shield and thrust forward his spear with a defiant scream. Gaius trod on the *angon* and pulled up his shield, snapping off part of the shield-rim. On the front-line he adopted the stance. Stared at the men opposite him who were shouting and screaming.

He heard the booming voice of Ursinus; 'Help us!' A thousand voices thundered in unison, 'O God!'

'Help us!' Again the response, 'O God!'

It was mesmeric. A wavering of the lines. A hesitation. Then action. Here and there, men ran out of the Gothic line with axes, and they threw them with all their force at the Roman front-rankers. They thumped and cracked into the shields, Gaius heard shrieking, to his left he heard shouting. Trumpets also sounded to the left. The Cornuti were replying with their own axes and the whole regiment was charging into battle.

'Charge!' The front rank began to trot toward the Goths, Gabinius was in front of an axeman who had tripped on the furrows and he speared him in the armpit. The barbarian squealed and writhed. Gaius stopped running to be next to Gabinius. The Goths were on them! Shields were bent backwards and men were shouting and yelling at the top of their lungs. Stab the spear, stab the spear. Keep down under the shield. With a mighty heave, Gaius was pushed back and he tripped over rough ground, his spear came out of his hand. From behind a push that jammed him shield to shield with a blonde Goth, pigtails lashing around. He was desperately tugging his *spatha* from its scabbard, he could hear himself wailing in fear. The Goth was nose to nose, blue eyes, flaring nostrils, staring into Gaius' eyes – and then he vanished, his shield pulled down by Severus' *spatha* chopping down. Both were side by side, Gaius had his sword out and his shield up. Blood was pouring across his eyes from the shield cut, but he could see enough. Faces were his target, and arms that came out at him wielding curved axes. He chopped and hacked. Backing down under his shield, at times. Roman spears flashed past him on both sides, turning a Goth face to pulp.

He was pushed forward again, and the barbarian in front fell under him out of sight. He felt the man thrashing behind him as a butt-spike finished him off. Gaius was pushed again. He held onto his shield and spatha with grim determination. Stop pushing! He realised he was still screaming in fear, and stopped himself. Between his oval shield, and the Gothic shield in front of him suddenly sprang an iron helmet with a red horse-hair crest. Gabinius. Another push from behind and Gabinius was forced forward. Axemen seemed to rise above their green shields and even in the terrific din of the battlefield, Gaius could hear his squad-leader's scream. Blood sprayed over him and as he blinked he was looking at Gabinius' helmeted head upside down, looking at him – his neck cut by a single axe-stroke, pushing his head back, attached only the skin of the throat.

Gaius thrashed his *spatha* at the edges of the Gothic shield wall, staying down so that the spears of his comrades could do their work. Several times *plumbatae* and *veruta* were thrown over his head into the dense mass of Gothic warriors.

The pressure dropped, Gabinius, who had been dead for several minutes, fell away from Gaius' blood-soaked shield. The barbarians were retreating. Some were glancing to their right from where a tumultuous din arose. Now they backed off and some began to flee.

The trumpets screamed and the legion charged. Gaius' racing heart lifted him forward with the rest of the front rank toward the backs of the fleeing barbarians. Easy targets. No shield wall, no harsh array of iron blades. After a few paces Gaius stumbled and crashed into the soft earth, tripped by a furrow, or a discarded shield or a corpse. He gasped for breath, and wiped the sticky blood out of his eyes.

He was alive.

A field of corpses lay around him; lately walking and talking men. Now twisted and bloody, each man rent open in awful and unnatural ways. In a stupor Gaius gazed at gore and guts, spilled out into the furrows, body parts he had never seen before.

A Goth, impaled by a *spiculum*, laying on top of a Roman, also transfixed by the same weapon, his nose and ears bitten off in the frenzy of close combat. Another Goth, sat upright against a body, staring blankly into space, his entrails in his lap. Yet another of the barbarians, writhing in the bloody mud with a knee twisted madly out of position, clutching the stump of his right arm and spitting defiant words at the Romans milling around. Bodies, stretching eastwards in a long line where Roman and Goth had clashed, had fought and had died. The groans and the shouts of the dying brought tears to Gaius' eyes, such concentrated human misery on one small patch of ground.

He found Severus, unharmed but dazed and bewildered, walking back an hour later from the Gothic camp clutching a leather bag and a tiny, gold-plated statuette. Amongst other things, the bag contained a generous amount of silver coins. He learnt to his great sadness that *centenarius* Ursinus had been killed leading that charge into the axemen. He'd died when the fighting became confused and the butt-spike of a Roman *spiculum* had gone straight through his throat. A good man. Justinus, trusted friend of the *Dux Britanniarum* survived, and led his cohort to victory. The battle had been won, despite losses, and the Gothic camp had been raided.

The Goths had run away… but they would one day be back.

A day later, many of the soldiers were back in camp, resting and tending the wounded, while others (Severus included) assembled a column to pursue the Goths in their flight eastwards. Gaius remained in camp, with two black eyes, a broken nose and a fractured cheekbone. He would be one of those soldiers returning to Mediolanum to reinforce the garrison there. Modesta and Flavius were with him.

CHAPTER X

Post-Script: The Fall of Rome

Away with delay, Alaric; boldly cross the Italian Alps this year and thou shalt reach the city.

Claudian, *The Gothic Wars*

The battle of Pollentia, a crossing point on the river Tanarus, was fought on Easter Sunday, AD 402. Alaric was defeated; his baggage train and camp were overrun by the Alan general, Saul, who was killed in the assault. Saul was a scarred Alan veteran, and his death from a sword blow put the Alan cavalry into confusion. They would have retreated in disorder had not Stilicho brought up a legion to exploit the general's success. The Goths fled, but the Roman troops did not immediately sack the camp as was normal, but pursued the barbarians, eager for more blood. Stilicho had inspired his troops, promised them revenge on the Goths for the depredations they had inflicted on Greece and for the casualties inflicted on the field armies in the past few years. To hinder the pursuit, the Goths began to throw down booty collected during their sack of Greece, gold and silver, purple garments, statuettes and other treasures. But the Roman legions sought vengeance, not wealth, and pushed on. Within the barbarian camp

185

the army was able to free many captives, slaves taken by the Gothic warriors as they plundered their way through Greece and Thrace.

Claudian, extolling Stilicho's successes to the stars in his work *The Gothic Wars*, claimed Pollentia as a fabulous victory: 'Thy glory, Pollentia, shall live for ever; worthy is thy name to be celebrated by my song, a fit theme for rejoicing and for triumph. Fate pre-ordained thee to be the scene of our victory and the burial-place of the barbarians.'

However, the battle of Pollentia was not the final stand of the Goths. Alaric survived, as did many of his warriors. It may even be that Stilicho had no intention of destroying them utterly, since it seems that an armistice was declared later in the year. After trapping the retreating Gothic army in the foothills of the Alps, the Roman commander made a deal with Alaric, of which we know little. Claudian, tells us that Alaric broke the treaty: 'Here, as once again he breaks his bond, and driven by his losses risks all in the attempt to change his present fortune, Alaric learned that his mad treachery availed him nothing and that change of place changes not destiny.'[111]

Never discussing directly what happened that year, the florid poetry of Claudian suggests to the modern historian that Alaric cut a deal with Stilicho and may have made a move to leave Italy. The treaty broken, the Goths were back in northern Italy by early AD 403 – Claudian mentions in passing a significant defeat at Verona, a Roman city at the foot of the Alps. This final defeat pushed Alaric and the straggling remnants of his army out of Italy. The king of the Goths fled back to Illyricum where he tried to rebuild his forces through plunder. Many of Alaric's men had deserted the Gothic cause and joined the Romans, including some of the king's commanders along with their warrior hosts.

The crisis over, the Emperor Honorius moved his court from Mediolanum to Ravenna on the east coast of Italy. This city was well protected from the hinterland by treacherous marshes, and protection was needed. City walls and large armies did not seem reliable enough. Should Alaric return, Honorius could continue to govern safely from Ravenna, and be resupplied by sea. But Ravenna was a retreat, whereas Mediolanum had been a forward centre of control and communications – a battle centre. Rome was on the back-foot.

Alaric would be back. In AD 404, Stilicho actually made another treaty with his erstwhile enemy, it was a treaty which would allow the western empire to annexe parts of Illyricum at the expense of the east. In this way Alaric became the powerful pivot between the see-saw politics of east and west. Both halves of the empire would like to have seen the Goths unleashed upon one another.

In AD 405, the treaty was wrecked when another Gothic horde poured into northern Italy and Stilicho marshalled his forces once again to finally defeat and enslave them in AD 406. No sooner had that been done than a massive incursion across the under-manned Rhine frontier forced yet more desperate fire-fighting. Germans, Vandals and Alans defeated local tribes of Franks friendly to Rome, and devastated large parts of Gaul. What was more, Constantine, a general from Britain, was in Gaul claiming the imperial throne! The crisis was deepening far faster than the army could effectively cope with. To free up his field armies and allow them to campaign in Gaul against the barbarians, without leaving Constantine unchecked, Stilicho now struck a deal with Alaric. As a military commander wielding the authority of Rome, Alaric would lead his Goths against Constantine's rogue legions. Stilicho's popularity amongst the Roman people was waning fast.

Arcadius, who had ruled the eastern empire for thirteen years, died in AD 408. Stilicho suddenly saw this as an opportunity to reunite east and west under a single military command, and planned to travel to Constantinople to establish authority there. Unfortunately, with victories seeming to count for little and his propensity for making deals with the Devil, Stilicho was arrested by enemies at court. He was executed in AD 408 and a campaign to undo his work began in earnest. Part of that 'undoing' was the massacre of families of his loyal barbarian soldiers. This included thousands who had been captured at Pollentia, Verona and during the huge invasion of AD 407. Alaric is said to have recruited up to 30,000 disgruntled Goths directly from Stilicho's armies in the west.

Alaric demanded payment for his services against Constantine, but the senate refused to acknowledge the agreement that had been made between Stilicho and the barbarian king. This led Alaric to bring his Visigoths, now stronger than ever before, back into Italy. Within two years, he had led these men to the gates of Rome and sacked the city, taking by force what he had been promised – with interest.

Yet Honorius still ruled safely from Ravenna – Rome had not fallen. Alaric died later in AD 410 only months after plundering Rome. His successor led the Goths north into Gaul where they attempted to establish a kingdom, although this was not realised until AD 418.

Did the sack of Rome mean the end of the Roman Empire? Ravenna was the seat of power, Mediolanum still a strategic centre, Rome was huge, cosmopolitan, central to the Christian church – but if it fell, Rome would continue. And it did. Further barbarian incursions ravaged Gaul and Spain, until parts of the western empire were given over to settlement and the establishment of kingdoms. The western empire, much reduced, still operated, but continued to fight for its survival. While the eastern empire thrived, despite facing the Huns from AD 441 onwards, the west was bound in by the growing power of independent barbarian kingdoms created out of old Roman provinces. Finally, the last Western Emperor, Romulus Augustus, was deposed, not by a jealous usurper as had been the norm in Roman history for centuries, but by Odoacer, a Germanic general. He set himself up as king. The office of the western emperor had been dissolved, the western half of the empire had ceased to be.

When Constantinople mounted an invasion of the Italian peninsula in AD 535 it did not lead to a resurgent Rome, independent and free, liberated by the legions of the east. Instead it led to Rome, Ravenna and Italy becoming part of the eastern Roman Empire: minor provinces within a greater state.

Constantinople continued to be the seat of the Roman emperor. In a true sense, there was no fall of Rome. The empire survived, Constantine the Great had shifted the capital to the east, and this event over a century ago had saved the empire from destruction. The eastern Roman empire could now look forward to a long and glorious history of its own.

What of Roman Britain? What became of the Roman cities, the roads, the businesses and craftsmen? What became of those remaining soldiers and their families left behind in the echoing forts? These are difficult questions that go far beyond the scope of this book, although a great body of literature has developed that seeks to answer them. A small number of books dealing with the immediate post-Roman period in Britain can be found in the bibliography.

Finally, what became of Gaius and his family? The year AD 403 marked exactly twenty years since he first joined the legions back in AD 383. After twenty years of service a legionary was able to retire with an honourable discharge (*honesta missio*) and as a mark of his status was awarded a discharge certificate. Any veteran with an *emerita missio* (twenty-four years' service) could actually claim exemption from poll tax for both himself and his wife. As a veteran retiring from the legion, Gaius would have been granted a plot of land (probably on abandoned or marginal land) for him to farm, a pair of oxen and 50 measures (*modii*) of each type of locally farmed grain.

Perhaps he and his family settled further to the west, reclaiming farmland near the city of Augusta Taurinorum (modern-day Turin). In this corner of the Piedmont region of Italy they may have lived out happy and peaceful lives, untouched by Alaric's return in AD 410 and by the Goth's flight into Gaul following Alaric's death.

In AD 411, following his eighteenth birthday, Flavius would be called up to serve in the legions. He would probably join a unit in the Italian field army. When Attila brought his rampaging Huns into northern Italy in AD 452, even Flavius would be an old retired soldier with sons of his own. Perhaps these sons, also destined for the legions (by imperial decree) would be some of those soldiers who harassed the Huns and helped the Roman general Aetius, who drove them from Italy for good.

Appendix:
The Remains of Gaius' World

Gaius, Severus, Modesta, Ursinus and the other characters in this book are fictional, but all of the locations, buildings and settlements are historical. Whilst the Late Roman world described in this book has long-since vanished, it is still possible to visit some surviving fragments of that world, to stand within the same spaces as Gaius and his comrades, to touch the same door posts and descend the same steps. And in some places it is possible to look out across the countryside from one of these Late Roman ruins and to gaze upon the landscape as soldiers like Gaius certainly did.

The list that follows provides a brief description of each site, with an emphasis on architectural details that relate specifically to the late fourth century. Additional information includes the modern location of the site as well as the building or location that it corresponds to within *The Last Legionary*.

Eboracum (York, North Yorkshire)

The modern city of York overlays much of Roman Eboracum, although a few gems can still be found. In the Museum Gardens the western-most corner tower of the legionary fortress still survives to a height of 5.8 metres (with medieval additions). It is sign-posted as the Multiangular Tower. An 11-metre stretch of the fortress wall runs north-west from the tower (and still stands 4 metres high). Missed by many visitors is the Anglian Tower, a rectangular interval tower built into the surviving Roman wall. This seems to have been a fourth-century construction that replaced an older tower suffering subsidence.

Remarkably, fragments of the legionary *principia* have been unearthed beneath the Minster, which stands at the centre of the fortress layout. The visitor must pay a reduced entry into the Minster to visit the Undercroft. The remains all date from the fourth century and consist of several column bases (which held up the roof of the vast cross-hall) as well as part of the cross-hall flagstones and a functioning drain. Particularly fascinating are surviving fragments of an elaborate wall-painting that decorated one side of a private room that may have been the residence of the *Dux Britanniarum* (including of course Magnus Maximus, if he held that office).

One of the massive *principia* columns was excavated in full and has been erected outside the entrance to the Minster. Standing 7.7m high it only hints at the size of the *principia* cross-hall, the roof of which could have been almost as high as the Minster's nave today!

Perfectly placed underneath a pub called Roman Baths, in St Sampson's Square, are the remains of a huge suite of Roman baths that were built for, and probably by, the Sixth Legion. They were built within the fortress walls. The remains are in the pub's basement and the archaeological level on display is dated to the fourth century. Certainly worth a visit.

Praesidium (Bridlington, East Yorkshire)

As explained fully in Chapter 2, no Roman fort has ever been found at Bridlington and there are no extant Roman remains. It is the author's contention that if Praesidium existed here, it was on the site of the present-day harbour, or a little way out to sea. Two Roman coin hoards were found in the harbour area, along with, surprisingly, two Greek coins from the second century BC – suggesting that the port was in use long before the Roman invasion.

The coastline may have retreated somewhat but the view from Bridlington harbour is essentially as Gaius would have seen it, standing on the fort's wall-walk. Wide Gabranticorum Bay, with the low coastline of Holderness stretching off to the right, and the white chalk cliffs of Flamborough Head out to the left. The gleaming white 1674 lighthouse that stands on the Head gives more than a passing resemblance to the high Theodosian signal tower that warned of sea borne raiders. The visitor must imagine a pillar of smoke rising from the chalk Headland, followed by a dozen more signal fires lighting up the low Holderness coast – and on the horizon, heading straight for the harbour – longboats!

Ocellus Headland (Flamborough Headland, East Yorkshire)

Flamborough is extremely likely to have been the site of a signal station, although no remains have been found. From Flamborough, the headlands of Filey, Scarborough and Ravenscar are all visible on a clear day. The vista northwards is dramatic and evocative; the crashing waves and wheeling seabirds capture some of the flavour of fourth-century military life, watching with trepidation for Saxon boats on the horizon.

'Two Bays' (Scarborough Signal Station, Scarborough, North Yorkshire)

The remains of the signal station on Castle Cliff are only accessible through Scarborough Castle. The stone foundations are clearly visible (unlike those at Filey, Ravenscar and others), although a portion has vanished over the cliff side due to erosion. It is easy to imagine the small garrison of 'Two Bays' weathering stormy nights up on this inhospitable headland. The view out across the Mare Germanicum is spectacular.

'Villa Claudius' (Rudston, East Yorkshire)

The Villa Claudius at Red Stone, that features in Gaius' life, represents the Roman villa at Rudston village, west of Bridlington. No remains of the villa are visible in situ, although mosaics from the site can be viewed at the Hull and East Riding Museum, in Kingston-upon-Hull. Of course the imposing Neolithic monolith (7.7 metres high) which dominated the landscape in Gaius' life, and still dominates the graveyard of Rudston church today, can be seen.

Arbeia (Arbeia Fort, South Shields, Tyne & Wear)

The local authority has invested in a scheme of architectural recreation at Arbeia which has made the site a very inspiring one to visit. Besides the excavated remains of the fort themselves, and the accompanying museum, the site boasts a replica barrack block and commander's house (wonderfully furnished and decorated). Arbeia is perhaps most famous for the replica gateway which dominates the site. Home in the fourth century to the Numerus Barcariorum Tigrisensium (the 'Tigris Boatmen').

Vercovicium (Housesteads Roman Fort, Northumberland)

Although Housesteads fort does not feature in the narrative, it is a fort of around the same size and dimensions as our conjectural Praesidium. The plan is easy to follow and the majority of the buildings within it have been excavated and are on show to the public. Barracks, hospital block, *principia* and latrines are all well preserved, and are a wonderful illustration of a typical fort layout surviving into the fourth century. Home in the fourth century to the First Tungrians.

Lavatris (Bowes Roman Fort, Durham)

This fort guarded the eastern end of the Stainmore Pass, within which the Praesidiensis fought their fictional battle with the Picts in AD 398. The ditches of the fort can still be seen, although much has been obscured by the church and castle moat. It was the home of the Numerus Exploratores ('Scouts').

Lavatris Watchtower (Bowes Moor/Durham)

This watchtower was burnt by Picts during the fictional battle of the Stainmore Pass. It is north of the A66, near the Bowes Moor Hotel. The timber tower has left no trace, but the surrounded bank and ditch (enclosing a compound 14 by 18 metres in size) is clearly visible.

Rutupiae (Richborough Fort/Sandwich/Kent)

Rutupiae is one of the so-called Saxon Shore Forts, and the massive defence walls still surviving give an impression of the threat that they were built to counter. The site has been arranged so that ditches from the earlier AD 43 invasion camp can be viewed, as well as the foundations of the huge triumphal arch that was erected at the centre of the town. Third-century ditches are visible around these foundations. When looking at Richborough as it appeared the fourth century, these features must be ignored. Part of the site has vanished into the sea, and the sea itself has gone! Silting eventually blocked traffic to Rutupiae, and filled in the waterways to the north; the sea is now far from the fort remains. Home, in the fourth century, to the Secunda Britannica ('Second British Legion')

Mediolanum (Milan/Regione Lombardia/Italy)

Milan is one of Italy's greatest modern cities and completely overlays its ancient Roman foundation. Yet some parts of the Roman past have survived. The Colonne di San Lorenzo is located at the front of the Basilica of San Lorenzo and is a square flanked by columns, this Roman temple or bath-house architecture is second century in date, but placed here sometime during the fourth. Behind the colonnade stands the church of St Lorenzo, which was initially constructed in the fourth century but has been extensively added to since then. The chapel of St Aquilino within the church is a former fourth-century mausoleum.

Milan's greatest fourth-century relic is the body of St Ambrose, the influential bishop of Mediolanum who was advisor and conscience of Theodosius the Great, and who died in AD 397. His resting place can still be seen in the crypt beneath the church of St Ambrogio! This church also holds the so-called Tomb of Stilicho (a fascinating tomb made up of third-century Christian and pagan fragments), as well as the chapel of St Vittore. This chapel dates from the fourth century, but is decorated with stunning (but often difficult to see) mosaics of St Ambrose and other saints of the period.

Bibliography

Ancient Sources

Ammianus Marcellinus
Aristophanes, *The Acharnians*
Aristophanes, *Peace*
Claudian
Codex Theodosius
De Rebus Bellicis
Gildas
Herodotus
Josephus, *The Jewish War*
Livy, *The War with Hannibal*
Maurice, *Strategikon*
Notitia Dignitatum
Peri Strategikes
Polyaenus, *Strategemata*
Procopius, *History of the Wars*
Scriptores Historiae Augustae
Sidonius Apollinaris
Sueronius, *The Twelve Caesars*
Syenisius, *Epistulae*
Tabulae Vindolandenses
Tacitus, *Histories*
Thucydides
Vegetius, *Epitoma Rei Militaris*
Xenophon, *Agesilaos*
Zozimus, *New History*

Modern Sources

Alcock, J.P. 2001, *Food in Roman Britain*. Stroud: Tempus.
Birley, A.K. and J.D. Thomas. 1983. *Vindolanda: the Latin Writing-tablets*

(Tabulae Vindolandenses I). London: Britannia Monograph.

Birley, A.K. and J.D. Thomas. 1994. *Vindolanda: the Latin Writing-tablets (Tabulae Vindolandenses II)*. London: Britannia Monograph.

Birley, A.K. and J.D. Thomas. 2004. *Vindolanda: the Latin Writing-tablets (Tabulae Vindolandenses I)*. London: Britannia Monograph.

Bishop M.C. and J.C.N. Coulston. 2006. *Roman Military Equipment*. Oxford: Oxbow.

Bowman, A.K. 1994. *Life and Letters on the Roman Frontier - Vindolanda and its People*. London: British Museum.

Cameron, A. 1993. *The Later Roman Empire*. London: Fontana

Campbell, B. 1994. *The Roman Army, 31 BC–AD 337 A Sourcebook*. Abingdon: Routledge.

Croom, A.T. 2000. *Roman Clothing and Fashion*. Stroud: Tempus.

Crow, J. 1995. *Housesteads*. London: B.T. Batsford/English Heritage.

Dark, K. 2000. *Britain and the End of the Roman Empire*. Stroud: Tempus.

De la Bédoyère. *The Buildings of Roman Britain*. London: B.T. Batsford.

Diehl, E. (ed.) 1925–31. *Inscriptiones Latinae Christianae Veteres*. Berlin: Weidmann.

Elton, H. 1996. *Warfare in Roman Europe AD 350–425*. Oxford: OUP.

Fink, R.O. 1971. *Roman Military Records on Papyrus*. Cleveland: CWRU Press.

Faulkner, N. 2000. *The Decline and Fall of Roman Britain*. Stroud: Tempus.

Fuentes, N. 1992. The mule of a soldier. *Journal of Roman Military Equipment Studies 2*. Oxford: Armatura.

Goldsworthy, A. 2003. *The Complete Roman Army*. London: Thames and Hudson.

Grainger, S. 2006. *Cooking Apicius*. Totnes: Prospect Books.

Grant, M. 1999. *Roman Cookery*. London: Serif.

Hanson, V.D. 1989. *The Western Way of War*. Berkley and Los Angeles: CUP.

Hartley, E., J. Hawkes, M. Henig and F. Mee (eds.). 2006. *Constantine the Great*. York: York Museums and Galleries Trust.

Johnson, S. 1980. *Late Roman Britain*. London: BCA.

Jones, A.H.M. 1964. *The Later Roman Empire*. Oxford: Basil Blackwell.

Lee, A.D. 2000. *Pagans and Christians in Late Antiquity*. London: Routledge.

Mason, D.J.P. 2003. *Roman Britain and the Roman Navy*. Stroud: Tempus.

Ottoway, P. 1993. *Roman York*. London: B.T. Batsford/English Heritage.

Renfrew, J. 1985. *Food and Cooking in Roman Britain*. London: English Heritage.

Rich, J. (ed.) 1992. *The City in Late Antiquity*. London: Routledge.

Salway, P. 1993. *The Oxford Illustrated History of Roman Britain*. London: BCA.

Santosuosso, A. 2004. *Storming the Heavens*. London: Pimlico.

Scullard, H.H. 1979. *Roman Britain*. London: Thames and Hudson.

Southern, P. & K.R. Dixon. 1996. *The Late Roman Army*. London: B.T. Batsford.

Stephenson, I.P. 1999. *Roman Infantry Equipment: The Later Empire*. Stroud: Tempus.

Turcan, R. 1996. *The Cults of the Roman Empire*. Oxford: Blackwell.

Van Berchem, D. 1952. *L'Armée de Dioclétien at La Réforme Constantinenne*. Paris: Geuthner.

Van Driel Murray, C. 2002. The Leather Trades in Roman Yorkshire and Beyond. *Aspects of Industry in Roman Yorkshire and the North*. Oxford: Oxbow.

Van Driel Murray, C. 2000. A late Roman assemblage from Deurne (Netherlands). *Bonner Jahrbuch 200*, 293-308.

Van Driel Murray, C. 2001. Footwear in the North-Western Provinces of the Roman Empire. *Stepping through time. Archaeological footwear from prehistoric times until 1800*, by O. Goubitz, C. van Driel-Murray, W. Groenman van Waateringe and W. Stichting. Zwolle: Promotie Archeologie.

Vermaseren, M.J. and C. C. Van Essen, 1965. *The Excavations in the Mithraeum of the Church of Santa Prisca in Rome*. Leiden: Brill.

Wacher, J. 1974. *The Towns of Roman Britain*. London: BCA

Wacher, J. 1978. *Roman Britain*. London: BCA.

Ward-Perkins, B. 2005. *The Fall of Rome and the End of Civilization*. Oxford: OUP.

Webster, G. 1981. *The Roman Imperial Army*. London: A&C Black.

Wellesz, Emmy. 1960. *Vienna Genesis (Library of Illuminated Manuscripts)*. London: Faber and Faber.

Williams, D. *The Reach of Rome: History of the Frontier of the Roman Empire*, London: Constable, 1996

Williams, S. and Gerard Friell. 1994. *Theodosius – The Empire at Bay*. London: B.T. Batsford.

Ordnance Survey. 1956. *Roman Britain 3rd edition*, 1:1 000 000 scale Historical Map.

Ordnance Survey. 2001. *Roman Britain.* 5th edition, 1:625 000 scale Historical Map.

Re-enactment and Experimental Research

There are a small number of organisations in Europe that are engaged in practical reconstructions of Late Roman clothing, equipment and military drill. Few have established offices, most must be contacted via their websites. The following groups are particularly noteworthy, or have assisted the author in his own research:

Comitatus. Based in the UK www.comitatus.net

Quinta. (Cohors, Quinta Gallorum). Based at Arbeia Roman Fort, Baring Street, South Shields, Tyne & Wear, UK, NE33 2BB. www.quintagallorum.co.uk

Fectio. Based in the Netherlands. www.fectio.org.uk

Herculani. Based in France & Belgium. www.herculiani.fr

Foederati. Based in France. http://monsite.wanadoo.fr/foederati

References

1   The legions of the fourth century were much reduced in size from the 5000-man legions of the second and third centuries, down to around 1000 men. Hugh Elton, *Warfare in Roman Europe AD 350–425*, (1996), has estimated that legions stood at 1200 men or less. Zozimus, in his *New History*, V.45, relates how five legions were redeployed to Rome at the start of the fifth century, and that they numbered a total of 6,000 men. This equates to around 1200 men per legion.

2   20 Roman miles equals 18 modern miles, 658 yards (or 29.57 km).

3   Very little is known about these sub-units other than the titles of junior officers and a few hints in Vegetius 2.8. My suppositions, for the purposes of creating a coherent narrative, take this fragmentary information and apply it to earlier Roman military practice.

4   Vegetius 2.15.

5   Ammianus Marcellinus 16.2.

6   Ammianus Marcellinus 27.10, describes how the Emperor Valentian lost his helmet, gold-plated and studded with gems, in a swamp when his chamberlain (who was carrying it) fell in and was lost.

7   One method that archaeologists use to help them classify helmets as either 'cavalry' or 'infantry' is the existence or absence of cut-outs for the ears, since it is thought that the infantryman had a need to hear spoken or shouted orders, while the cavalryman did not. Although this may have influenced the *design*, I do not think it influenced the *use by soldiers*. However, the Deurne four-piece ridge helmet certainly *was* a cavalry helmet: the name of the owner's cavalry unit was inscribed on it!

8   Ammianus Marcellinus 1.2.

9   A.H.M. Jones (1964, *The Later Roman Empire 284–602*, Oxford: Basil Blackwell, 2 vols) calculated an annual legionary pay of 600 *denarii* from the Panopolis papyri of AD 298–300. This figure was subsequently reinterpreted by Richard Duncan-Jones in his article 'Pay and numbers in Diocletian's army', *Chiron* 8 (1978), 541–560 to give an annual pay of 1,800 *denarii*. Regardless of the exact value, it was certainly a pittance in 400 AD. It is known that the *stipendium* continued into the late fourth century (Ammianus 20.8).

10 *Tabulae Vindolandenses II* 181.
11 Traditionally named Coel, or Coel Hen ('Old Coel'), this legendary High King of Britain has been posited as the last *Dux Britanniarum*, ruling the northern province from York until the end of Roman Britain. Old King Cole became enshrined in popular folklore as the 'merry old soul who called for his fiddlers three'. Caelius is a suggested Latin form of his name.
12 True purple was, and always had been, prohibitively expensive often associated with the emperor's own household. Of course this made purple extremely desirable and in the fourth century there were many cheaper (and less effective) alternatives.
13 *Tabulae Vindolandenses III* 604.
14 Tactitus, *Histories* 3.50 refers to this bonus as *clavarium* (*donativi nomen est*), and its character as a donative suggests an irregular payment that might easily be put to other uses by the canny soldier.
15 The 8-man *contubernium* is a feature of the infantry cohort prior to the fourth century. Maurice, in the sixth-century *Strategikon* 12.B.9, also describes how files of 16 men were able to split into 8-man squads, and how these 8- and 16-man units fitted into the military formation arrayed on the battlefield. Vegetius, writing around AD 390, instead refers at 2.13 to 10-man infantry squads, which is at odds with both the earlier and the later system. Consequently, I have taken Maurice's 8-man squad as the standard organisation for legionaries in the fourth century.
16 M.C. Bishop and J.C.N. Coulston, *Roman Military Equipment*, (Oxbow, 2006), pp. 263–266.
17 *Tabulae Vindolandenses II* 316.
18 *Tabulae Vindolandenses II* 154.
19 *Tabulae Vindolandenses II* 155.
20 R.O. Fink, *Roman Military Records on Papyrus* (Cleveland 1971).
21 *Tabulae Vindolandenses II* 344.
22 Syenisius, *Epistulae* 129.
23 *Codex Theodosius* 7.4.28.
24 Procopius, *History of the Wars III*, 13.12–20
25 *Codex Theodosius* 7.1.2. It is unlikely that the law was introduced to protect the rights of legionaries, but instead to prevent avaricious commanders denuding their garrisons of able-bodied men for extended periods of time.
26 *Tabulae Vindolandenses II* 174.
27 *Codex Justinianus* 12.35.13
28 A quern from Maryport, Cumbria was marked 'tenth mill of the century of …' which suggests that a century had several quernstones, and in the case of Maryport, one per *contubernium*. A large mixing bowl (*mortaria*) for preparing bread dough was discovered at Usk, south Wales, it was inscribed with 'mixing bowl for the *contubernium* of Messor' This again suggests that bread making was handled at

the squad level. However, other querns found on Hadrian's Wall are inscribed with the name of the centurion commanding and the possibility still exists that milling and baking was conducted at the century level by designated members of the unit.

29 Metal bread stamps have been found on some fort sites. From modern experiments, they seem to work only on unleavened breads. They leave an imprint which marks the loaf as belonging to a certain legion, sometimes baked by a named soldier.

30 Suetonius, *The Twelve Caesars* 2.24, records how the Emperor Augustus introduced barley as a punishment ration: 'If a company broke in battle, Augustus ordered the survivors to draw lots, then executed every tenth man, and fed the remainder on barley bread instead of the customary wheat ration.'

31 Patrick Ottoway, *Roman York*, (Tempus, 1993), p. 103.

32 A hoard of legionary cooking utensils with a grid-iron was discovered at Newstead in Britain. All of the pans had been heavily used, and some had even been repaired with patches of bronze plate. Such was the usefulness and the value of these pots and pans!

33 Josephus, *The Jewish War* 3.86

34 There is a precedent for the legions of a defeated usurper being renamed and redeployed. In the 350s Constantius II dispatched the rebellious legions of Magnentius and Decentius to Syria (Ammianus 18.9). Regarding the lost soldiers of the Sixth Legion, the Duke of Thebes (the *Dux Thebaidos*) who controlled all forces in southern Egypt had a pair of legions on his rolls, Legio I Valentiniana and Legio II Valentiniana. They are both likely to have been established in the name of the young Valentinian II who was the legitimate Western Emperor when Magnus Maximus made his bid for the throne. Legio II Valentiniana may well have been a *vexillation* of the Legio II Augusta, originally based in Britain, but brought across to Gaul in Maximus' army. Likewise, the Legio I Valentiniana may have originally been those troops taken from Eboracum. As is the way of Roman military usurpers, Maximus may have renamed both *vexillationes* as Legio I 'Magnecensium' and Legio II 'Magnecensium'. Once defeated by the military might of Theodosius, the memory of Magnus Maximus would need to be expunged and the legions renamed and redeployed far from their homeland. That Theodosius renamed the legions after his young ward, Valentinian II, would fit very much with Theodosius' personality. So little is known of the *Notitia Dignitatum*, however, that other interpretations are possible. This particular theory is based on the writings of A.H.M. Jones and of Luke Ueda-Sarson.

35 Southern and Dixon, *The Late Roman Army*: 'There seem to be no radical changes in the garrisons of most forts, but after 370 the vici probably ceased to be occupied and the inhabitants perhaps migrated to the forts.'

36 Philip Katcher, *Armies of the Vietnam War 1962–75* (1980), and Lee E. Russell, *Armies of the Vietnam War 1962–75 (2)* (1983), Osprey Books.

37 Gildas, the sixth-century British writer, records that there were three wars fought against the Picts before the mid-fifth century. The first of these is said to have occurred after Maximus had invaded Gaul. Gildas is not entirely reliable, but it would not be surprising to find that continued raiding across the northern frontier had occurred, particularly when it is thought that the *dux* took several military units away with him. Coin finds from Hadrian's Wall indicate that the northern defensive line did not collapse entirely after Maximus' departure, but there may certainly have been localised attacks.

38 D. Van Berchem, *L'Armée de Dioclétien at La Réforme Constantinenne,* (Paris: Geuthner, 1952), p. 87, dates the reorganisation to between AD 311 and 325.

39 Although most of the *limitanei* regions were commanded by a *dux* (plural *duces*), according to the *Notitia Dignitatum*, eight of them were actually commanded by a *comes* (rendered in modern English as a 'Count'). An entire stretch of defensive forts on the south coast of England, the Saxon Shore Forts was under the command of the Count of the Saxon Shore – certainly a highly defended border area. The Count of Isauria, responsible for two infantry legions in southern Turkey, is also referred to as a Duke, which seems to show that although the title or rank might change in name, the duties of border security remained the same.

40 Anonymous, *Peri Strategikes* 9.3–8

41 Maurice's *Strategikon* 9.5 also mentions the capture of Roman deserters by patrols and also the welcome given to enemy troops deserting to a Roman patrol.

42 Hugh Elton, *Warfare in Western Europe AD 350–425*, p. 206.

43 Ammianus Marcellinus 22.7.7.

44 *Tabulae Vindolandenses II* 164.

45 The identification of possible naval bases on the East Coast is problematic. A likely candidate is Brough-on-Humber, not just due to its location on the Humber estuary, but also because of the titles given to a unit once stationed there. The Numerus Supervenientium Petuariensium (garrisoned in AD 400 at Malton) was once stationed at Brough-on-Humber (Roman Petuaria) and the word '*superventus*' has an established naval meaning. Vegetius uses the word in his discussion of the British navy (4.37); it means 'descent' or 'coming down from above'. This cavalry force would form the landward component ready to ambush raiders who were trapped onshore by the Roman warships. The problem, however, lies in the fact that Brough was heavily silted up by around AD 350 and plainly useless as a port and naval base. It does not appear in the *Notitia Dignitatum* as part of the British defences.

At South Shields, however, there is evidence that the fort and its attendant maritime activity, which had been burned down in the late third century, was now thriving once again. Early in the fourth century a unit called the Numerus Barcariorum Tigrisiensium is recorded as the new garrison. Literally meaning Tigris Boatmen (*barca* was a small boat used to ferry cargo from ship to shore), this force may have transported supplies from the harbour at South Shields up the Tyne to the forts on Hadrian's Wall. However, the Wall forts had already been supplied for 150 years without the help of dedicated units like the boatmen. A more likely proposition is that these skilled sailors from the other end of the empire were able to handle light-weight boats both on rivers and inshore, and could provide a useful naval patrol force for the vulnerable stretch of coastline south of the Wall.

46 Sidonius Apollinaris *Ep*.8.6.14.
47 Vegetius 4.37.
48 Gildas, *De excidio et conquestu Britanniae*, 16–17.
49 Maurice, *Strategikon* 9.5.
50 Maurice, *Strategikon* 9.3.
51 Maurice, *Strategikon* 12.B.20.
52 Maurice, *Strategikon* 12.B.20.
53 Maurice, *Strategikon* 9.5.
54 Maurice, *Strategikon* 9.5.
55 Maurice, *Strategikon* 7.11.
56 Maurice, *Strategikon* 9.2.
57 Maurice, *Strategikon* 9.5.
58 Conversation in April 2006 with a US Army captain, company commander of a Basic Training and OSUT company at Fort Benning, Georgia.
59 Josephus, *The Jewish War* 3.133
60 *Codex Theodosius* 7.13.3. This reduced the minimum height for Italian recruits from 5ft 10in (Roman) to 5ft 7in (Roman); that is, from 1.77m to 1.64m.
61 Vegetius I.19. The Roman pound is equal to 0.7219lb (avoirdupois), or 327.45g. Note that the US Marine Corps recommended that its Vietnam-era troops carry a maximum of 50lb (avoirdupois) of equipment. This equates to 22.7kg, or 69 Roman pounds, which comes close to Vegetius' recommended fighting load.
62 *Scriptores Historiae Augustae* 47.1.
63 For references to rations carried on the march, see the *Codex Theodosius* 7.4.11, also Vegetius 3.3, *Scriptores Historiae Augustae* Hadrian 10.2, Ammianus Marcellinus 17.9 and Avidius Cassius 5.3.
64 M. J. Vermaseren and C. C. Van Essen, *The Excavations in the Mithraeum of the Church of Santa Prisca in Rome*, (Brill: Leiden, 1965), p.157.
65 Maurice, *Strategikon* 5.4.
66 Ken Dark, *Britain and the End of the Roman Empire*, (Stroud: Tempus, 2000), discusses this problem in relation to the mixed Saxon and

Romano-British communities in eastern England.

67　*Inscriptiones Latinae Christianae Veteres*, ed. E. Diehl (Berlin: Weidmann, 1925–31). An inscription from Lyons, dated to the fifth or sixth centuries.

68　Ammianus Marcellinus 20.4.18

69　Vegetius 2.7. Vegetius also describes how the chief standard of the entire legion was the eagle, and that each cohort had its own dragon-standard (*draco*).

70　Maurice, *Strategikon* 7.1.

71　Maurice, *Strategikon* 12.B.16.

72　Peter Salway, *The Oxford Illustrated History of Roman Britain*, (BCA, 1993).

73　It was at this point in the fourth century that the Roman forts began to be abandoned for good. Some had already emptied out their garrisons earlier in the century. Arbeia was abandoned 'around AD 400'. The British field army appears to have been garrisoned inside the walled cities of the province, it was composed of nine comitatenses units under the command of the Comes Britanniarum. In the *Notitia Digitatum* many of these units also seem to appear in other army lists, in Britain or in Gaul. The evidence suggests that the British field army had a presence in Britain sometime between the early 390s and the 420s. Peter Salway (1993) suggests that the field army originally came across the Channel after the revolt of Magnus Maximus, and that it was the removal of this 'task force' that may have led to the barbarian unrest of 398 and 399. I have followed this line of thinking to help explain the events of 398–399.

74　Vegetius 3.6.

75　Maurice, *Strategikon*, 1.2.

76　Vegetius 3.3.

77　Ammianus Marcellinus 25.2.1.

78　Ammianus Marcellinus 15.4.8.

79　Ammianus Marcellinus 19.5.2.

80　Ammianus Marcellinus 18.2.11.

81　Josephus, *The Jewish War*, 3.5.

82　Other uses for the tool have been suggested. The length of the wooden haft that attached to the metal blade is unknown, perhaps the half-moon blade was used to strip bark from tree trunks, or even (with a very short handle) to cut leather. A traditional leather cutting tool still used today bares a remarkable resemble to the Roman 'turf-cutter'.

83　Derek Williams, *The Reach of Rome: History of the Frontier of the Roman Empire*, (Constable, 1996).

84　Claudian, *On the Consulship of Stilicho*, 2.

85　Claudian, *The Gothic War* 26.

86　Ken Dark, *Britain and the End of the Roman Empire*, (Stroud: Tempus Books, 2000).

87 Richard Reece, 'The end of the city in Roman Britain' in *The City in Late Antiquity*, ed. John Rich, (Routledge, 1992).

88 Neil Faulkner, *The Decline and Fall of Roman Britain*, (Stroud: Tempus, 2001).

89 Peter Salway, *The Oxford Illustrated History of Roman Britain*, (BCA, 1993).

90 Claudian, *The Gothic War* 26. This florid and unlikely speech is actually ascribed in *The Gothic War* to Stilicho.

91 Maurice, *Strategikon* 12.B.9.

92 There is some confusion of terminology in the *Strategikon*. In 12.A.7 the *foulkon* is static, with shields and spears planted in the ground. However, later on (12.B.16) the text describes a different *foulkon* formation that sounds exactly like the traditional Roman *testudo*. Reluctant to begin renaming the Roman *testudo*, I have opted for the meaning of the word '*foulkon*' which describes an anti-cavalry shield-wall.

93 Maurice, *Strategikon* 12.B.16.

94 Ammianus Marcellinus 18.8.

95 Thucydides 5.10.

96 Vegetius 1.19. As discussed in Chapter 6, this military step refers to a length of stride used to pace the speed of the soldiers on the march.

97 Maurice, *Strategikon* 12.B.16.

98 Aristophanes, *Peace* 241 and 1176ff.

99 Polyaenus, *Strategemata* 3.4.8.

100 Herodotus, *Histories* 7.224 and 9.62.2, and Ammianus Marcellinus 31.13.

101 Xenophon, *Agesilaos* 2.12.

102 Livy, *The War with Hannibal* 22.5.

103 Ammianus Marcellinus 16.12.

104 Ammianus Marcellinus 31.13.

105 Ammianus Marcellinus 16.12.

106 Ammianus Marcellinus 18.8.

107 Ammianus Marcellinus 31.7.

108 Ammianus Marcellinus 16.12.

109 Livy, *The War with Hannibal* 22.51.

110 '*Silentium. Mandata captate. Non vos turbatis. Ordinem servate. Signa sequute. Nemo demittat signum et inimicos seque.*' After Maurice, *Strategikon* 12.B.14.

111 Claudian, *Panegyric on the Sixth Consulship of Honorius*.

Index